From Set Shot to Slam Dunk

From Set Shot to Slam Dunk

The Glory Days of Basketball in the Words
of Those Who Played It

CHARLES SALZBERG

E. P. Dutton   New York

Published in the United States by E. P. Dutton,
a division of NAL Penguin Inc.,
2 Park Avenue, New York, N.Y. 10016.

Published simultaneously in Canada
by Fitzhenry and Whiteside Limited, Toronto.

Library of Congress Cataloging-in-Publication Data
Salzberg, Charles.
From set shot to slam dunk.

1. Basketball players—United States—Biography.
2. National Basketball Association—History. I. Title.
GV884.A1S25   1987   796.32'3'0922   [B]   87-623
ISBN 0-525-24555-3

COBE

Designed by Michele Aldin

1 3 5 7 9 10 8 6 4 2

First Edition

Grateful acknowledgment is made to Alfred A. Knopf, Inc.,
for permission to reprint an excerpt from Rabbit, Run by John Updike,
copyright © 1960 by John Updike. Reprinted by permission of the publisher.

With luck he'll become in time a crack athlete in high school; Rabbit knows the way. You climb up through the little grades and then get to the top and everybody cheers; with the sweat in your eyebrows you can't see very well and the noise swirls around you and lifts you up, and then you're out, not forgotten at first, just out, and it feels good and cool and free. You're out, and sort of melt, and keep lifting, until you become like to these kids just one more piece of the sky of adults that hangs over them in the town, a piece that for some queer reason has clouded and visited them. They've not forgotten him; worse, they never heard of him.

JOHN UPDIKE, *Rabbit, Run*

The ball is round and the floor is smooth.

RED AUERBACH, *explaining why basketball is a simple game*

Acknowledgments

There are several people I should like to thank, without whose help I would have been lost. They are, in no particular order, Dorothy Marcus, Caroline, Jim, and Maria Ross, Sandra Bedgood, Josh, Brooks, and Sam Brand, Phyllis Ricci, Liz Lawson, Connie Hilliard, Mark Levine, Bernie Pincus, Chris O'Rourke, and Irene Salzberg. A special thanks to Janet Kirby, Elliot Ravetz, and my editor, Leslie Wells, without whom this book would not have been possible.

Contents

Preface   xi

Chronology   xv

Moe Goldman   1

Sidney "Sonny" Hertzberg   15

Nat "Feets" Broudy   33

Robert Davies   45

Slater Martin   61

"Easy Ed" Macauley   79

Dolph Schayes   103

Nat "Sweetwater" Clifton   123

Bill Sharman   135

George "the Bird" Yardley   147

Norm Drucker   171

Johnny "Big Red" Kerr   191

Cal Ramsey   209

Jerry West   225

Preface

In comparison to all the other major American professional-league team sports the National Basketball Association is the new kid on the block. First established in 1946 by a group of arena owners as the Basketball Association of America, it underwent a name change to the National Basketball Association in 1949 when it merged with the rival National Basketball League.

Previous to the formation of the BAA there were, of course, other professional basketball leagues, all regional in nature, as was the American Basketball League, which, comprised primarily of teams in the Northeast, began in 1925 and finally, after a few stops and starts, disappeared forever in 1963; and the NBL, which was established in 1937 and was made up mostly of teams from the Midwest.

But even in those early years the notion of a professional national basketball league was the dream of men like Eddie Gottlieb, who coached and was part-owner of the Philadelphia SPHAs (South Philadelphia Hebrew Association) of the ABL, a team that was the forerunner of the Philadelphia Warriors.

That dream finally became a reality with the creation of the NBA, a league that in its first year consisted of a somewhat bloated field of seventeen teams with names like the Anderson Packers, Indianapolis Olympians, Chicago Stags, St. Louis Bombers, Tri-Cities Blackhawks, Sheboygan Redskins, and Waterloo Hawks, in addition to the familiar Knicks, Celtics, Pistons, and Lakers. The next year, the league shrank to eleven teams and by 1952 it had settled in at ten.

Those early days of the NBA were a time of struggle, a struggle for existence, not only for the league itself but for the individual franchises and the players. The money paid to the players was minimal by today's standards, and the travel and playing conditions were occasionally substandard. Still, the league survived and later flourished, as did the game, which underwent some subtle and some not-so-subtle changes over the years. For instance, there were new rules, like the introduction of the 24-second clock in 1954, and the widening of the foul lane, a direct result of the play of Minneapolis Laker center George Mikan, the first superstar in the game and the most dominant player of his era.

But then the game has been evolving ever since it was invented by Dr. James Naismith, an instructor in the YMCA Training College (now Springfield College), in the winter of 1891/92, when there were nine players on each team. In fact, it was only fifty years ago that there was a center jump after every basket, discontinued dribbling with two hands, and a lot of extracurricular activity under the boards.

This book represents an attempt to create a picture of what life in the NBA was like from the time it began in 1946 up through its initial growth period of the 1950s and 1960s, by tapping into the memories of those who were there.

Of the fourteen men interviewed for this book, eleven played in the National Basketball Association, and the majority of them are Hall of Famers. The other three, Moe Goldman, Nat Broudy, and Norm Drucker, offer other views of the NBA. Goldman, a star center at City College of New York in the early 1930s, played in the American Basketball League and provides a unique look at basketball as it was played in the early 1930s through 1942. Norm Drucker was a referee in the NBA and presents yet another angle of vision; whereas Nat Broudy, never a player himself, has been a part of the game for over forty years, as a scout and timekeeper for Madison Square Garden. Each was chosen not so much for what he accomplished, though in every case it was substantial, but for the piece of the picture of the early years of the NBA he could provide.

Today, the NBA is predominantly black, but in the 1950s, after Chuck Cooper and Sweetwater Clifton broke the color line in 1950/51, and even into the early 1960s, there were very few black ballplayers in the league. Upon undertaking this book, it was decided not to interview any players who already either had their own books or were extensively in the public eye, which eliminated players like Bob Cousy, Wilt Chamberlain, and Oscar Robertson. This, coupled with the fact that there were few black players in the early days and that those contacted preferred not to take part in this book, explains why there are only two black men represented here: Sweetwater Clifton and Cal Ramsey. Nevertheless, a good part of the game's success is undoubtedly due to the participation of black players and so, whenever possible, their experiences have been related through the eyes of white players who played alongside them.

The method was rather simple. I sat with each of these men, with only a tape recorder between us, and we spoke about their lives in basketball, from the time they first began playing the game until the time they retired. Most, I visited in their homes or offices. With others, like Nat "Sweetwater" Clifton, this was not possible because his "office" is the yellow cab he drives in Chicago. Instead, we met in a park on the North Side, sitting opposite each other over a chess table, while drug deals went down behind us. Bill Sharman cannot give interviews because of a serious problem with his vocal cords; so he offered to give written answers to questions I provided. Ed Macauley was more comfortable interviewing himself; so he asked that I send him a blank tape and all the questions I could muster. He was so informative that he wound up having to provide an extra tape of his own.

Each man was asked questions not only about himself and his experiences in the league, but also about those whom he had played with and against. They were also asked how they feel about the game as it's played today and, in some instances, what they might suggest in the way of changes.

I wish to thank all those who participated and gave so generously of their time. I am thankful for their patience, articulateness, and cooperation, especially as I found all to be decidedly modest men who were never quite comfortable talking about themselves.

Chronology

American Basketball League (ABL): 1925–32, 1934–46, 1961–63.
National Basketball League (NBL): 1937–49, 1950–51.
Basketball Association of America (BAA): 1946–49.
National Basketball Association (NBA): 1949 to the present.
American Basketball Association (ABA): 1967–76.

Initial members of the Basketball Association of America (1946):

Boston Celtics
Chicago Stags
Cleveland Rebels
Detroit Falcons
New York Knickerbockers
Philadelphia Warriors

Pittsburgh Ironmen
Providence Steamrollers
St. Louis Bombers
Toronto Huskies
Washington Capitols

Initial members of the National Basketball Association (1949):

Anderson Packers
Baltimore Bullets
Boston Celtics
Chicago Stags
Denver Nuggets
Fort Wayne Pistons
Indianapolis Olympians
Minneapolis Lakers
New York Knickerbockers

Philadelphia Warriors
Rochester Royals
St. Louis Bombers
Sheboygan Redskins
Syracuse Nationals
Tri-Cities Blackhawks
Washington Capitols
Waterloo Hawks

From Set Shot to Slam Dunk

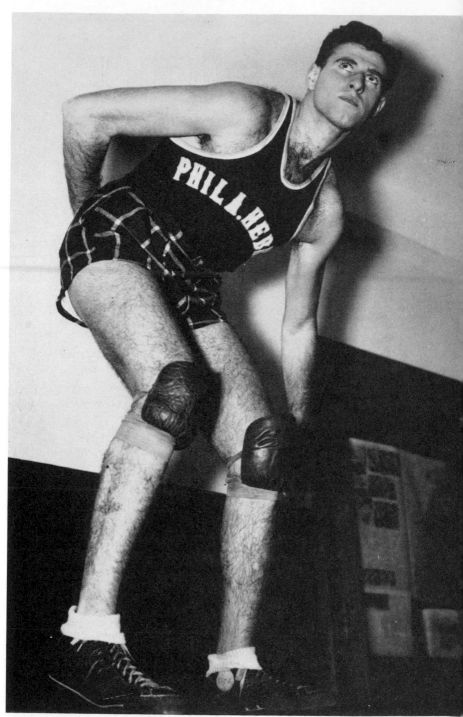

Moe Goldman

Moe Goldman

Moe Goldman, a star basketball player at CCNY in the early 1930s, under the coaching of the legendary Nat Holman, played professional ball from 1934 to 1942, before the establishment of the NBA. He played what was then called "the center man" for Eddie Gottlieb's team, the Philadelphia SPHAs (South Philadelphia Hebrew Association), the forerunner of the Philadelphia Warriors. Goldman, at six feet three inches, was certainly one of the shortest centers playing. At that time, statistics were kept haphazardly, if at all, so there are no career figures for him. Today Moe Goldman, who after his retirement from the game taught in the New York City school system and was eventually named the commissioner of high school basketball for the New York public school system, lives in southern Florida with his wife and says that he "must be one of the oldest pros left alive."

I grew up in Brooklyn and never played too much basketball. I went to a school called Franklin K. Lane high school and it seems that in 1928, over the summer, I suddenly grew very,

very tall. When I came back to school, the basketball coach took one look at me and said, "Oh, you've got to be a basketball player." So, in '29, I joined the team, and the funny part was we went on to win the city championship that year. And that was my beginning as a basketball player.

After high school, I went to City College in 1930 and played there until 1934. In 1934, I was captain of the team, and if it were today I would probably be chosen as a number-one draft choice. I was about six-three and the center man, and I made the All-Metropolitan team for three years. I also made All-America in 1934, and then came professional basketball.

It's all different today. Today they have the draft. For me it happened when we played Temple in Philadelphia. We beat them, which was very unusual because in those days each home team got their own referees. There was no such thing as a referees' association. They assigned referees. In fact, the man who refereed our Temple game never refereed for Temple again because we won. He was a fellow named Doc Sugarman. Anyway, that night, after the game, back in our hotel, a man came to me and said that Eddie Gottlieb wanted to speak to me. Well, not knowing anything about professional basketball, I didn't know who Eddie Gottlieb was. He said, "He owns the SPHAs," and I didn't even know who the SPHAs were. I said, "Okay, I'll see him." Eddie Gottlieb took me aside and said, "Look, Moe, how would you like to play for Philadelphia?" I said, "I don't mind if I can make some money." He said, "All right. Tell you what. I'll give you thirty-five dollars a game." And I accepted, because it was good money, comparatively speaking.

It was the end of the college season, and we were playing our final game against NYU on a Saturday night, and this was the way I was introduced to professional basketball. Eddie had told me in Philadelphia, "You live in Brooklyn and we're playing the Wonder Five from St. John's"—who played as the Jewels. "Sunday night, we're playing the Jewels in Brooklyn. You come to the game. We'll meet you there and have a uniform for you." So I played Saturday night at City College, and Sunday night I took a bus by myself to what we called Arcadia Hall. I got to the gate and the gate people wouldn't let me in. They said, "Who are you?" I said, "I'm gonna play here tonight." Finally, they got Eddie Gottlieb out and he said, "Yeah, he's one of my players." I got a uniform and I figured I'd go upstairs and watch them play. But after we warmed up, Eddie says, "Okay, at center, Moe Goldman." I'd never even played with those fellows before. But I'll tell you this much, it didn't matter. You can always break in with a team if you know some of the fundamentals.

In those days the American League had a split season. The winner of the first half played the winner of the second half for the championship. That year the first half was won by the Trenton team. I started with the Philadelphia team at the beginning of the second half of the season and we won fourteen straight, and then went on to win the championship, so I must have helped them. In fact, up in the Hall of Fame they have it written down that we won fourteen straight, going undefeated for a whole half season.

The league was composed of all eastern teams. There were the Philadelphia SPHAs; a team from New Britain, Connecticut; the Brooklyn Jewels; a team from Trenton, New Jersey; Newark had a team; so did Union City; there was the Brooklyn Visitation; and the Kate Smith Celtics. She owned a team that played at the Hippodrome, and Ted Collins was the manager. The Hippodrome was in the center of Manhattan. It was a theater. You played on a stage.

We played two games a week, one at home, one away, and we usually had off during Christmas week. Christmas week, Eddie had a big car and we'd all go out West, because the East played the East and the West had their own organizations. At first, they were not professional teams out there, they were industrial teams. They had an industrial league with teams like Phillips 66, Akron, Oshkosh, and if you joined the team they'd offer you a job and you could stay with the firm for the rest of your life. It was a good deal. In fact, for the

3

1936 Olympics, which was the first time they had basketball, you know how they picked the team? There was nobody from the East, no colleges were involved. They took the industrial league, had a postseason tournament, and the team that won it, they took their first five men and a couple of All-Stars from the rest of the league. I think there was only one college man picked for the 1936 Olympics, and they won anyway. No contest.

So Christmastime we'd leave Philadelphia right after a ball game and go out West. This would be what Eddie called his western tour. We'd stop at Harrisburg, Cleveland, Akron, and end up in Oshkosh, Wisconsin. We'd make this trip up and back, and you know how much we made for it? One hundred dollars each. That's what we made. And I'd ask him, "Eddie, why do we have to go out? Why can't we take the week off?" And he'd say, "Because you are the pioneers for a big league someday." That's right.

Actually, you know, he's the father of professional basketball, of the NBA. Without him they may have had a league but it would have taken a lot of years longer. He really put it together. He always had this vision of professional basketball. Eddie Gottlieb was the man behind the whole thing. He was behind the ABL [American Basketball League] and all the rest of it. During the war years, he would make sure they continued playing and that they wouldn't drop out. In fact, he supported a couple of teams in order to keep professional basketball going during the war. Eddie Gottlieb was quite a man.

But in those days it was entirely different. We played in dance halls and had dances after the game. We traveled by car. Many of us played in more than one league. For example, I would play for the Philadelphia team in the American League, but during the week I played for Wilkes-Barre, in the Pennsylvania State League.

I was teaching physical education during the week and there were three of us from New York, myself, Shakey Gotthoffer, and Red Wolfe. We'd take the train on Saturday

4

night, sleep over on Saturday, and usually play on Sunday. It was usually a weekend thing, though occasionally we'd play during the week. Eddie really kept us busy. He had exhibition games all the time. He'd put us up, and you'd get the $35 a game, plus expenses.

In Philadelphia we played at the Broadwood Hotel. We had a nice place and we'd draw between two thousand and twenty-five hundred. They charged about $1 for a ticket, which included the game and the dance afterwards. I bet about fifty people met and got married out there.

In those days, incidentally, like in baseball, there were no colored ballplayers in the league. So naturally, as they did in baseball, the coloreds became one team. The best of the coloreds played for the Renaissance team. We used to play them maybe thirty, forty times a year. Hell of a good competition. Later on, out West, the Harlem Globetrotters developed. You know, they started as a regular team. They saw that it didn't mean much, that they couldn't draw too many people, so Abe Saperstein changed them into the act they do today.

As I said, I used to run twice a week up to Wilkes-Barre, all after school. I'd go down, get the Lackawanna Railroad, go to Wilkes-Barre, then take the sleeper back. In the morning, I'd get back to Hoboken, take the railroad across to New York, and go back to work. And I'd probably have to go again the same afternoon. They paid more than Eddie did. I got $75 plus expenses. If there was any conflict, though, the American League would take precedence, because that was the big league. In between, I also had exhibition games. I also played Sunday afternoons for the New York Hebrew Club in Newark, New Jersey. For a while, I played in Albany for the New York State League, twice a week. I usually had about seven games a week.

It was different from the game today. At the beginning, you know, we jumped center after each basket. There was no such thing as taking the ball out. Also, at the beginning, we played what we called a *double dribble*. You could dribble,

5

discontinue, and then dribble again, and we did it with two hands. That's another rule they had in the thirties. And nobody knew anything about a one-handed shot, and the shooting was nowhere near what it is today.

It was a rough game. Fouls were not so prevalent. You had to get killed to get a foul. There was a rule that the only time you got a foul was when you had possession of the ball and you were hit. You could end up in a crowd quite often. Scoring was very, very low. It would be a 20-, 24-point game, or less. College was the same. At City College we once played a school from Virginia where in the whole game only a couple of fouls and one basket were scored. If you scored 8 or 10 points, you had a good game.

We had one fellow who did most of the shooting for us, outside of me. A Philadelphia fellow named Cy Kasselman, who never went to college. He could shoot from anywhere, a two-handed set shot, and he was high scorer; and after him everyone had a piece of the business. There was continuous movement toward the basket, continuous passing. Today, it's an individual game more than a passing game. A few teams have it, but in our day it was all passing. You tried to get under or near the basket. Your shots were taken near the basket. Occasionally, they were taken from a distance. Of course, today the shooting is so tremendous you can't compare the two.

The game took longer, but there was no stalling as such. During my era they made the *ten-second* rule. Before that, you could keep the ball. You could score two baskets and then stay way down at the other end of the court.

Now this really happened. Mayor Jimmy Walker, during the Depression, made a request of sportswriters to see if they could get some money together in order to help people out. So they got the Garden and had a triple-header there. We played Fordham that night, and there was no ten-second rule. Fordham played a zone defense, and we made 6 or 8 quick points, and then we just passed the ball up and back. We were very impatient. We wanted to go. But Nat Holman, our coach, said, "You stay there until they come out." And the crowd just sat there. And after this they decided they'd better get that ball up over the line within ten seconds.

The game was of different lengths. For example, in the American League we played three fifteen-minute thirds. In college, you played ten-minute quarters. In high school, it was eight-minute quarters. You played the whole game. You were substituted for only if you got too tired to play. We carried maybe seven men. It was very, very rare that you didn't play a whole game, unless you were hurt. College was the same way. No substitutions unless you were way ahead, and then the whole second team might play.

The game did change while I was playing. They went from the two-handed dribble to a one-handed dribble. Then, after a while, they eliminated the center jump, so that you took the ball out-of-bounds after a basket, as it's done today. I think they also got tougher on the fouls. In the beginning, we had only one official, who had to take care of everything, and one body who all he had to do was toss the ball for the center jump. It was difficult.

At some places in the Pennsylvania State League, we played in a cage. There was no out-of-bounds. You just went up against the cage. You'd come out after the game with scratches and marks all over your body.

We got into some fights, but not too many. In Union City, New Jersey, one time we had a whole mob scene. There was no dressing room as such, so during the breaks you'd sit around wherever you could. At this game in Union City we were sitting around at the end of the first third, and somebody came along with a bottle and hit Harry Litwak, who used to be the coach at Temple University, on the head, splitting it wide open. Then there was a whole general fight.

At the Brooklyn Visitation, they'd sit in the front row with no supervision, no cops or anything. They could throw a drink at you as you went by, or touch you with a lighted cigarette as you stood there to take the ball out. Little things like that. But they were good days, very good days.

I played with some guys who later went into the NBA. I

played a team that George Mikan played for. I tell you, I could go by him. I was the first center man in those days who could run and shoot. The rest of the center men were tall, gangly, and couldn't run. All I had to do was fake and go. I could shoot if they stayed back. So I would say, without trying to be boastful, that I revolutionized the center position. I think I was the first center to be able to run and shoot, to dribble and pass, to do all those things. Whereas, in the past, the center man would just stand there, tap the ball, and then stay out of the way. At that time, they didn't bother with the pivot. They just stood back. I think most of the boys would tell you that I was the first because if I went through all the names of center man at that time, very few would run and do what I did.

I played George Mikan in Newark. He also couldn't run. If they gave me the ball in the center of the court, I could just dribble right by him. Of course, he'd come back, he was so big. I played against him and against Red Holzman. Red was smart. He came out of City College. Red was a good, smart ballplayer.

All the boys who played at the beginning of the NBA had two-handed shots. There was a ballplayer who wasn't known by anybody, he just played with me at Newark, who they used to call Hooker Cohen. He's the only one who came around with a one-handed shot. After Joe Fulks, who played for Eddie Gottlieb at Philadelphia, came along with that one-handed shot everyone had to learn it. See, a one-hand shot is so much easier. And it's also so much more difficult to stop.

Eddie Gottlieb was the coach, the manager, the promoter, and the owner of the SPHAs. Then, when the NBA came along, he took the Philadelphia Warriors and did a good job. He was a very nice guy, very considerate. You could talk to him. He was one of the boys. Later on, he ran the whole schedule for the NBA. When he sold his team to San Francisco, he was asked by the NBA to come back and make the schedule. They'd tried it one year with machines and were unsuccessful, but he did it without machines. He was quite a man.

8

He was one of those who used to choose for the Negro Baseball Hall of Fame. He was involved in baseball, too. He had a Philadelphia team in the black baseball league.

If I had to, I would say that Willie Smith or Tarzan Cooper of the Renaissance team were two of the best players I ever played against. In their case, they both jumped center, so one would take me for a while, then the other would take me. I had both of them. And I think they were two of the best. They were taller than me. I have large arms, but Tarzan's were even larger. Smitty was much bigger. The rest of them on that team were also outstanding.

I scored approximately 6 to 8 points a game, sometimes more. But not a record was kept then. The game was played, you went home, and that was that. The season ran about five months, and before the season we'd play exhibition games, playing all different kinds of teams. I bet we were close to the number of games they play today, what with the championships and all.

I suppose there are a number of incidents that stand out from my playing days. For example, there was the time we played the Brooklyn Jewels. They came out to our place and they had a ballplayer who was a very peculiar person. Before the game started I see him in the shower and I say, "Why are you taking a shower now?" He says, "Well, after the game I gotta run off, so I'm taking my shower now."

I wasn't involved in this story, but there was a center man for the Jewels, named Matty Begovitch, who became a very famous referee later on. He played with the St. John's Wonder 5. And there was another center named Stan Entrup. This Entrup was the worst. Strong, with incredibly large arms. When I got through with a game with him, I'd have black-and-blue marks all over my body. He wouldn't do anything in the game, just jump center, stand there with his arms out and dare you to go by him. Well, one day Entrup and Begovitch were going to play against each other. Entrup never scored. So Entrup says to Matty, "Tell you what we do. You let me go down to the first basket and you let me go by. I'll make a basket, then I'll let you` go by for a basket. Okay?" Matty says, "Fine," as long as Entrup won't hit him. Well, the game starts, Entrup goes in, Matty lets him go by, he makes a basket, and the crowd goes wild. Then Matty says to him, "Okay, Stretch, it's my turn." Entrup says to him, "You dare go by me and I'll break you in half." And Matty looks at him and says, "Why?" And Entrup says, "I got mine, I'm not worried about you."

Some of the players used to drink quite a bit; however, I didn't indulge as much as the others. I had to run back home after the games. But I know the others used to drink. In fact, there was a center named Tiny Hearn, who played with Trenton, one of the real old-timers. He and Rusty Saunders were drinking one time and they get back in the car, going somewhere, and suddenly they have an argument. Tiny Hearn always had a long coat. He was a big fella, biggest one we had, must have been six-seven, six-eight, or six-nine, something like that. Rusty takes the back of his coat and *zzttt*, tears it right up the back. They were both that drunk.

We'd get a lot of anti-Semitism when we went to some places. Our traveling uniform had the name SPHAs in Hebrew on it. If we traveled to the Brooklyn Visitation, in an area where they were all Catholics, we'd have some trouble. And in Union City there was a lot of anti-Semitism. For that matter, they didn't allow blacks in the league, so you see, it worked in reverse, too.

I don't think there was too much anti-Semitism among the players, although there could have been. Over the years, while I was playing, the outstanding basketball players were Jewish, so you really can't say much about anti-Semitism within the teams themselves. I do know that when Milty Trupin, who played at City College, started playing with the Visitation, they'd say, "oh that Jew this and that Jew that." So

10

there had to be a problem there. And I think that when we went out West we hit some problems.

Out in the West, by the way, they had a different style of play. They were more offensive-minded and they were also more physical. They were always in there for the basket and they didn't play much defense, which I think is happening now in the NBA.

When the NBA started, Red Auerbach was at Norfolk, in the service, at the training station, and they had all his ballplayers. That station had a hell of a team. I was there for a while, but then I said, "Let me out. That's all I'm doing is playing basketball." Anyway, when they first started talking about the new league, Red wasn't supposed to be the coach of the Washington team. The one who was supposed to be coach used to play with the Brooklyn Jewels. He had a lot of experience, a fellow named Max Posnack. I don't know exactly what happened, but somehow at the last minute, Auerbach got the job. Red was tough. Since then, he's come a long way. I knew Red as a kid in Eastern District High School. He wasn't much as a player. He coached a private school in Washington for a while before the war, then he went into the service, and when he got out he got this coaching job with the Washington team. Actually, what made him was getting the right players at the right time. He was lucky a lot of times. How about that Ed Macauley deal that got him Bill Russell? St. Louis wanted Macauley in the worst way. He came from St. Louis University. So Red took Russell and it made his team. A couple of other times he got ballplayers he didn't necessarily want. [Bill] Sharman was one. Somebody else was supposed to get him.

I had to stop playing ball because I got hurt. In those days once you tore your cartilage, doctors couldn't do anything. It wasn't like today where you have your operation and a couple of months later you're back playing. I had a knee injury in a game and then they removed the cartilage and I tried it again, and that's when I knew I was finished. I think that if it hadn't been for that I would have been playing for many, many years more. I think I could have played in the NBA if I had a leg. But when it went, I decided I was going into the Navy and I did, and that was that.

After I got out of the service I went on to officiate games in high school and college. I worked for the ABL for a while. I used to referee all the games at the Garden. I couldn't stay out of basketball, but I never went in for the professional game.

But today I think the pros are great. Their ability to move—those tall fellows—is phenomenal. And their shooting. But I think they're not too smart when it comes to the game. You get a smart ballplayer and he's going to be outstanding. The smartest ballplayer today, and he doesn't really have the physique for the game, is Larry Bird. He's the smartest player around today because he thinks all the time. He will get rebounds like nobody else. It's only because of the rebound position he puts himself in. You've got to watch him, the little things he does. And remember, he's not the tallest and he's not the fastest, but he's the greatest of them all. He has the sense to be able to be at the right place at the right time. He has good peripheral vision where he can give off the ball. So today, if you have that ability, you've got to be a real good ballplayer.

I think when the NBA first started they were better basketball players. Not better physically or better shooters, but they had more basketball sense than they have today. Passing, shooting, defense, team play, and all that. Today they make up for that because they have size and a better ability to shoot and score. They don't care if a man scores on them that much. It doesn't matter. "If he's going to make one, I'll try to make two," that's what they think. Whereas years ago you always said, "Let's keep them down. Defensively, we gotta take our man, we gotta do something with him." Of course, today, they could shoot your eyes out. They're that good.

Sidney "Sonny" Hertzberg

Sidney "Sonny" Hertzberg

Sonny Hertzberg's professional basketball career began with the New York Gothams of the American Basketball League, but once the NBA was established he was signed by the New York Knickerbockers. Later, he was traded first to the Washington Capitols and then to the Boston Celtics, where he ended his career in 1951. He now works as an associate managing director of Bear, Stearns, a New York brokerage house, and lives on Long Island.

I grew up in Crown Heights, Brooklyn, and started playing basketball as a kid by shooting through the rungs of a ladder attached to a fire escape, using a stocking hat stuffed with paper as a basketball. There was no dribbling, of course, just passing and shooting. Later on, I played in elementary school and by the time I was fifteen or sixteen I started playing in high school. At that time, the school gyms would be open in the evenings and we'd play there. The ceilings were not that high, so you had to be a good shooter, since the trajectory of your shot was kind of low. I think the reason why New York players were all good ball handlers, good dribblers, and good passers was because of the small, narrow gyms they played in.

I went to City College and played under Nat Holman. At CCNY, I played on two metropolitan championship teams. In fact, we never lost to any metropolitan team in the years I played guard on the varsity. I am six feet tall and at the time my backcourt partner was Red Holzman. He went into the service when I did. Red went into the Navy, and I went into the Army. In later years, we played against each other: he with Rochester, and I was with the New York Knickerbockers, Washington Capitols, and the Boston Celtics.

Professionally, I started playing while in the service, with the New York entry in the American League. First we were the New York Jewels and later the name was changed to the New York Gothams. I led them in scoring for several consecutive years until the NBA [actually the BAA] was organized in 1946. The teams in that American League were the Philadelphia SPHAs, Trenton, Wilmington, Paterson, Saratoga, and New York. We played mainly on weekends. I got $50 a game and we played either two or three games a week. Most of the men had regular jobs and they probably earned more in those years in basketball than they did in their five-day employment.

I was in the service at the time, but I was fortunate enough to be stationed in New York and I had permission to play pro ball. I was married and was given permission to sleep off the base. After Army duties, I had free time to do what I wanted.

Most of the games were in arenas that were two to two and a half hours away, so I could get out, play the game, and come back the same evening. The only time we slept overnight was if we played a Saturday-night game in Philadelphia and then a Sunday-afternoon game in Wilmington, which meant we'd be back Sunday night. Fortunately, I was able to get weekends off.

The American League didn't use a 24-second clock, of course, and it made for a better defensive game than they play today. It was also a lot rougher, because the men who played the game were all experienced college ballplayers but were

16

not in top condition because they were working at different jobs and didn't have time to practice. So there was a great deal of holding, shoving, and body contact. If you took a shot, you'd get fingers in your eyes, accidentally or on purpose. And the rules in the American League were a little bit tougher than the current rules. There were rules that you couldn't keep your back to the basket more than three seconds, which eliminated some of the pivot playing and the maneuvering for good body positioning.

For that game, incidentally, you had to be strong physically because these fellows who were earning $150 a week playing three times a week would not give up that income. So, if you were a new kid in the league, you had to take your lumps, show them you could put up with everything. And if you couldn't, word spread around the league that "this new kid isn't so tough, you can bang him around." There were plenty of fistfights and you had to take care of yourself and prove your ability and stamina.

It was a good game, because in order to score you had to really know your basketball, every phase of the game. Whereas today you're a specialist in either jump shooting or the fadeaway shot, or a good defensive ballplayer, or a terrific dribbler. In those days you had to be proficient in boxing out your man, setting up plays, in addition to all the rest. You couldn't be weak on defense or else they'd take advantage of you because you could hold the ball offensively as long as you wanted. Now, with the 24-second clock, you get it up the court and shoot, whereas then they could take advantage of anybody who was a weak sister, work on him long enough until he made a mistake, a bad step, crossed his feet, or something of that nature. I found that it was real tough basketball. When you finished a game, you knew you had played hard and earned your pay.

They didn't keep statistics as they do today, but I averaged about 12 or 13 points a game, and that was a lot. I think I still hold a record for a forty-minute ball game in Paterson, New Jersey, when I scored 38 points. I don't even know if I led the league in scoring, since there wasn't that type of statistic publicized. There wasn't, for instance, a publicity office to put out that type of information. I do know I led my team in scoring. The length of the season varied. Sometimes, the arenas would cut a schedule short, but I think we averaged about forty to sixty games a season, including the play-offs. Depending on the arena, we'd get anywhere from one thousand to three thousand people watching us.

As I said, it was a physical game and a slower game, because you always had someone holding you or slowing you up with a fist in your chest. The players knew every dirty trick and clever maneuver that could be pulled on the court, short of drawing a foul.

There were a few big men, six-seven, six-eight, jumping center. But height was not that important because everybody knew how to box out a man. I could hold a man six-six out from getting a rebound. City College had a pattern of offense called *five moving pivots,* where everybody was actually a pivot man. You didn't have to be six-seven. You could be five-eight, just so long as you came out of the corner to set up for a bounce pass coming into you or a chest pass, you were a pivot man.

Concerning the creation of the NBA, it started as an arena-owned franchise. Madison Square Garden owned a franchise with the Knickerbockers; Walter Brown, who owned the Boston Garden, owned the Celtics; and so on. Since they owned the arenas, the owners weren't really going out on a limb financially. They could just place the nights that were available for them for basketball. If there was no ice show or boxing match, they could fit in pro basketball. In the American League, the owners of the teams would rent arenas because they were promoters.

The first NBA team to approach me to play for them was Washington. Red Auerbach, who'd just gotten the job as coach in 1946, asked me to come down and play for them. But I had played my high school and college and pro ball in New York prior to the NBA, my wife was pregnant, and I was involved in business in the city after I got out of the service. I was an optician. So I figured if I stayed in New York rather than traveling out of town I could still devote time to the business. I signed with the Knickerbockers, earning less money than I would have if I'd signed with Washington. But I figured business came first, and basketball was always a sideline. I enjoyed playing and if they didn't pay me I'd still have played somewhere.

I signed with the Knickerbockers that first year for $4,500. But in salary discussions with Ned Irish, who was president of the Garden at the time, he said he didn't know how the thing would develop, but he thought I would be able to maintain my job in the optical business while playing. It so happened that the schedule was too rough and I was able to spend little time in the optical business and so he promised me a bonus at the end of the year, which he fulfilled. I think it was $1,500, so my entire salary was $6,000 that first year. I could have made more with Washington, but I was at home, which was important to me.

I was high scorer with the Knickerbockers that first year, and the team went to the play-offs. We lost to Philadelphia in the semifinal round, and they wound up winning the championship. At that time it was not yet called the NBA, but the BAA, the Basketball Association of America. It took a couple of years before they changed it to the National Basketball Association.

The second year with the Knickerbockers Joe Lapchick, formerly of St. John's, became the coach. I guess I didn't fit into his style, or there was something awry there, because I was sent to Washington. It wasn't a trade of bodies, just money, the waiver price of $1,000. I went to Washington and played for Red Auerbach for two years. We went into the finals of the play-offs against Minneapolis while I was there.

Washington had the best record in the league my first

year there, although we didn't win the championship. We also had the best winning streak going—it was in '48/'49—which was recently broken by Boston. I think we had eighteen or nineteen wins in a row. We had a real good ball club. There was Bob Feerick, of Santa Clara, who held the best league shooting percentage; and Freddie Scolari, who also came from San Francisco. He was a great scorer. Bones McKinney, from Wake Forest, who later coached there, was also on the team. That was a big, fast-moving club. Good ball handlers, good shooters, and good rebounders.

Auerbach as a coach was the same as he is as a general manager. He recognized talent better than anybody I ever played for, and I played for quite a few coaches, some of the best. Red never wasted time in being the cheerleader, never said, "Let's go, let's fight." It was always corrective criticism. "Sonny, your guy goes to the right, play him a little bit to the right." "Feerick, your guy is slow, go up an extra six inches." It was one comment after the other, always corrective. He saw all ten men on the court, and I think he could review the entire game when it was over, how the scoring went, where the mistakes were made. If you were out there, you didn't dare take it easy because you knew Red would recognize your loafing, or when you did something wrong. And he has that extra sixth sense, something that most coaches do not have. Nat Holman, my college coach, was in my opinion the greatest teacher of basketball. He could develop a ballplayer to do things. He would teach the game, but he could lose sight of the score at times because he was so intent on teaching. Red was cognizant of everything that went on at all times, and I feel that was his claim to fame.

Joe Fulks was the first good jump shooter. The one-handed shot started with Hank Luisetti before I started college, so that shot was popular, but jump shooting was not. But once Fulks started using it, it was something that everyone started developing. If you could hang in the air a half a second longer than your opponent, you could get in closer to the basket and on your way down you could release the ball and get off an easy jump shot. So the fellow who could jump higher or hang longer had a distinct advantage.

I didn't attempt the jump shot because I was fortunate enough to be shifty enough and had enough experience that I didn't have to do that to get off a shot. This was mainly used by the big men closer to the boards. My scoring was done on a drive, or a set shot from far out. Maybe I made two jump shots in my entire career, but that was maybe against Slater Martin or Ralph Beard, somebody a head shorter than me.

After two years in Washington I was traded. Red had lost his job at Washington, too. The owner of the arena had fired Red and made Bob Feerick coach. Red went out to Tri-Cities [this team eventually moved to St. Louis after a short stay in Milwaukee]. I never found out what the reason was, but anyway, the owner appointed Feerick coach of the Capitols. Bob and I were roommates, but the thorn in his side was that his team was knocked off that first year by Chicago, who had the tallest man in the league, Charlie Halbert, who was six-eleven. He dominated the boards when Washington played Chicago during the season and he knocked them out of the play-offs. By this time Boston had acquired Halbert, and during the off-season after my second year at Washington, Feerick traded me to Boston for Halbert. I think he felt that if he kept the team the way it was and he'd won the championship it would have been considered Red's team. This way, if he made some changes, it would be considered Feerick's team. Washington ended up in last place that year and that was the end of the franchise.

Washington was a one-hour plane ride from New York and Boston was the same, so the trade really had little effect on me. If I was going further west, I probably would have packed it in. But I was able to get home on off days, contribute some time to the optical business, so it was fine.

Boston was not a very good ball club in those days. I joined them in the '49/'50 season, after they'd had a very poor year. The coach was Doggie Julian, who formerly coached at Holy Cross. He was not a well man and after a year he couldn't take the traveling so he retired. Walter Brown, the owner, who was quite a gentleman, also interested in international sports, by the way, asked me about a new coach. I recommended Red Auerbach. Fortunately, Boston signed him. I don't know if I was the big influence in Boston's getting him, but I did suggest Red for the job.

That year with Julian we had a pretty good team, and over the season we improved considerably. That year we got Ed Macauley, who was my roommate. And then there was a breakup in the league that year, several teams folded, and there were three backcourt ballplayers available. We had to pick out of a hat to see who we would get between Max Zaslofsky, Andy Phillip, and Bob Cousy. We got third choice and wound up with Cousy. He was a substitute in the backcourt when we started that year. Eddie Leeds started playing with me in the backcourt, but then Cousy won his job.

Cousy wasn't that good in the beginning. He was a phenomenal passer, a great team ballplayer, but he was not that good a shooter. I think he realized that to be a hundred percent ballplayer and not a ninety-five percent ballplayer, he had to develop his shooting. Also, he was a little too fancy for the pros. In college ball, you have one or two good defensive men on a team, but in pro ball all five men are experienced. Instead of giving a player a direct pass if he was free, as we did, Cousy would get up and do a pirouette or something fancy and then get him the ball. By the time he received the ball, the man either had someone on him or it wouldn't be an easy shot. We had to tell him to cut out the whip cream and just make it bread and butter. He learned very quickly. He was a smart ballplayer and he knew the game. It was just a matter of developing with better ballplayers than he'd played with in college in order for him to become a star.

Cousy was about six-two, but he had extraordinary hands.

With the ordinary man, the wrist breaks here, but Cousy's wrist broke two inches higher. The effect was that he had a dangling hand. He had wonderful control of the ball, and great peripheral vision, which allowed him to spot a free man and get a pass to him. He developed into a tremendous pro ballplayer by the end of his first year.

Red never forgot the abilities of older ballplayers. If he could pick up an experienced ballplayer, he would get something out of him at the tail end of his career. Red never looked at a box score to see who was scoring or who got the most assists. He wanted five men to fit together, and if he could get something out of a ballplayer that could help the cohesion of the ball club, he used him and gave him an extra year in the game before retirement.

We had the first black man in the league that year, Chuck Cooper. He was a delightful guy. Coop was about six-seven, a good ball handler, very good rebounder, though not an excellent scorer. But he was a real team player who would give you forty-eight minutes of hard play.

My last year was 1950/51. My wife was pregnant with our second child, and the game was not that important to me. The salary was not that much. I think I was earning $10,500 or $12,500 at the time, and I was considered in the top echelon of players. But I wanted to retire.

There was a problem. Walter Brown had written me several letters when I told him I wasn't coming back. He said something like, "You Jewish athletes, you and Auerbach, together, you're both stubborn. Come to terms." I said, "No, it isn't worthwhile for me to come back." Red spoke to me and tried to convince me to return, but I stuck to my guns and retired.

There's a story here about Bill Sharman coming to the Celtics because of my retiring. Red said I'd be at training camp and I said I wouldn't. They thought I was holding out for more money, but I just had no desire to play anymore. I had played enough years. My family and I had just had our fill of traveling. I was twenty-nine years old, I'd had one of my best years with Boston, scoring a little over 10 points a game. The 24-second clock wasn't in force at the time, so maybe you could double that because you didn't take too many shots in those days. But still, I decided I'd had enough. They were stuck. They hadn't drafted any backcourt men because they were sure I was coming back. I spoke to Auerbach about Sharman, who had started with Washington but had a poor year. Bill had said that he would probably stick to baseball, that his career was there. I said to Red, "Why don't you offer him a contract?" Red said, "He doesn't want to play and he's property of Fort Wayne, anyway."

We had a ballplayer named Bob Kinney, who originally came from Fort Wayne, and he said he was hanging up his shoes, too. Red worked out some sort of deal, giving Fort Wayne the right to Kinney, while Boston got the rights to Sharman. Bill called me up and asked me all about Boston. They offered to pay his transportation and give him some extra money—he wasn't getting much then, maybe $7,500 in Washington. He said no. They influenced him and he finally said, "All right, I'll try it one more year." And that one more year of playing with Cousy developed into a sensational career. So, in reality, I was quite instrumental in getting Auerbach involved and in getting Sharman involved in coming to Boston.

That was the beginning of Boston's dynasty. After that, Red got Russell and Heinsohn and the rest of them. It was a team that lasted for many, many years winning championships.

After retiring from the game, I started to do some television work. Ned Irish, of Madison Square Garden, asked me to be assistant coach of the Knickerbockers. I had to get permission from Boston, a release. But they wouldn't give it to me, because they thought I was still a decent ballplayer and they were afraid I was going to play for the Knicks. This condition lasted for years, that they wouldn't give me my release. But

24

they did give me permission to do television work, be assistant coach, or scout, or whatever.

I scouted for the Knicks for two or three years. I picked up Richie Guerin, who became All-League, and he wasn't a first choice. I also picked up Gene Shue, who also became All-League. Neither of them were heralded ballplayers by any means, but I think it was Holman's teaching and Auerbach's eye that helped me to recognize talent, and I was very fortunate that nobody drafted them before I did.

I also did some announcing. I worked with Bob Wolf, who I'd met in Washington when he was doing the Senator baseball games. He had gotten an invite to come up to New York to do basketball, and he wasn't that familiar with the game. Since I was retired and knew Bob, he asked me if I would help, so I did some of the color for him and analyzed the game. I think I was probably the first professional ballplayer to assist an announcer. Now they have former athletes in every sport. At the beginning, I used to whisper to Bob. I wasn't on the air and he would make the comments. Later, I did interviews at halftime. I did analysis, and I enjoyed that. I had to stop because I became a partner in a New York Stock Exchange firm, and they frowned on my working on television. So that was really the end of my being associated with basketball.

That first year out of the game was very difficult for me. I would go to a game and I'd be perspiring because I would be twisting, making moves in my seat, watching somebody make mistakes, and so on. I kept thinking who should have shot, who should have done this and that. But that only lasted for a year.

I had a good time while I was playing and, as I said before, I would have played somewhere, even without getting paid. I just enjoyed the game. But I don't know how the current ballplayer feels about that.

Getting back to the ABL versus the NBA, it was a big change for the ballplayers. The players in the ABL, as I said, had jobs. They were strong and experienced. When you came to the NBA you went to a training camp for a month and you had to be in tip-top shape physically. The ballplayers in the American League could not stay with the ballplayers in the NBA. It was a much faster game. It was a cleaner, more youthful game. I would say that fifty percent of the ballplayers in the old American League also went to college. They were just tough, good pros. But when it came to forming the NBA, I would say that ninety-five percent of the players had college experience, and there were very few who did not attend some college for some period of time.

Some of the players that stand out in my mind include Max Zaslofsky. Max started with Chicago and I played against him twenty or thirty times. He was a great ballplayer. He was very offensive-minded. He had a good touch and he was a good competitor. He was deceiving in his size, about six-three. There wasn't a phase of the game that he wasn't proficient in. He was court-wise. For a fellow who had only one year of college experience, he was just outstanding.

Max was one of the better guards I ever played against. Johnny Logan was another. Bobby Davies was a great backcourt ballplayer. Ralph Beard became an excellent backcourt player, and so did Angelo Mussi of Philadelphia.

George Mikan, who played for Minneapolis, was a great pivot man. I don't know whether he would do as well in today's game, because the seven-foot man today is much faster than George was in his day. George's scoring was done from the pivot. He didn't face the basket and he was strong enough to ride somebody on his back and then turn and make the score. He was a very good rebounder. He'd plant himself close to the keyhole, the ball would come into him and he would maneuver for the shot. They had an enormous team: Jim Pollard, who was about six-seven, [Vern] Mikkelson, who joined the team a little later on, as tall as George and a little more agile. So they had three good rebounders and they dominated the league for quite some time.

As for particular games that were memorable, I don't remember scores or statistics too well. I do remember the games where I had fights. They stand out. But one particular game I recall when I was with Washington and we were playing against the Knicks in the play-offs. I had a phenomenal night. I think I made every field goal I attempted and every foul shot, too. I just didn't miss a shot. And it wasn't that many points, maybe 18 or 20, something like that. It was a night when we knocked the Knicks out of the play-offs and Joe Lapchick came over to me and said, "You're probably the biggest mistake I've ever made in basketball." It was the previous year that he'd traded me away from the Knicks, and I appreciated that comment. So that game stands out.

Other games that should stand out, where I might have made a foul shot when time was running out, or a winning basket with no time left, are just a blur. But the fistfights and that particular game against the Knicks do stand out.

One day we were playing Minneapolis in Washington, I think this was the fourth or fifth game of the play-offs, and I was having a very hot hand and Mikan wasn't doing too well. Mikan had been knocked down, fractured his wrist, and had to play the rest of the play-offs with a cast, which made him quite dangerous. Anyway, Mikan had a friend who played with him, who probably wouldn't even have been a pro player if it wasn't for Mikan. We had played Minneapolis for two or three years and this player was on that team but he never guarded me. Anyway, he came into this game of the play-offs to guard me and he was so pent up, so upset that Mikan was hurt, that the first shot I threw up he slapped me in the face. No foul. "What's that for?" I said. He said, "Mikan broke his wrist." Something like that. And the second time he did the same thing. I said, "The next time you touch me I'm going to deck you." And he did, and I decked him. We were both fined something like two or three hundred dollars. In those days that was big money. So I had my fights. Those days are gone but remembered.

When I was playing, the league had a rule: You could fly, but if your plane was canceled you had to be able to get there by train. So many of the trips were made by train. Some of the tough trips, of course, were flying to Chicago and then going to Minneapolis. We'd fly to Chicago, then take a train to Minneapolis. We had trips to Toronto, St. Louis, Indianapolis, and many of them were by train. We would read, we'd play cards, but there wasn't much gambling because we couldn't afford to lose much. And then there was storytelling time to pass the traveling hours.

Most of the time, though, we slept. We were tired, because those were very difficult trips. I remember one trip to Toronto where we had played a game. We had to go to a small town near Toronto to catch a train after the game. Three cars picked us up to drive us to the outlying station. Going there, the last car had the starting five because we were the last to get dressed after showering. Our car broke down. We were stuck in the mountains of Canada and had to hire several cabs to get us to a railroad. It was an all-night affair, but we got to Providence the next night just in time for the ball game.

We ate sandwiches, peanuts, whatever we could. We had many bad experiences traveling, and a lot of funny situations, or maybe they just seemed funny because we were overtired.

One time, leaving Toronto, the customs agent asked what we were taking out of Canada. This was in the middle of the night. They'd wake us up to ask us. Leo Gottlieb, who is no longer with us, had a keen sense of humor. He was upset that they woke him and he told the customs inspector he took out a malted. The customs man said, "What'd you take out?" And Leo said, "A malted." The customs man said, "Show it to me," and Leo said, "I can't." We were hysterical for several minutes.

Bones McKinney, who played with me at Washington, would not fly. He said, "If He'd meant me to fly, He'd have given me wings." That was the first time I'd heard that expression. We'd leave for Indianapolis a half day after Bones because he'd travel by train. This particular evening Bones didn't make the meal we'd always have together before the game. We were on the court practicing when Bones walked in with a patch over one eye and using a cane. The train he was on had had an accident, and the cabbie he'd paid extra to rush him to the arena also had an accident. It was a harrowing experience for him.

The players were very close back then. On the road, we were always together, eating, going to the movies. We knew each others' families, our wives would sit together at the ball games. There was a close association. I still speak to Ed Macauley, as well as some of the other old-time ballplayers, coaches, and referees. We still get together. Red Auerbach and his wife and my wife and I are still friendly.

The only injury I had in all the years I played was a broken nose. I was out for maybe two or three games. That was an unusual experience. We were playing at the Armory on Lexington Avenue. We didn't play all our games at Madison Square Garden, you see. We must have been 20 points ahead of Cleveland in the third quarter. It was a cold, snowy, winter night. I lived in Manhattan Beach at the time. I dove for a loose ball and a fellow tried to kick the ball away and kicked me in the nose. My wife was pregnant at the time and she was sitting in the first row. The players all ran over to her instead of me. There was no doctor at the game. I had to go back to Madison Square Garden to see the doctor, who was covering a fight. Here I am, no shower, my wife has a big stomach, and we have to grab a cab to the Garden. The doctor said, "This is nothing, Sonny. I see these all the time." And he snapped it back in place. "Go over to St. Clare's Hospital and get an X ray." I did, and it was negative, no concussion.

It was a snowy, miserable night, and we had to go back to Manhattan Beach. We got on the BMT subway. You have to see this picture. A fellow with two black eyes, broken nose, all perspired, shirt and tie open, and this woman with a big stomach, sitting on the train. I was carrying a Knickerbocker bag, so everybody probably assumed I was a basketball player. But I won't forget that night. We got to Manhattan Beach and I was a mess.

My game strength was court savvy. I could set up plays. Red Auerbach called me his second coach on the floor. Cousy said the same thing. I could tell somebody that his man was weak here or there, capitalize on what was going on. I was a very good shooter. When my defensive man played close to me, it was very easy for me to get around him. I wasn't fast, I was quick, and my getting around my man would cause someone else to switch over to me. I was also a good passer. Macauley loved me. He'd say, "Drive some more," instead of shooting. His defensive man would come up and take me and I'd give him a bounce pass and he'd have an easy lay-up. Scoring didn't mean anything to me. The assist didn't mean anything to me. It was the win that was most important.

The 24-second clock started the year after I stopped playing. I think it was a great addition for the spectator. If you're brought up in a basketball environment, you can appreciate good ball handling, dribbling, and passing, but ninety percent of the people go to a ball game to be entertained and the 24-second clock makes for marvelous entertainment. I think it's a great thing for the game to have scores of 150 points— and the shooting percentage is phenomenal. Today's players are much better scorers than we were. The old players didn't shoot as much, and the more you shoot the more proficient you become. Average scores when I was playing were in the eighties and nineties. I'd go through some games and make six or seven baskets out of nine attempts, where these fellows today take that many shots in a quarter. These players today want to shoot often, and they can shoot within ten seconds, so you don't even need a 24-second clock. They're so fast, their strides are so long, they're down the court in two seconds, and the ball goes up within five or six seconds. All they need is for someone to stand in front of their defensive man. They take one step, hang in the air, and the ball goes up.

30

I have always enjoyed the game. I find ex-athletes, especially basketball players, sharp and alert and pleasant to be with. They have good dispositions. They know how to lose and how to enjoy winning, and they don't take unfair advantage of people.

Nat "Feets" Broudy

Nat "Feets" Broudy

Nat "Feetsie" Broudy is seventy-two and has been a bas-
ketball "junkie" for most of his life. His association with
the game began before the establishment of the NBA and
includes a stint as a scout as well as working in the pub-
licity department of the league. For the past twenty-eight
years he has been the timekeeper for both the NBA and col-
lege games at Madison Square Garden. He lives in down-
town Manhattan, no more than a bounce pass from the
South Street Seaport, and his apartment has the appear-
ance of an annex to the Springfield Hall of Fame. There
are the awards and certificates he's received, including a
life-size gold basketball from the NBA, a score of auto-
graphed copies of books pertaining to the game, and a
large ceramic ashtray made by Maurice Stokes. But per-
haps the item he's most proud of is an autographed towel
that hangs, framed, above his bed. "Bill Bradley," he ex-
plains, "like all ballplayers, was very superstitious. He
used to come out of the locker room with a towel in his
hand, wiping his perspiration, and as he ran past me sit-
ting at my table he'd always throw me the towel and I'd
use it to rest my elbows on. Before his last game he took
a new towel and signed it to me and my sister, Evelyn. He's
a great fellow."

I was born and raised in Brooklyn. My name is Nat but in Yiddish it's Nisel and when I was growing up kids started calling me *Nisel fissel*. *Fissel* means feet in Yiddish, so naturally they began calling me "Feets." My mother hated that name, but it stuck and even today some of the ballplayers don't know my real name.

I first got involved in the game after friends of mine who played basketball for LIU graduated and signed with the Philadelphia SPHAs, which stood for the South Philadelphia Hebrew Association. I used to travel to Philly to see their games and I became very close with Eddie Gottlieb, who was like a godfather to me. In 1946, when he was part-owner of the team, I used to sit on the bench with him and keep the fouls. It wasn't long before he had me scouting for him in the New York area.

Later, Eddie bought the team from Pete Tyrell, who owned the arena they played in. In those days each arena was for a team, like Pittsburgh, Philadelphia, Toronto, they all had their own arenas. That year there were eleven teams in the BAA, which stood for the Basketball Association of America. The next year the league was down to eight teams and eventually they merged with the National Basketball League, which was mostly made up of teams located in the Midwest.

I'll tell you how that happened. The game was starting to get very popular. There was an Armory on Park Avenue and 34th Street, now it's a school, and the teams used to draw very well down there on open dates. All eleven teams in the BAA were owned by fellows who owned arenas. So all the arena owners met and decided to have a league with Mr. Maurice Podoloff as the commissioner. He didn't know much about basketball, but he was a lawyer who owned the New Haven team and the arena they played in, so they figured that was good enough.

At that time they had a salary cap, which is why someone like Dolph Schayes, who played for NYU, ended up with Syracuse rather than the Knicks, who would have had him as a territorial pick. You see, they'd reached their cap. As it was, the Knicks tried to get all the New York–area ballplayers like Ossie Schectman, Leo Gottlieb, and Ralph Kaplowitz, who played for the SPHAs, and Sonny Hertzberg, who played for the New York Gothams. All the teams tried to maneuver so they could get ballplayers from their area.

For instance, Eddie Gottlieb got the assistant coach from Penn, Howie Dallmar, since he was already in Philadelphia. He also got Joe Fulks, who was, to my mind, the first jump shooter. He came from Kentucky and he used to shoot and you just couldn't stop him. He was about six-five and a terrific leaper. "Jumpin' Joe" Fulks, they called him. You know, in those days you never saw a jump shooter, although years ago in a Newark YMHA there was a fellow we used to call "Hooker" Cohen. He used to shoot one-handed like Hank Luisetti, and people were amazed in those days because everything was done two-handed in the eastern area. But Joe Fulks was really the first I ever saw do it in the pros. Everyone was amazed because he got his shot off so fast, and he was tall so you couldn't block it. He was six-five and he could jump a foot and a half off the floor, which means he was close to eight feet when he shot the ball. And they weren't shot blockers as they are today. I once saw him score 63 points against Indianapolis, which was tops at that time.

That one-handed jump shot caught on very quickly. Bud Palmer, who played for the Knicks, started shooting one-handed and leaving the ground on his shot, but he didn't get as high as Fulks. And then Carl Braun of the Knicks started shooting one-handed. But Fulks wasn't an all-around player. He was a great offensive ballplayer, but on defense you had to help him out. Because, you see, in the Midwest and West they never really played defense. Everyone was shooting, shooting, shooting. Out there it was strictly an offensive game. Of course, in the East you knew the player was going to shoot with two hands, which gave you an opportunity to block the shot. But people can shoot further with two hands. To this day sometimes you'll see fellows take a long shot from half court with two hands, because you can shoot further that way. In fact, there was a fellow named McDermott in the old American League who used to shoot from the center of the court with two hands.

In the early days my main job was to scout the New York area, which meant seeing every team that came into Madison

Square Garden. By this time—1951—Eddie Gottlieb had bought the team, which was now called the Philadelphia Warriors, and made one of his ballplayers, George Senesky, the coach.

I remember scouting a fellow named Walter Davis, but not the Walter Davis playing today. This Walter Davis was a high-jumping champion in the 1952 Olympics. He played basketball for Texas A & M. We drafted him and then, later, he played for the championship St. Louis team. He was a white fellow who could really rebound. I recommended him and Eddie signed him. I also scouted Larry Costello and Eddie drafted him, but he was homesick so Eddie traded him to Syracuse. You recommended a lot of ballplayers, but sometimes you couldn't get them for various reasons, including the territorial draft.

To this day I've always thought the highest of Oscar Robertson. I always said that Oscar was the best basketball player, pound for pound, in the game. But now, you see, I'm leaning towards Larry Bird, because Larry does everything— pass, shoot, rebound, play defense. Oscar was so talented. He used to go through the first half of the game just watching his team and then gradually he'd see what he could do for them in the second half. If he needed points in the second half, he'd go out and get them. He used to feed Jerry Lucas and Wayne Embry. But Oscar was territorial, so we couldn't get him. Jerry was territorial, too. Incidentally, George Steinbrenner had Jerry's contract when he owned the Cleveland team in the American Basketball Association.

Of course, there were some surefire successes that turned into failures. There was Paul Hogue from Cincinnati, for instance. He never really made it in the league because he was too slow. But you couldn't always pick that up from college play because they don't use the 24-second clock. I also remember a tall kid that the Knicks drafted who couldn't see. John Condon, who was the announcer at the Garden, and I were sitting at the table during a game when this kid comes over to check in and he asks us, "What's the score and how much time is left?" He couldn't see that far. But he also just didn't have the ability to play in the pros. There was also a guy named Workman from West Virginia who played for three different teams as a first-round draft choice, but he never made it either.

I'll tell you how I started timing. I used to sit there and watch games from the bench. One day, in the Garden, one of the timers saw me just sitting there. They'd just found out that one of the regular timers had been gambling on games, so this other fellow comes up to me and says, "Why don't you do the job as timer, Feets, you're sitting here anyway?" So I did it. I worked the 24-second clock. Eventually, this fellow retired and I became the timer from 1971 through now. I've been timing at the Garden for twenty-eight years now.

I did the timing for the first 24-second clock game in New Haven. The 24-second rule was originated by Danny Biasone of Syracuse. It came after that Fort Wayne–Minneapolis game that ended 19–18. He figured that without a clock the game was lost because teams would hold the ball and they'd just foul the other guys and walk the foul lines back and forth. He had a scrimmage in Syracuse and he decided that 24 seconds would be just enough time. A pro team could get the ball over the line in ten seconds and then there'd be enough time in the remaining fourteen seconds to shoot. As we used to say, "They'll end up with arthritis in their arms from shooting too much." So they tried it out in 1954/55. Maurice Podoloff was then president of the league and he had an arena in New Haven where they used to play some exhibition and some league games. Philadelphia was playing Baltimore up there in an exhibition game, and I did the 24-second clock and it worked perfectly. The rule went like this: If I take a shot and I don't hit the backboard or the rim, the clock still goes; but if I take a shot and hit the backboard or the rim, the clock starts over again. There was some confusion that first game, but not too much. It worked very well, considering it was a new rule. But at times the ballplayers were a little bewildered because when the horn rang and the ball was in the air, just as the clock ran out, they thought the half was over, but it wasn't. I don't care what they say, there's no question in my mind that the 24-second clock saved pro basketball.

I've seen some pretty good ballplayers and some pretty good
teams over the years. Bobby Davies, who played for the
Rochester team, was the first to use the behind-the-back dribble. I remember when he was playing for Seton Hall in college against LIU. Clair Bee [the coach of LIU] was so smart.
He knew Davies was going to go behind his back on the
dribble, so he had his man playing on the right side, and then
he had a man on his weak side running to his left so that if he
went to his left on the dribble this guy would box him out.
The Royals were a good passing team, which I enjoyed. They
were also a smart team. They had Davies and Red Holzman
and Bobby Wanzer.

The Lakers of that era were also a good passing team. Jim
Pollard was very good. He played on that Mikan Laker team.
That team used to play the game of waiting for Mikan to go
into the pivot. Mikan played with a six-foot lane, he never
played with the sixteen-foot lane, so he was closer to the
basket and he was very strong. That team always moved off
the pivot because that's where Mikan was. That team was a
great one because they had Vern Mikkelson, Mikan, and
Pollard: six-ten, six-nine, and six-six. But Pollard could jump
like a six-eleven guy. It was an enormous team for its time.
They didn't have the 24-second clock then, so they would wait
until Mikan got to his offensive basket with his back to it. That
team was responsible for widening the lane to sixteen feet.

Max Zaslofsky was another great one. He died of cancer
recently. He played one year for Joe Lapchick at St. John's
and then the new league started and he went to the Chicago
Stags. He was one of the top scorers that year. He was about
six-two and he had a very good shot and he was quick.
He wasn't fast but he was quick. He went well off a dribble.
If the guy played him too close, he used to go around him.
And he had a good, soft, one-hand jump shot. He didn't go
up that high, but he had a good shot. He played close to ten
years and had nothing to show for it because there was no
pension back then. I remember he came to the Maurice Stokes
game just before he died. He was so weak we had to help him
out of the car. We played that game that year so he could

have some money to help him pay some of his bills.

The 1955/56 championship Philadelphia team was a good one. They had quite a few Philly boys: Tom Gola, Paul Arizin, Neil Johnston. Johnston was originally a baseball pitcher for the Philadelphia Phillies. They had good team play, with two good scorers like Johnston and Arizin. Johnston had one of the best hook shots you'd ever want to see—either way. He was always a scoring leader. But when Bill Russell came into the league it was a different story, and I'll tell you why. No one mentions this too much, but Russell was a lefty. Now on hooking, a player will go right into Russell's left hand. And he was six-nine, six-ten. That's why he was so great. Johnston had to go out and develop a little jump shot. Russell changed the game entirely because there are so many right-handed ballplayers. Another thing, when you're a lefty in the pro game it does so much for you. Why? Because the right-handed ballplayers are moving to their right. Now, if you're a lefty you've got the whole left-hand space. You're out there on your own.

Then, with Russell, naturally the Celtics took over. They lost one year to the St. Louis Hawks, but I think that was the year Russell was hurting. There's no question about it, the Celtics were the greatest team. They didn't invent the fast break, it was always in the game, but they certainly honed it. Rochester used to use the fast break a lot because they didn't have too many big players. Arnie Risen was six-ten and they used to have a guy named Arnie Johnson who could get them the ball. Once you get the ball you can fast-break. Without the ball you can't. Syracuse, too, the year they won, had a good fast break. Johnny Kerr was a good ballplayer for them. He used to have an expression: "If not for basketball we'd have the biggest elevator operators in the business."

Tom Gola was a better player in college than he was in the pros, but he was steady. He'd always help you out on defense, which doesn't show in the box score. Paul Arizin was a great offensive player. It was because of Arizin and Neil Johnston that Philly won the championship that year. [Bob] Pettit was an incredible player. He could do everything. Pass, shoot, defense, a great team player. [Dolph] Schayes, too. At one time he had a cast on his right hand so he became a left-handed shooter.

Now Wilt [Chamberlain] was a funny ballplayer. He could have been so much better if he'd have gone to the basket more. You see, his shot was going away from the basket, that fadeaway shot. Now teams, as soon as he went to bounce the ball, would double-team him. But he was the strongest player I ever saw, I don't care who they have now. I once saw him nearly take Johnny Green of the Knicks into the basket. He was dunking the ball and Johnny Green wanted to stop him and Wilt nearly stuffed him into the basket.

I was at that game where he scored 100 points. It was in Hershey, Pennsylvania, and he made twenty-eight out of thirty-two foul shots, which was unbelievable for him. You know, the Knicks tried to hold up the ball so he couldn't get it, but Guy Rodgers just kept feeding him. He was so hot. Just consider that he made twenty-eight foul shots. They were playing in Hershey because Eddie [Gottlieb] used to play some regular season games there because he trained there. He wanted to give them the satisfaction of seeing one or two games a year. It was not only the crowd, which was only about four thousand, but the team itself that was excited as he kept scoring. Philadelphia did something smart. They let the Knicks score so they could get the ball back. The ballplayers themselves couldn't believe it when Wilt hit that one hundredth point.

But Boston always had a better team than Philly. To this day Wilt will tell you that if he'd been with Boston and Russell had been with Philadelphia, it would have been a different story. One thing I'll say, Wilt is his own man.

Slater Martin, who played with the Knicks, the Hawks, and the Lakers, was a great defensive ballplayer, quick as a cat. He had great basketball sense and nowadays you don't see much of that. Dennis Johnson has it. Isiah Thomas has it, but not too many. They figure their ability is enough. You hardly ever see someone boxing out. They figure they can jump over everyone and they'll get the ball. But it doesn't work that way. If the ball bounces a pickle away, they're lost because they're going straight up. But if they'd been boxing out, they'd get the ball. Dick McGuire also had that innate basketball sense. So did Larry Costello, Bob Cousy, and Bill Sharman.

The best ball handlers I ever saw were Cousy and McGuire, although Oscar controlled the ball better than anyone. He was so big and broadly built. But they were quick, although Cousy shot off the wrong foot. Cousy was a great passer, but remember he had the team behind him: Heinsohn, Russell, Sharman, and Ramsey.

Russell had more impact on the game than Wilt because defense wins games. Everyone can shoot. You see in the playgrounds everyone is shooting. That's why I enjoyed the sixties and seventies Knick teams, because they played defense. They thought Frazier was a great defensive ballplayer because he took a lot of gambles. But guys like DeBusschere and Reed would be there to help. It was the same thing with the Celtics. K. C. Jones took a lot of gambles, but remember he had Russell in the background. Tommy Heinsohn took a lot of gambles, but he had Russell in the background. In my mind, that's what basketball sense is. They knew their teammates would maneuver, that they'd switch off. Nowadays you don't see that. Kareem's a great ballplayer, but he doesn't switch, he doesn't get the rebounds he should.

I used to rate the pro ballplayers for *Basketball* magazine. The only thing I used to take off the stats were the foul-shooting percentages. Everything else was my own opinion. I gave ratings to each player in the league. Four was perfect for each category: driving, shooting, playmaking, defense, and foul shooting. Oscar was the only player I gave a perfect score of 20. Elgin Baylor got a 19.5 one year. The players took it very seriously. In fact, I was once doing the timing of a game in the Garden when I was served with a subpoena to appear in Cleveland. Why? Because I didn't rate Dick Barnett. I only rated NBA players and he'd jumped to the ABL so I didn't rate him. Eventually, though, the lawyer for the NBA settled it out of court.

There are differences between the game today and back in the late forties and fifties. For one thing, the biggest difference is the 24-second clock. Secondly, the fellows today are far superior athletes. They're so superior they don't look for their teammates as much as they did years ago. "I'm doing my shtick and let someone else do their shtick" is what they think. Also, the balls are much better molded today. I think then the ball was a little larger. Also, now the seams are wider than they were so you can grip the ball better at the seams.

There's another difference today and the difference is like night and day. Today the guys are very selfish, but the old guys would do everything for you. I'll tell you a story about that. Today they don't know about Maurice Stokes. They figure they got all the money in the world and they don't have to worry about someone else. Years ago I used to hold the Stokes game and I would have some thirty-odd players offering to appear. Nowadays, if I get eighteen I'm lucky. One year Wayne Embry wanted to shoot me because I didn't bring enough extra uniforms with me. I'm very close to the ballplayers today, but I'll tell you I don't go into the dressing rooms much anymore. The ballplayers of yesteryear were very close, even with opposing teams. Oh, you have some today who are close, but it isn't like it was years ago. Then they used to go out to a bar and drink beer and talk about the game. Today they run, as soon as the game is over they run. And today they don't talk basketball. And also there's the drugs now. Years ago they didn't know about it. They didn't know anything about it.

But I'll tell you, that championship team of the Knicks in 1969, they were very close. They even had nicknames for each other. Walt Frazier was Clyde from the movie *Bonnie and Clyde,* because he was so well dressed. And we used to have a nickname for Dave DeBusschere: "the Pole," because that's what keeps up the tent, because he did all the rebounding. They used to help each other out. Like they helped out Bradley, who wasn't such a good defensive player.

Nowadays, in my mind, the players are much more talented individually, but years ago it was a team game. I enjoyed basketball years ago much more. Like now everyone's looking to shoot, but years ago they'd turn their heads to see who was free under the basket and pass it to them.

As I mentioned before, I do the Stokes game every year. Maurice Stokes was a great ballplayer. He did everything. Got the ball off the boards. Scored. A great, great ballplayer and a great fellow. He had what they call sleeping sickness. He got hit in a ball game, and Jack Twyman took charge of him, took care of all his expenses.

Haskell Cohen, who was the publicity man for the NBA, and Milt Kutscher decided they had to do something for a fellow like Stokes, so they got together with Twyman and brought up the idea of a memorial game. I used to be very close to Haskell Cohen. I was a part-time worker for the NBA at that time; I used to strip the papers and cut out articles for the publicity department. He said, "All right, Feets, you pick the teams." So I've been picking them for twenty-eight years now. The players really took to it. One time Wilt chartered two planes and he still got there late. Pettit came one day from summer camp in Vermont. He got held up and finally arrived late by car from New York. As soon as Red Auerbach saw him he said, "He's on my team." He was the All-Star player that day.

Usually, the games are close the first half. The resort wants the game to end in time for the evening show, so I run the time for the second half accordingly.

One year I picked the teams for Red Auerbach and Red Holzman. Now Auerbach didn't have a good record there. So he says to me, "I want this player." I said, "All right." Holzman says, "Why are you making trades for me?" I said, "Red, don't worry about it. You'll win." And sure enough he won it in overtime. But it's a good-natured game. Years ago they came from all over to play. And near the end, if it's a close game, they take it very seriously. They'll call time-outs just like a regular game. I try to make the teams as fair as possible.

All in all, I love what I'm doing. I'm getting paid for something I love. How many people can say that? I finished my twenty-eighth year last year and I'll keep going as long as they want me.

Robert Davies

Robert Davies

Bobby Davies joined the Rochester Royals in December 1945, while they were still members of the old National Basketball League. Three years later, the team was absorbed into the new Basketball Association of America, which eventually became the National Basketball Association. Davies played for the Royals until he retired after the 1954/55 season. During that period he established himself as one of the premier guards in the league. It is generally acknowledged that Davies originated the behind-the-back dribble, while playing his college ball at Seton Hall. Today, after having worked for the Converse Rubber Company for twenty-seven years, he is retired and lives in southern Florida with his wife. They have three sons and one daughter.

When I was ten years old and living in Harrisburg, Pennsylvania, we had one basketball court at City Hall. However, it was seldom available. To improvise, we played in the alley, tacked a five-gallon paint can to a telephone pole, and used a tennis ball as a basketball. We would shovel snow out of the alley in the winter in order to play.

Never giving basketball a thought, other than something to do in the winter months, when I was twelve years old a playmate said, "Why don't you go out for the junior high basketball team?" I said, "Do you think I can make it?" He said, "I think you're as good as the star of the team." I said, "Maybe I'll give it a try," because sports were my life. I made the JV team. We were undefeated that year and I was the second highest scorer. I was very small, which made me quite quick. I was able to do a lot of things as a result of our playing in the street games, which taught me all the jukes, feints, and moves needed for basketball. Those games were an unbelievable teacher.

My varsity year in junior high school I was benched because I was so small. I played maybe two or three minutes. When I went into high school as a blond, blue-eyed kid, they kept me on the JV squad as the fourteenth man. After that, things started to progress. I don't know exactly how it happened, but by the end of the year I became the number-one reserve, then captain of that reserve team, and even played in a varsity game for about ten seconds as a tenth-grader. What a thrill!

My confidence was now confirmed, but it was back in the ninth grade where things were nurtured. When I was down my father had said to me, "Stop fretting and pitying yourself. Just go out there and get to work." I loved my father and he was right.

I went to high school at five foot, 90 pounds, and grew to five-eleven, 142 pounds, as a senior. Today, I'm over six foot and weigh 175, my playing weight. I went to college at Franklin and Marshall for one year. We had a great team and were undefeated, but a lot of promises were made to me which were not fulfilled. While at Franklin and Marshall, which didn't have a baseball team, I was also playing semipro baseball. That summer, the Boston Red Sox scout saw me and signed me to an option to play with them when I graduated from college. I received a bonus and went to Seton Hall on a full baseball scholarship. I was an infielder, a shortstop, but coach Al Mammaux made a second baseman out of me.

46

At Seton Hall, they were unaware that I was a basketball player. After leaving Franklin and Marshall and having that good year, I knew basketball was my better sport. In baseball, I was able to run, field, steal bases; but my hitting was suspect.

I made the freshman basketball team at Seton Hall. They didn't know who I was, being from Pennsylvania and all, which meant that I played a different style ball from the New Yorkers. For some reason, the priests liked me, so I made the starting team and things progressed from there.

We played the pros when we were freshmen at Seton Hall. We played Kate Smith's Celtics, with Bobby McDermott, Davy Banks, and company. We beat them by 15, 20 points, just running. We ran them into the ground. My teammates joined me with the midwestern style of play, which was run and go. That was forbidden in New York, and the pros just couldn't keep up with us.

In the Midwest, which was considered just outside of New York, it was full-court basketball. In the East, they were bringing the ball down slowly, which made it half-court basketball. When I was a kid I couldn't afford to pay to see the high school team, so we would look through a crack in the door. The only thing I could see was the foul-lane area and the basket on the other end of the court. I'd see these great black players jump in the air, throw the ball, hit somebody with a pass, or shoot the ball, and I guess that stuck in my mind. I think that's what helped me to become a playmaker. I always figured that it was best just to get the ball down the court, get there first, and get in a two-on-one situation where I could pass off for a goal rather than score myself.

When I first arrived at Seton Hall, they played a slow game which lost me. It seemed that the faster I could make things happen, the more I was at an advantage and my opponents were at a disadvantage. So I would just take off. My roommate was from Akron, Ohio, and played that way, too. The other three players were from New York, but it didn't take long for them to join us.

We beat the varsity that first year and, as I recall, we

47

only lost one game that whole year. We were undefeated my sophomore and junior years, and I think that our style of play made the difference. Kids outside the city were all uninhibited and gung ho. The city kids were very wary and very cautious, which I think explained their slow style of play.

My coach at Seton Hall, Honey Russell, was a Hall of Famer, and he was the ideal coach. I couldn't have been more fortunate than to have played for him. They once asked him what offense he used and he said, "I gave the ball to Davies and that was my offense." Of course, that hurt us sometimes.

The idea for the behind-the-back dribble came to me after I saw a movie with Hank Luisetti and Lloyd Bridges, made about 1938, just after Luisetti graduated from Stanford. I saw Luisetti come down the sideline and put the ball behind his back and then go to the middle of the floor on a ninety-degree move to the left. When I saw that I immediately said, "If I could do that at full speed and dribble through a whole team, I could be the greatest basketball player in the country." I was, you know, only fifteen years old at that time. So I used to lay in bed at night and visualize myself dribbling down the floor and one person trying to come at me, to stop me. I'd just take it behind my back. Then another opponent would come up and I'd take it behind my back again and I'd beat him, too. I just dreamed of beating every opponent and walking in and laying the ball up for the hoop.

During my junior and senior years in high school, I would practice dribbling the ball behind my back. It's really very easy, but just like the jump shot or the dunk, nobody ever thought about it in those days. So I worked it out and it wasn't very difficult. The hardest thing was when somebody came at me to steal the ball. I'd have to get up ahead of the ball to get it behind me in a fraction of a second, or in a reflex act.

I practiced when I was fifteen, sixteen, seventeen years old, and I didn't actually use it until I was eighteen. It came to the forefront in 1941 in Madison Square Garden when we played Rhode Island in the NIT [National Invitation Tournament]. Many fans knew I was using it while I was at Seton Hall. I always tried to use it once against every team we played, and some of my opponents who used to play against us in '39 and '40, who I've seen since, said they knew it was going to happen and they were wary about guarding me because they thought it would embarrass them. But it was in that game against Rhode Island that the behind-the-back dribble really came to the forefront.

The reaction to it? Well, I've said this many times and it's been in print. One priest was winding his watch—this was told to me by priests from Seton Hall—and he had it off his wrist and when he saw that move he just threw his watch up in the air. And I was told that another priest died of a heart attack just at that moment. I question that, but they say it really happened. That's not one of the happier moments that transpired, but that was a reaction. And, of course, we beat Rhode Island by 19 points and that sealed my popularity, so to speak, in the New York area, and as New York goes, so goes the country.

The Red Sox didn't pay for my education. They gave me a bonus and my only agreement with them was an option that if I decided to play professional baseball I would play for their organization. It was now the spring of '42 and instead of being drafted I enlisted in the Navy and went to Great Lakes where I played for the Great Lakes Naval Training Station. We had a great year, going 34 and 3. I guess we were the best service team in the country during the war.

That fall, I played in the All-Star game in Chicago against the National League pro champions, the Oshkosh All-Stars. We won the game and I was selected the MVP and that set me up as far as the pros were concerned. We didn't give the pros much thought at that time because there was only the old National League. However, in 1945, on my way home after picking up this MVP award and being discharged from the Navy, a Seton Hall teammate of mine was asked by Les Harrison, the owner of the Rochester team, whether he knew of any good ballplayers. This friend told him that he knew the best offensive player in basketball—don't forget, this was 1945. Les asked him how to get in touch with me. My friend said, "I think he's in the Navy, overseas."

49

*   *   *

I finally got word in Chicago that someone was looking for me and I talked to Les. At the same time, other friends of mine were playing for Sheboygan and Youngstown. They also contacted me, so I had an opportunity to go with any one of three teams. It was like being a free agent, so to speak. I looked at the records and saw that Rochester was 8 and 0. I knew the players, people like Red Holzman and Fuzzy Levane. I knew they were good and so I said, "That's my team."

When the owner, Les Harrison, asked me how much money I wanted, during a phone call, I gave him a figure and suddenly the phone went dead. Finally, Les said, "Let me talk to my brother, Jack." Eventually, they said okay.

Otto Graham, Chuck Connors, and Del Rice were also on that team. In those days, the season was something like forty-four games, in addition to forty or fifty exhibition games, because whenever you had an open date they'd book an exhibition game because it meant more money.

The following year, I went to Seton Hall as a basketball and baseball coach. I had all of Honey Russell's great prospects and great players. Bobby Wanzer was one. We went 24 and 3 that year, and at the same time I was coaching I also played ninety-five pro games in the National League. Whether it was a league game or an exhibition game, I received $100 a game. That year, I became the MVP of the National League and Les gave me a bonus of $2,000. He also paid my income tax, which was part of the deal, so that year I made roughly $15,000, which was by far the highest ever. Recently, when I was talking to some of the best hockey players in the NHL, they told me their top pay during that period was only $5,500.

By the way, this was probably the only time anyone ever coached a top college basketball team and played pro basketball at the same time. It was my best year coaching and my best year playing. But thirteen straight nights on a train, a sleeper, whew! Don't the present-day pros have it rough!

Anyway, Les wanted me to be higher paid than George Mikan, so that year I think I did make more than he did. After that, I signed a four-year contract for $50,000.

Other than Mikan, that was probably one of the highest contracts in the league. Most of the players were getting only $7,000 or $8,000 a year. In those days, we had two contracts. Two contracts were drawn up because the maximum salary could only be $7,500, so I had another contract for the summertime. I'd talk to one or two people about an ad for the program, and that would account for the extra money.

In 1948/49, the NBA was starting and they wanted the three solid teams from out of the NBL. These teams were the Rochester Royals, the Minneapolis Lakers, and the Fort Wayne Pistons. We had the players, the BAA had the arenas, so we joined them. Teams like Oshkosh and Sheboygan were upset, because they thought we ran out on them. But anyway, we went with the BAA. The next year, they changed the league name to the NBA.

When I started playing with Rochester it was either us or Minneapolis who would win it all. They had the big men and we had the good little men. That was the difference in a nutshell.

Of course, George Mikan would always beat us. Originally, George played for the Chicago Gears after he graduated from De Paul. He only played with them at the end of one season and then the Gears became the Minneapolis Lakers.

We managed to win the division in 1951 when Mikan had a hairline fracture in his foot. But that was the only time we beat them out. And whoever won that division would always beat the other division champions.

But Mikan was the difference, just like Bill Russell was with the Boston Celtics. It was murder playing against Mikan because when they needed two points, he'd get the two points. One year we held the other Lakers to four field goals, and we beat 'em. We just let Mikan get the ball all the time, while the other players were neutralized. Later on, this ploy didn't work so well.

With Minneapolis, our set shooting was our one asset. But they'd come up on us, force us around and into the big men, and we couldn't get set up to shoot, and that did make the difference.

51

George Mikan cost me a lot of money in advertising, too. He got all the endorsements. Jim Pollard and I had one endorsement for Wheaties and this did put us on the backs of some comic books at that time.

While I was playing pro ball the coaches and players would not let me put the ball behind my back. They'd say, "You're making the other players look bad and we don't want that." So I was limited in my style of play. I'm sure that, above all, Les Harrison is sorry that he curtailed what I did, because it's an asset to today's game and it's show business. If you can do something and do it well, exploit it. And it did take a big part of my game away. Players today are not limited in the pros, though they are limited in what they can do while playing in college.

When the 24-second clock came in, our team was starting to age. I think what precipitated the 24-second clock was the Rochester Royals team of Franny Curran and Red Holzman. Curran was, at that time, the best dribbler in the game. He was from Notre Dame and he could dribble it forever and no one could take it away from him. With a lead of 8 or 10 points in the middle of the third quarter of a game in New York City, coach would put Frank and Red in the game and they'd just dribble until the final whistle. It was the big stall, and the other teams couldn't take the ball away. Of course, this deep freeze, taking place in New York as it did, upset the fans, upset management, and upset the sale of tickets, I'm sure, so the league had to do something. Danny Biasone of Syracuse gets much of the credit for the clock, although we all thought a 30-second clock would be better.

There were other modifications, too. Mikan was responsible for the twelve- or fourteen-foot foul line. This didn't change the game much, I don't think. If it did, it was negligible and no one noticed it. As far as the 24-second clock was concerned, it just meant that Franny and Red couldn't save the game for us.

The introduction of the jump shot into the game was very disturbing, because to guard someone like Joe Fulks was very difficult. Suddenly, you had to guard someone shooting on the move. This was next to impossible when we first saw it. I played against a player from Rhode Island, Howard Shannon, in 1949, who was the first opponent I played against to use the jump shot. He wasn't the greatest jump shooter in the business, but he could score and he did present a problem. I never really had to play against that many jump shooters because I retired in '55 and they were just beginning to come into the league in the early fifties. But when I did, it was an ordeal.

I never thought of using a jump shot. In fact, I spent four years learning the set shot at Seton Hall. When I came out of Pennsylvania, we had never seen a two-handed shot. I'd do all my scoring beating my opponent and getting lay-ups, on the fast break. When I went to Seton Hall, my teammates shot those long set shots. This bothered me, but I practiced and practiced and watched Bobby McDermott, who always faked and stepped backwards before shooting, so I was able to develop that shot. McDermott played for the Fort Wayne Pistons and he was far and away the outstanding set shooter of our day. He could shoot from thirty feet and he was very, very accurate. He had that high arch on his shot. Freddie Scolari, who played for the Washington Capitols when Red Auerbach coached the team, once said that Bobby Wanzer was the most accurate of all the two-handed set shooters of all-time, and he added that I was the fastest, the quickest two-handed shooter. I wasn't as accurate as Bobby Wanzer, but the set shot was good to me. The Lakers said we were the only team able to fast-break to a set shot.

The toughest player I had to play against was Bill Sharman of the Boston Celtics. I'd have relished playing against Bob Cousy because he gave up the ball one out of every three or four times down the court. But Sharman, when he got his hands on the ball, would always set up to shoot. He was by far the most accurate basketball shooter of all time.

Cousy, of course, was the best dribbler. Trying to take the ball away from him was very difficult. George Senesky, who played for St. Joe's and was the top scorer in the country

53

in college, was the toughest defensive player that ever played me. If I'd try to go around him he'd stick his arm out, and he was so strong I just couldn't get by him.

But nobody was as good as George Mikan. If you beat George you did a great job. But I think the greatest moving pivot I ever saw was Alex Groza. He was mobile, he'd get the ball in the pivot, he could dribble it under the basket, and then get the lay-up. The fastest player I ever played against was Ralph Beard. Beard was like a swarm of bees. I'd give him a fake, he'd be over against the wall, and before I could shoot it—and I shot it pretty quick—he was back in front of me again. He was six foot and built like a fireplug. Beard and Groza were from that Wonder 5 from the University of Kentucky. They went into the National League in toto as the Indianapolis Olympians.

My biggest game was against New York on Christmas Eve, 1949. I've even got the film of the game. At the end of the game, the score was tied and I was isolated against Dickie McGuire. I had to either shoot the ball or draw him in and drive around him. So I faked him and went around, but he's got me locked and I'm going out of bounds, and as I go out of bounds, in the air, I use a Frisbee-type throw with my left hand and the ball goes in the basket and we win the game. I scored 33 points that night, by far my best scoring game ever.

I remember that game. My arms were tired because I never shot that much. But the game did go two extra periods and that helped me get a few more points. Luckily, I have the film.

My best college game was against Baltimore University. Baltimore has the ball out-of-bounds with five seconds to play and they're ahead by one point. They throw the ball in bounds, and I was lucky enough to steal it, go down and make the basket just as the buzzer went off, to preserve our thirty-six-game winning streak. Another game that meant a lot to me was at Great Lakes when we played in the Sugar Bowl and beat Stanford, who had been the NCAA champs the year before. I got the MVP award and that was the highlight of my service career.

As far as travel was concerned, we had it rough because we traveled by train. We'd leave Rochester for Minneapolis at say 10:30 on a Saturday night, rushing to get from the end of the ball game to the train on time. Sometimes, they even had to hold the train for us. We'd get on an all-night sleeper to Chicago. We'd get up at 7:00 A.M., and then at 9:00 A.M. we'd catch the *Hiawatha* to Minneapolis. We'd get there at 3:30 and play at 7:30, and then rush to catch a train at 10:30 back to Chicago, so we could get on to the next game.

The only difficult thing for the present-day players is the time-zone changes. When you eat four meals a day and sleep fifteen hours a day, and you work at most forty-eight minutes a game, how can it be a rough life? I don't understand the present-day ballplayers who complain about work and travel. We played as many games as they play today, except many were exhibition games. I used to gain weight during the season and lose it in the summertime. That was because we'd sleep fifteen hours a day, eat four meals a day, and play only forty minutes a game. Traveling on trains, we'd either sleep or play cards. We'd play a lot of pinochle. You could read, but not many of us were readers in those days.

There were a few characters. There was Chuck Connors. We'd play in Sheboygan or Oshkosh and we'd be in the hotel tavern that night and Chuck would make the band and everybody stop playing and dancing so he could get up and recite "Casey at the Bat," or "The Face on the Barroom Floor." They wanted us to go on radio shows, but we were not receptive to that. But Chuck said he'd go only if he could recite his poems. There was a closeness in those early days that we didn't really enjoy later on. You can't forget that in the earlier days the war had just ended and everybody was so happy that the war was finally over. It was a celebration time for the years of 1946, '47, and '48. Later on, it became more of a business. But in those days there was an athletic camaraderie. Today everybody seems to go his own way.

You might call me a loner, really, because, though I can't say why, I didn't like to sit in barrooms and drink beer. That wasn't for me, but the other guys would go and that's where trouble might start. A little envy might creep in insofar as what some guys might be making in the way of salary. But I liked to stay away from that.

There were fights during those days. I remember when I got involved, a player would hit me and I'd say, "Did you really mean that or was it an accident?" He'd say, "No, I meant it," and then real trouble erupted. Other times, you'd get into little ruckuses, but they were mostly harmless and accidental.

The fans could be pretty rough. In Syracuse one night at halftime a spectator came onto the floor and said, "Davies, if you don't lose this game you're not getting out of here alive." But I took it with a grain of salt. Not today, though.

Another time we were playing in Anderson, Indiana, where the Anderson Packers played in the old NBL. The fans were pretty rabid there. We were the top team in the league and I remember I'm at the foul line and—bingo!—a paper clip hits me and sticks in my hand, just as I'm getting ready to shoot the foul.

The Syracuse fans were very vociferous. The Fort Wayne crew used to holler and boo me, but they did it in a respectful way and they were some of my favorite fans, really. I remember when we played the 1953 all-Star game out there and I scored 9 points in the last quarter to win the game, they were clapping for me. It was like I had played for Fort Wayne all my life. They even gave me a nice retirement gift when I played my last game there.

As all pros do, I loved it when the fans booed me in the other towns. Our fans in Rochester were great, really high class. They would come in fur coats, the whole first ten rows were very affluent people, and they loved us. We were really close-knit. We could only seat four thousand. Rochester's not a city like New York, but in those days most of the towns were like ours: Fort Wayne, Oshkosh, Toledo, most of them were the same size.

In the early years, our big rivalry was with Fort Wayne

because they were the National League champs prior to the entry of the Rochester franchise. By the way, the reason that Syracuse and Danny Biasone formed a team was because Les Harrison of Rochester had one. They said, "If they can have a team in Rochester, then we gotta have one of our own in Syracuse," and that's when they hired Al Cervi away from us to be their coach. We were bigger rivals for them than they were to us, because they were fledglings, so to speak, and new in the league. But they came on as one of the better clubs in the league, and later they were NBA champs.

I had a very good relationship with Les Harrison, the owner of the team. I never had a contract dispute with him. He gave me everything I ever wanted, and he's been very generous throughout the years, even today. He was the owner/coach of the team, but with Les it wasn't so much that he was a coach as he was an owner. He looked after his own like George Steinbrenner looks after a lot of his people today. But what Les said went.

I always had problems with referees. Right now, though, I am very close with all the referees that worked the games when I played. We, as players, sometimes make mistakes and sometimes the refs make mistakes, too. My favorite story concerning a referee was with Sid Borgia. He was quick. He had his own rules and a lot of people didn't like him, but I liked Sid because he was quick and I thought he was the best of the officials. If something happened, he always understood what it was. One game in particular, Bob Brannum was coming down the center of the court—he was big, but not as agile as some of the other players. I got in front of him and he went up in the air and I caught him on my back and as I caught him, I looked to Sid and he was ready to call a foul on me. In my mind I'm saying, "Sid, I'm helping him or he'll get hurt." Sid looks at me and he doesn't blow the whistle. Instead, he shook his head and gave me a look that said, "I understand." I thought, what other referee would be that quick to realize what had happened? We had communicated in a thousandth of a second. Yeah, he was a character. There were a lot of good referees, but to me he was the best.

*   *   *

I had a good year when I was thirty-four, but I found that at
thirty-five years of age I just couldn't play the night game and
then be ready for a game the next night. I was just washed
out. The recovery factor wasn't there. Unfortunately, I was
the playmaker, so that drained me, too. I had to control the
game and the ball, so to speak, and it just wore me out. Like
a pitcher in baseball, I needed two days' rest. When you slow
down and lose that step, sports are not as much fun as they
once were, because now you're just half the ballplayer you
were ten years before. Age was a factor, and there was the
recovery factor, too. I finally said, "It's time." We were losing. We weren't the ball club we once were, and it's not fun
when you've been winning all your life and you were able to
take charge and control the situation. No longer could I control the game and this took the fun out of it for me.

Over the years, I was pretty lucky with injuries. The
worst was to my left knee and today, because of it, I can't play
tennis. It was 1949 in Chicago. We were playing Sheboygan
in one half of a doubleheader. I fell and a six-ten center fell on
my knee. I rolled over, but my lower knee didn't roll at all. I
played the rest of the game, but the next morning I couldn't
bend my leg. It was ripped up pretty good and it was six
weeks before I could play again, and when I did come back I
was a step and a half slower. A newspaper writer said I was
finished, but I knew better. I did come back and had a lot of
good years after that.

The other serious injury I had was to a finger. In Fort
Wayne, I sustained a compound fracture of the little finger on
my left hand, tore all the extensors and flexors. I was shelved
for three or four weeks with that one.

But back then it wasn't like the crazy injuries they have
today. A strained back, a pulled hamstring. I don't understand the injuries today.

Today it's not the same basketball game we knew when I
was playing. We used to play the game below the basket and
now it's played above the hoop. When we played we'd maneuver for shots and the game was an aesthetic game, great to

watch. Now a player just takes the ball and jams it in the hoop. I don't know who can stop them.

It's quite different today. When you think about it, it's the only game where the players are better than the game itself. It's a paradox, because it's the hardest game to play for little leaguers, yet it's the easiest game to play for the pros. You can't say that about any other game. In little-league baseball, the kids look good. In major-league baseball, the game is better than the players, otherwise you wouldn't have players batting only .210 or .220, and the pitchers would all be winning thirty games. In basketball, the players are just too good, it's too easy for them.

After retiring, I went to Gettysburg College and coached there for two years, then joined the Converse Rubber Company, where I worked in sales and promotion for the next twenty-seven years.

Overall, I'd have to say I was very pleased with my playing career. I was inducted into Basketball's Hall of Fame, won an NBA Championship, three National Basketball League Championships, had four or five undefeated seasons in high school and college, helped beat the pro All-Stars, was voted MVP in the league, MVP in two ball games that featured the top players in America. About the only thing I regret is losing three seasons, 1942–1945, during World War II. Otherwise, basketball has been very good to me, and to think this all started shooting marbles in grammar school.

Slater Martin. Knicks versus Minneapolis, November 11, 1955; Martin is the man on top, diving for the ball. (N.Y. Daily News Photo)

Slater Martin

Slater Martin was drafted by the Minneapolis Lakers in 1949 and played for this George Mikan–led Championship team until 1956, when he was traded first to the New York Knickerbockers, for whom he played for only a matter of weeks, and then to the St. Louis Hawks. He retired in 1961, after having won five NBA championship rings, four with the Lakers and one with the Hawks. A perennial All-Star, Martin was known primarily for his tenacious defensive play. Today, he lives in Houston, where he was born, and runs Slater's, a restaurant and bar.

I started playing basketball right here in Houston, in junior high school. I went to Jeff Davis High School here and had a coach named Roy Needham who was really well versed in the fundamentals of basketball, shooting and defense. He was a little bit ahead of his time, did a lot of defense and made you work at it. That's where I got my background in defensive basketball.

I was very small. In high school, I was like five-seven. I was skinny, but I was always quick and fast. I graduated high

61

school in 1943 and entered the University of Texas, but then I went into the Navy. When I was in the Navy, I grew to the size I am now, five-ten, and weighed about 165, 170 pounds, just about what I am now.

After I was discharged, I played a year of basketball and we won the Amateur State Championship. A lot of coaches saw me play and so I got a few scholarship offers. But I was like Darrell Royal [former football coach at the University of Texas] in that I was gonna dance with who brung me, so I went back to the University of Texas. I spent three years there under coach Jack Grey, who had been a commander in the Navy. When I was at U.T. before the Navy, I'd played a couple of preseason games and they counted that as a year of eligibility. When I came back, the coach tried to get me an extra year, but he wasn't able to do that, so I had just three years left on my scholarship.

By that time, I was five-ten, which was as big as I got. I was a scorer. Like everybody else, I learned to come up shooting. Everybody in basketball is a shooter. They don't practice defense. I was schooled in defense, so when I got to U.T. the coach spotted that trait in me and so I always had to guard the leading scorer on the other team. In those days, he might be six-four, but I'd just have to play him, that's all. It was something I could do and I liked it.

My last year at the University of Texas, I made All-American. That was 1949. I had no dreams of going into the pros, though. My dream was to play with Phillips 66, Oklahoma, which was in the industrial league and owned by Boots Adams, who was Bud Adams's father. You could get a job there and have a lifetime deal.

By that time, I was married, and me and my wife took a trip up to Bartlesville, Oklahoma, to talk to them. They were gonna hire me, no problem there, but they wanted to put me behind a desk for eight hours a day. I'm not a desk man, I'm an outside boy, and I told them that if they'd let me stripe the softball field and dig pipelines, whatever they do outside, that would be all right, I'd play for them. But I couldn't work inside. But they told me, very politely, that their people were all inside people. I said I'd think about it, but I turned them down.

Instead, I went up to Minneapolis. A scout had seen me play at the University of Texas when we'd taken a trip up to New York to play some of the teams up there. He recommended me to the Lakers. There was no contract talks. They sent you a contract in the mail and you either accepted it or not. I imagine if I was six-ten, I could have dickered with them, but at five-ten I just wanted to see if I could make it.

The contract was for $3,500 and if we won the World's Championship I got a $1,500 bonus, which would make it $5,000. But what I didn't understand about that contract at the time was that if we won the World's Championship we got the $1,500 anyway, because it was the bonus for the deal, for winning. So they screwed me, excuse my language. Therefore, every year I held out for more money and they didn't like that at all. But I got more money every year from the Lakers, every year I played—seven years in all, except for the year they traded me.

My wife and I packed up our '49 Ford—it was a little coupe—with everything we had, and went up to Minneapolis 'cause I just figured I was gonna make the team. We got us a room in a motel for $3.70 a day.

We practiced at the Minneapolis Athletic Club, and there was nobody even close to my size. That year, there were three rookies that made the team: myself, Vern Mikkelson, and a boy named Bob Harrison from Michigan. Herm Schaefer was the old steady hand at the game. Herm was about six-two, an All-American at Indiana in like 1939, paunchy, fat, very smart, slow, but he was a good passer. We had Arnold Ferrin, from the University of Utah. He was about six-five. And Bob Harrison, who played guard at six-four. There was also Billy Hassett and two boys from the University of Minnesota, Tony Jaros and Don Carlson.

We had Jim Pollard. He could dunk the ball behind his back, over his head. He had tremendous leaping ability. We called him the Kangaroo Kid. Like Dr. J, he could leap from the line and dunk it. He was a tremendous player, very wiry, a skinny guy who played guard, forward, center; he could do it all. Jim was one of the best you'll ever see. Mikkelson was the lumbering type, but you couldn't out-rebound him. Bud Grant played with us, too [Bud Grant later became the coach of the Minnesota Vikings football team]. He came off the bench. A spot player who was a good, tough rebounder. He'd knock you around if you had to be knocked around. He was a good defensive player, who didn't take no crap from anybody. Bud could do anything. A tremendous athlete.

There was a guard before me named Don Foreman, from New York. He was a little guy. I played against him when I was at Texas and he was at NYU. He was probably my size, and why they let him go, I don't know. I never asked. I was just glad he wasn't there. I was just trying to make the team. I didn't think it was going to be that hard because I could guard everybody there with no problem. I was awfully quick. I could stop and start—I did have that attribute—and I was always in shape. I could run all day. Play two, three games a day. I didn't smoke, drank very little. You didn't really have time to drink, and you didn't have the money, either.

I could also shoot. I'd just come out of the University of Texas where I'd just got through setting the Southwest Conference scoring record of 49 points. But up there I didn't have to shoot the ball, which made my job easier. All they expected out of me was to hold Bob Davies or Bobby Wanzer or Bill Sharman or Bob Cousy to 12 points and then we'd win the game. If I got 6 or 8 points extra, I was home free. Besides, they found out I could pass the ball.

It was actually a very easy game for me. We played it very slow. It was just the opposite at U.T., where we'd run, run, run. But Mikan, even if you got a fast break, wasn't involved in it because he was back at the other basket.

The first time I met George Mikan he was very gruff. George was a tremendous competitor. He couldn't see, he couldn't jump, he had bad feet, his arms swung out opposite from what yours and mine do, elbows stuck out, and the arches of his feet were so bad he had to have supports in there to get him up. So actually, when he put on his shoes, he was about seven feet tall. But he'd never admit how tall he was.

I got along with George very well. We'd have team meetings all the time. If you'd get beat on the road once or twice, they'd say, "Let's have a meeting 'cause something's going wrong." They'd jump all over George because he got all the glory. He was the man. But he deserved everything he won. He always treated me nice. We didn't have any problems on our team at all. We had one player, I'm not going to mention his name, he had a wife that got on him a little bit. But that was only at home. On the road, he was tremendous. We were very close. We went out and ate together all the time.

I didn't like the weather up in Minneapolis, and my wife didn't like it either. But it was part of the life you had to go through to make a living, to do what you enjoy doing. I enjoyed what I was doing, playing basketball and practicing. I just enjoyed it. But I didn't like the long train trips we had to take. We'd play a game in Minneapolis one night, get on the train, go through Chicago, and wind up in Rochester. If the train was late out of Chicago, we didn't get in until three. We'd get into the city at six, have to go straight to the gym to play. We might have to catch the train right back and come all the way back to Chicago, then to Minneapolis to play again the next night and do the same thing, then go back to Syracuse the next day. I never could understand why we had to make that trip, when Rochester and Syracuse were only seventy miles apart.

We were in berths or had compartments. We'd play cards, if we were lucky enough to get a compartment. Of course, George [Mikan] had to sleep on the bottom bunk because he could set his suitcases up to put his feet on. That's the only way he could sleep.

On $5 a day, you couldn't eat too well on a train. My father was a stationmaster for the Southern Pacific Railroad in Houston for twenty-five years, and I'd been on trains a lot. He'd taught me that if you want any service on a train, you got to tip those porters or you don't get anything. Breakfast in those days on a train was like $3.25, so that blew most of your meal money for the whole day. So it was kinda rough getting a square meal. If we were playing Rochester, for instance, after the game we'd send the coach, John Kundla, to a little delicatessen down by the train, and he'd get all these sandwiches and milk, so we'd have something to eat.

Later on, we started flying and it was a little bit better, though flying out of Minneapolis was a problem, too. But we never did miss a game. I don't think any team missed a game because of the weather or anything like that.

When I first came into the league, I was wearing contact lenses. Gene Stump, from De Paul, also had contact lenses. I think he and I were the only ones in the league that wore 'em. I've been wearing them for thirty-seven years. In those days you wore big ones. Put water in them. Got a bubble in them, you couldn't see. You'd tell the referee, "Hey, let me change them," and he said, "Get the hell out of here and play." They didn't know what they were. You couldn't take a time-out. So when they had the time-out, I'd change them. I never lost them. They were so big they covered the whole eyeball. Took a mold of your eye; put clay in your eye, then molded it. Not like the little ones. I wore them just to play. I had the small ones for off the court. The bigger ones were just for play. You had to pick them out with your thumb. Gene Stump is the only one I ever saw in those days who had 'em. When I went to Minneapolis I had the small ones and he told me to get some of those big ones. I asked if the team would pay for them, they said no.

I never did find an easy player to guard. Every time I had to go out there it was tough for me. Cousy, with his ball handling and other skills, and Sharman were both tough. Cousy had a lot of guts as far as shooting. He might miss three times, shoot four more in a row, miss all of them, and then make the next one. Some of the players I guarded would take me in the low post. Of course, the line was narrower in those days. Like six foot across, and you could step across it. It was tough for them to drive against us. We had Mikan standing there. And Pollard might reach across and grab you.

They had some real tough players then. A boy from Fort Wayne, Curly Armstrong, and Frankie Brian, Freddie Scolari, Bobby Davies and Bobby Wanzer. And sometimes, like Davies and Wanzer, they were on the same team. If Cousy went out, I'd take Sharman. That was just as tough a job as guarding Cousy. Sharman was such a good shooter. From a certain area, he was deadly. He was a hell of a good competitor, tough as a boot. Hell, you'd hit him, he'd hit you right back, but that was part of the deal. It's a physical game. I thought the first year I went to pro ball with Minneapolis it was the most physical game I'd ever seen. They didn't care if you were six-eleven or five-eight, if you came through there, they'd knock your butt off. You weren't supposed to come down and try to make it easy.

In those days, you couldn't leave your feet. They'd just knock you into a wall. You didn't dare steal a ball, go up and dunk it, or they'd kill you. That was a show-off deal, and I couldn't dunk anyway, of course. I can't remember if Pollard ever dunked it in a game. I kinda remember him laying it in with two hands over the rim, but not any of this dunk stuff.

You get used to the physical part of the game, though. In those days we didn't have any doctor traveling with us, or a trainer. If you got stitches, the doctor had to come out of the stands. If you were in New York, you were lucky, because they had a doctor because of the hockey team. We had a doctor in Minneapolis, but he might not be there all the time. We had a trainer at home, but he couldn't sew you up. I remember getting stitches at the halftime, with whatever they had there. Japanese doctor in New York sewed me up several times. In those days you got a patch and came back. If you dislocated a finger, you'd put on a piece of tape. The next day, it swells up, but you still gotta play or somebody will get your job.

We had quite a few fights, but nobody held any grudges. It was just a situation, and afterwards, you'd go back to playing. Our fans in Minneapolis were great. We played in the auditorium there, and when we couldn't play there we had to play at the Armory, which was just like the Armory in New

York. The floor was built on concrete and so it was just as hard as playing on concrete, except there's a floor there. That wasn't easy when you fell, because it didn't give.

The fans at home were great. In Syracuse and Philly the fans were bad. In Philly, they'd throw things at you. In Boston, too. But I never did see that in Minneapolis. I think they were an older group, more sophisticated people up there.

Fans are funny. One time when I was with St. Louis we were playing Detroit or somebody in Madison Square Garden, the first game of a doubleheader. We were winning by 10 or 12 points. Players don't really pay any attention. Anyway, I stole the ball, made a basket, and as I was turning around, the guy on the other team threw it right to me. I just hooked it and kept running. When I came out of the game, the crowd gave me a standing ovation. It turned out it was because I'd made the point spread, but I didn't know that at the time.

Just like in every sport, every city wants their team to beat the champions, and they all wanted to beat Mikan. They'd boo us and him. But some people liked you. They'd talk to you on the sidelines. After all, you're there five, six years, so they'd get to know you. But they used to get on George wherever we went. Like in Fort Wayne, they found out Mikan didn't like smoke, so everybody came to the game in this little North Side gym and filled the place with smoke. They closed the windows and you couldn't even see. They were puffing smoke in there all afternoon.

I never really saw the fans get physical with the players. I had them pull the hair on my legs, though. But there's always a cure for things like that. They had a smart guy in Fort Wayne like that. We'd take the ball out, see, and since there wasn't much room between you and the fans, they could reach out and pull the hair on your legs. But the next time down the court, you'd just have a guy stand in front of him and then he'd move away real quickly and you'd hit the guy with the ball right in the face and that was over with.

It was hard to get up every night to beat a team, especially on their own court. When we'd go into Boston, they wanted to beat us so bad because we were World's Champions. They were trying to beat our brains out. The next night, you'd go to New York and they'd be the same way. New York had a real good ball club: Carl Braun, Sweetwater Clifton, Harry Gallatin, Vince Boryla, Connie Simmons, Dick McGuire, Al McGuire. Rochester had a good team, and they were in our division, so we had to beat them every year in the play-offs. Syracuse was hard to beat. Those fans would boo you like crazy. It was tough to beat Fort Wayne in Fort Wayne, in that little place they played in.

It was hard. You take a guy like Cousy, or one of them high scorers. He's got to maintain his average. For me, if I could get him below that, I figured we're gonna win the games. Or if he has a bad day, we're gonna win. He might get 25 points, but he'd still have a bad game. He might have shot twenty-eight times and made 6 and got fouled the rest of the time. In that way, the box score lies to you a lot. But he was a tremendous player. In Boston, at the third quarter we'd be ahead by 20 to 22 points and he'd have 10 points. Then he'd get 14 points in the last quarter, to end up with 24, and the sportswriters write about that. That made me mad.

The 24-second clock came in because of a Lakers–Fort Wayne game, which ended in a score of 19–18. We had played them the night before in Fort Wayne and just beat the devil out of them. We all got on the train, came to Minneapolis, to play them again. They had a coach named Mendenhall, and he just decided he wasn't going to try to run with us. So he just held the ball. We were leading the whole game till the last second and Larry Foust beat us; bless his soul, he died of cancer. Anyway, we get the rebound on a shot, but it slipped out of a guy's hand. There were three seconds left and Larry shot it. Made some kind of hook shot and rolled in off the top. Beat us 19–18. But during the game the fans were leaving. They wanted their money back. It was boring to watch a team sitting on the ball. People were reading their newspapers. They had to do something, 'cause if you're gonna hold the ball like that, you won't have any fans. They want to see you play. The guy from Syracuse, Danny Biasone, finally came up with a remedy which was tremendous for basketball. We had tried a lot of different things during the early years. Tried in the last two minutes if you made over two fouls to give the ball back. You got your choice, you could take it or give it over. It was just bad until they came up with the 24-second clock. I remember we played a game one time with a twelve-foot basket. They were always trying to make rules to get Mikan out of the game. That time the season was over. We were playing Milwaukee, who'd come in last. We experimented with this twelve-foot basket and we couldn't even throw the ball up there. From the free-throw line, you couldn't get it up there. You can't imagine how much arch you gotta put on the ball to get it up twelve feet. Besides, you couldn't rebound. Ball comes over, everybody is jumping, the ball's hitting you on the head. We tried everything.

But the 24-second clock didn't change our style of playing much. We just played slow. Pollard was very fast and Mikkelson was, too, but Mikan wanted to play slow, for us to wait until he got down there. He'd get the ball, hit you, bounce you around, then shoot it.

Mikan was a tremendous passer, by the way, and we had some good shooters on our team. We got Clyde Lovellette. I think he played one year while George was there. Then George retired and we went to the play-offs, but didn't win. I think Fort Wayne beat us in double overtime. Then, the next year, Mikan tried to make a comeback, but that didn't work, and they acquired some more Minnesota players, Dick Garmaker, Charles Mencel, and Ed Kalafat. Then they traded me because I wouldn't sign.

I was in Houston in '56 and I wanted more money. I was probably making $9,500, $10,000. I wanted probably $1,500, $2,000 more. We're not talking about nothing. It was a lot to me. But I'd never forgotten what they did to me that first year, and I played some good basketball for them. I wanted more money every year because I think I deserved it. Max Winter was the owner then, the same fellow who owns the

Minnesota Vikings, and there was another guy, Ben Berger. We corresponded about the contract, and talked on the telephone. They said, "Are you coming in?" I said, "Give me more money."

They wouldn't give it to me, so I opened a sporting-goods store here in Houston. The season had already gotten started, and I got a call from a sportswriter here in town. He says, "Would you go to St. Louis if they could get you a contract?" I said, "If they give me the money I'll go wherever." So he says, "Just sit tight."

In the meantime, Minneapolis traded me to New York for Walter Dukes. They didn't want to get me in the Western Division because they knew I'd beat them. Meanwhile, we'd made a deal with Mr. Ben Kerner [the St. Louis Hawks' owner]. He said to me, "You go to New York, stay for about a month, then I'll make a trade and you'll come to St. Louis." Over the phone he says, "How much do you want?" I said, "Mr. Kerner, we're two weeks into the season; can I get my back pay?" He says, "Sure. No problem." He says, "Can you win this championship for me?" I said, "Yes, sir. I'll do that. I'll see that you get one before you go." Took me two years to get it for him, but we got it.

I went to New York, played for three or four weeks, then they traded me to St. Louis for Willie Naulls. New York didn't know what was happening. There was only a couple of guys who knew what was going on: me, Mr. Kerner, and Ned Irish [owner of the Knicks]. I walked into Mr. Irish's office when I got to New York, we talked. He says, "You're gonna sign a contract." I said, "Mr. Kerner told me I'd get two weeks' back pay." "Oh, well," he says, "I don't know anything about that. Let's call him." We called and Mr. Kerner says, "Give him the back money." There was no arguing.

When I was playing in New York I liked it. It kinda went around that I was going to go to St. Louis, but it was just a rumor. They liked me in New York, and we were going great. Finally, we went on a western trip and we swung down through Fort Wayne. I got cut open real bad on top of my eye and they had to stitch me with a big ole stitch. My eye was all black. So I got to St. Louis the next day and I was calling my wife from the arena, and I'm all puffed up real bad. Mr. Kerner is walking up and down outside and I'm talking to my wife in Houston. I'm there maybe fifteen, twenty minutes on the phone, and I see this guy parading up and down. When I finally came out he says, "What's the matter with your eye?" I said, "I got cut last night." He said, "You gonna play tonight?" I said, "Why, certainly." He said, "Would you consider sitting out?" I said, "No way. You can't tell me what to do, I'm playing with New York." He said, "You'd be surprised what I can do," and then he said, "Okay, I'm going to let you play." We beat the hell out of them, we just killed them. Now we go to play them the next night in Milwaukee and he won't let me play. I don't get to play against St. Louis. But then we were going to Minneapolis, and he let me play there. All he had to do was call Mr. Irish and say, "I don't want Slater to play against me." So what could I do?

I was with the Knicks something like November to December fifteenth. I remember my first game with St. Louis because we opened up near Christmastime in New York against the Knicks. We had Pettit and [Cliff] Hagan, who was playing guard, way out of position. We also had Jack McMahon, who played with Rochester and was traded to St. Louis. He wasn't a real good dribbler; you could press him. So all we did was pick him up.

When I came to St. Louis Red Holzman was coach. Of course, with every team I'd ever been on, I'd run it. I said, "You gotta get rid of Hagan. He's a forward, put him down in the corner. So we put him in the corner and that was the end of that. He started developing into a tremendous basketball player. Ed Macauley was there, too. Kerner traded Russell for Hagan and Macauley. Mr. Kerner had the rights to Russell but he wanted the team to get started, to build it up, and he did by getting Hagan and Macauley for Bill Russell. They didn't know if Russell was going to play pro ball or not.

Ed Macauley was a good shooter, good rebounder, but he wasn't real physical. He didn't need to be, though. He could jump good, had a good competitive heart. He never quit on you, wanted to play all the time. I've seen some that had tremendous ability but wouldn't play a lick, didn't have the desire to play. I'd rather have the one with ninety-five percent desire than ninety-five percent ability who didn't want to play. Pettit wanted the ball. Mikan wanted the ball. All the good players want the ball.

I very much enjoyed playing with the St. Louis team. We were very close and we had a good ball club.

The first year I was there we played Boston. It was '56/'57 and they beat us in double overtime. We should have won that game, that series. Then we beat them the next year and they claimed Russell was hurt. They were using that as an excuse. Then they beat us again the next year for the Championship. So we played 'em like four years in a row for it. We could have beat them two out of the four years, since we took 'em to overtime. But they had a great team.

There are quite a few games in my career that stand out. I scored some thirty-odd points against New York in the World's Championship one time, in the old Armory. We beat them three in a row. They came to Minneapolis and beat us the first game, then we beat them the second, so we had to go to New York to play three in a row and we beat 'em three in a row.

Then there was the time I held Bobby Davies to no points one game. He didn't do nothing. I remember that quite vividly because he was so frustrated. He just had a bad game. It wasn't all due to my part. I just got going good and he got going bad, and he couldn't do anything right. I also held Cousy several times, defensive-wise. I had quite a few good ball games with St. Louis, 'cause I ran that club, too. I enjoyed it if I could make a good play, set a guy up, give him the ball, let him shoot, he'd make it, and that satisfied me just as much as making a shot myself. The main objective in the deal is to win, and that's what we did most of the time. I wasn't concerned with how many points I got, 'cause nobody was going to get on me about not getting 15, 20 points. If I happened to have a real good ball game, which I did many times, getting 18, 19, 23, 24 points, that was gratifying. But if you lose a game, it don't mean anything, scoring those kind of points. So those kinds of games don't stick with you. It's the ones you win and you might do something other people think, "What's so big about that?" Those are the things you remember.

I stayed around the same scoring average all the time—9, 10 points a game. And I never had a technical foul called on me in my life. I wasn't even-tempered—when I was coaching in the ABA, I got lots of technicals—but in the NBA you could talk to a referee. There wasn't no sense in me running up to him and making a big scene. Mikan would make a big fuss, 'cause you know he was a big star and if he got hit, he'd want a foul called. If I got hit and they didn't call a foul, I couldn't raise much Cain, because they would say, "I'm not gonna listen to you." So I never had any problems with referees because I just talked to them.

We had a few characters on the team. Larry Foust was a big jokester. I remember one time in Milwaukee when we were with Minneapolis. We all had one big room. That's what they'd get you. We'd all lay down on the floor to sleep. Well, Larry was in the bathroom shaving and he nicked himself. He was perspiring and he let the blood run all over his face. Got it mixed up with the lather. Larry was a big man, six-ten, and he came out of the bathroom, towel wrapped around him, and ran up beside Sihugo Green, who was a tremendous player. Sihugo looked at him. I thought he was gonna faint. Well, the rest of us looked that way, too. He had that blood everyplace and he just came out screaming and hollering.

When the jump shot came in, it was hard to play against it. You'd just have to play the man without the ball, try not to let him get it that much. Deny what you can. In the old days, you had to give and go, which they don't do much anymore. Now they do things down low. That's why you see them get the free baskets all the time, 'cause nobody's back.

They shot a lot of two-handed set shots above the head then, so you'd have to get up high. I remember I had to play against Carl Braun, who was six-four and a real good shooter. And Max Zaslofsky was a good shooter, too. You just had to get your hand up and do the best you could.

I played in 1960, but I got hurt. I was beginning, after eleven years, to get injuries. I'd never wrapped an ankle as long as I'd played basketball, never had a sprained ankle, never put a piece of tape on it. I could get dressed for a game in thirty seconds. I'd put on my jockstrap, slip on the jersey, and I was ready to go. I didn't have to wrap or do all that junk. But I did hurt myself in an All-Star game in St. Louis; pulled a hamstring. Ripped it and tried to come back too early. They needed me and I tried to play and I just couldn't. Then, during the play-offs, I pulled a muscle in the back of my leg and I was getting well; but we were going to Minneapolis to play and Mr. Kerner came to me and said, "Can you play?" I said, "Right now, I don't think so." He says, "Can you play if we give you some Novocain?" I said, "Oh, hell, anybody can do that." He said, "Will you do that?" I said, "If you want me to." So we got the doctor, went to Minneapolis, they stuck me with that thing and of course I couldn't feel nothing. We win the game, but I was out for the series. I had to have crutches, couldn't walk. Took me two, three weeks to get over it. I pulled everything, but I did what they wanted me to do.

The next year, I dislocated the bone in my leg, that was in '59, and then I played the '60 season. I was getting old. They wanted me to sit around on the bench and help. I said, "I'd rather go. Leave happy, like I am."

I coached in St. Louis for a bit. Mr. Kerner made me the coach when he fired Red Holzman, even though I didn't really want the job. I always thought that Red thought I came up there for that reason, 'cause he was always a little cool to me after that was over. Was no sense in trying to explain to him that I had nothing to do with it. Guy fired him, came by me, said see me in the office in the morning. I knew exactly what he wanted. I argued with him. I said, "You brought me here to play. I'll coach, but coaching and playing are two different deals." I said, "I'll help you out for a while, but if I see it's bugging me, can we find somebody else?" He said, "Okay." Now he didn't like Alex Hannum very much, but we finally came to an agreement after six or seven games. Alex and I would help him off the bench, a combination of the two of us. I went to Mr. Kerner and told him, "If you want to win this thing, you better let me play." I said, "I'll sit over there and coach, but if you want to win I've got to be out there." So he said, "I can understand that." So we changed it. I helped Alex while he coached. Mr. Kerner was big on that, hiring and firing coaches. I didn't want to do it, I couldn't do it, but I was under his power and he wanted me and that's why I did it.

I watch quite a bit of basketball now, but I don't go out to see it here very much. The game has changed. The players are bigger and better. They all shoot better and run faster. Got better places to play, better balls, better shoes. But I think the players are about half fruity. They seem like some want to play and some don't. And I can't understand dope at all.

One thing that bothers me is that they won't put the old-timers on the pension plan. They go back only to '64, I think. Nobody wants to get involved in this. They're scared, though I don't know why. I think you have to play five years before you're eligible. In my day, in '48 and '49, there weren't that many players who played that long. A lot are dead now, so you're not talking about picking up a lot of people or a lot of money. You're talking about taking care of people who could use the money. What really sticks in my craw is that they've got a player's representative on each team and they got a union, but they're not taking care of the older players. Do you think Abdul-Jabbar is gonna need a pension when he's sixty-five? He's making $2 million a year. You think Magic Johnson is going to need one? I have never found anybody with enough guts to bring this up. It's a shame, because most of the older players worked hard and got very little for it.

It wouldn't be so hard. I'd venture to say there's not fifty ballplayers who would qualify. And if you give them $1,000 a month, you're only talking about $50,000 a month and

$600,000 a year. That's only about one man's salary a year today. They could play a benefit game and get that much to take care of those people. After all, it was the older players that started this whole league.

I had a great career, but I've got to thank my beautiful wife, Fay, of thirty-nine years, for putting up with a boy playing a game he loved, and my two boys, Slater and Jim, for supporting and believing in me.

"Easy Ed" Macauley. (Courtesy Basketball Hall of Fame)

"Easy Ed" Macauley

Ed Macauley began his NBA career with the old St. Louis Bombers in the 1949/50 season, after being voted All-America at St. Louis University. When the Bombers folded, he signed with the Boston Celtics the next year and led the team in scoring with a 20.4 average. He spent seveal years with the Celtics and then was part of a trade that probably changed the history of the NBA, as Boston sent him and Cliff Hagan to the St. Louis Hawks in exchange for Bill Russell. Macauley finished out his career with the Hawks, coached the team for a while, then went into private business. He has also done some sportscasting—both football and basketball—as well as being in the cable TV business. Today he lives outside St. Louis and is, according to him, "semiretired, which is driving me nuts."

I started playing basketball in St. Louis when I was a Boy Scout. We didn't have a team in seventh grade, so we played at Scout meetings. Then, in eighth grade, we had a team at St. Barbara's, probably the worst team in the world. We did not win a game that season. We played thirteen or fourteen games and lost them all. We even played St. Francis Xavier, the best team in the city, and didn't score a point. Lost 33–0.

I went to St. Louis University High School, a private Jesuit school with a tremendous athletic background and reputation. My freshman year I didn't play on the team. I had a typing class from 3:00 to 4:00 P.M., and that's when the team practiced. But I liked playing basketball. I was shy. I was tall. And I was not too good with girls. So I guess I turned to basketball as something I could do, although I wasn't very talented.

We started playing outside school because we couldn't get into the gym, since the teams were practicing there. We actually did sweep snow off the court so we could play. As you'd play your hands would get chafed and sometimes your fingers would crack along the fingerprint line, and we really did put on gloves and play with them on.

I never had any goals in basketball. I just liked to play, and I guess my nature was that I just wanted to be as good as I could possibly be. That didn't include being an All-American, or playing in the NBA, or being an All-NBA player. I just wanted to be as good as I possibly could, which meant spending time in practice.

At the end of my freshman year, I was walking down the corridor and the varsity basketball coach, Jack O'Reilly, who was also a math teacher, was walking in the opposite direction. I was about six-five, and there weren't too many six-five freshmen anywhere. So we passed each other and nodded, and suddenly Mr. O'Reilly was walking next to me going in the same direction as I was. He said, "Son, did you play basketball here last year?" I said, "No, I had typing class." He said, "I really think you ought to play next year," and I did. I went right out for the sophomore team and that's when my success started, right? Wrong. As a matter of fact, I was a substitute on the team.

The regular, Larry King, had to quit school at the end of the first semester. His father had gotten sick and in those days there was no welfare or Social Security, so Larry had to go to work. So I got an opportunity to play, in a rather unfortunate manner.

In the second semester, I was a starter on the B team. I wasn't too good, but I did get some experience. I think during that time the techniques I used to become a ballplayer started. I began practicing a lot by myself, which I think is the way you have to learn any game. You have to spend time by yourself because if you don't, you don't get enough practice shots.

I'd go back to outside courts after high school practice and spend another hour or two trying to improve. The problems I had were the same any ballplayer had. In those days there was nothing to model yourself after, no TV, no pro basketball, no college basketball. All the guys were away in the service. So you just worked and hoped you did something right.

As far as I was concerned, I developed very slowly. I was not a very good ballplayer when I was young. I was skinny, weak, not very coordinated, and couldn't rebound very well. It used to astound me later on when I got the name "Easy Ed," and people would say, "I guess you got that name because of your ease, naturalness, and grace in basketball"—and it wasn't that way at all. The fact that I liked to practice and spend time at it was probably the difference as far as my career was concerned.

By the time I was a senior I was a pretty good basketball player. I was all-district and all-state and started to look upon the game as something I was good at. I was still shy. I didn't date much in high school, and spent a lot of time playing basketball. I had a few scholarship offers to Notre Dame, University of Kentucky, Boston College, Washington University, and St. Louis University. My father was an invalid, and I knew my mother wanted me to go to school in St. Louis, and the only place I could go was St. Louis University, because all the other Catholic universities in St. Louis were girls' schools.

So I accepted a scholarship to the University of St. Louis. But I wasn't convinced I was a great basketball player. A lot of players have tremendous confidence in themselves. I never did, not even as a professional ballplayer. I was always fearful

of my opponent. If we'd been playing a girls' school, I probably would have been fearful. As a result, I said to myself,
"You're going to have to be prepared because you're probably
not as good as these people," and that's why I spent so much
time practicing. I might go out and score 25 points, but I still
didn't have that confidence and felt I had to continue working. My physique wasn't in my favor. I was tall but skinny,
and got knocked around a lot, so there was a lot of work to do.

We lost three games my junior year, won the NIT, which
people said was bigger than the NCAA tournament, was voted
All-American, and was the MVP in the NIT [National Invitation Tournament], as well as getting the Gold Star Award as
being the outstanding player to appear in Madison Square
Garden. It was just a phenomenal year. My senior year was
another great one. We lost four games and went back to the
NIT. I was voted All-American, getting more votes, I think,
than anyone else in the polling.

So I wound up with an excellent college career, but I still
wasn't the most confident player. I worked best with a team
that had a system. I was a team player rather than a free-lance
player because I had not developed free-lance techniques. I
played in some All-Star games after my senior year, but I
wasn't that good because the individual players did a much
better job than I did.

When I graduated I was drafted by the St. Louis Bombers,
who had been in the old BAA for three or four years. The
league was pretty spread out at that time and not in good
financial shape with some very weak teams like the Chicago
Stags, the Bombers, the Sheboygan Redskins, and the Tri-
City Blackhawks (Moline, Rock Island, and Davenport, Iowa).

I signed a contract with the Bombers that turned out to
be a hell of a contract, I guess. They gave me a $10,000 salary
and $7,500 to sign, so I made $17,500 my first year as a
player. I found out this was an awful lot of money when I

learned that a fellow like Dick McGuire of the Knicks was making $7,500.

But the Bombers had to have me. Obviously, they felt the kid from St. Louis University, a college star, would come in and turn their fortunes around and they'd make a lot of money from me. But it didn't turn out that way. That was the worst team I ever played on in my life. We finished last in the division.

My first training camp wasn't like modern camps. We trained in Alton, Illinois, staying in an old hotel about forty miles from St. Louis. I didn't know the players that well. I was written up in the papers as the savior of the franchise, and, frankly, I didn't play too well. I wasn't that strong, or a good one-on-one player as yet. I relied on the organization of the ball club. If you could work the ball, get open, get me a shot, then I was tough. I could play defense, keep my man off the board, but I didn't dominate the boards. I wasn't that impressive and I'm sure the guys weren't that impressed with me. But I got along with them fine.

It wasn't anything like it is now. Compared to today, it was bush league. But that was as good as there was. You had an opportunity to play basketball. I was offered $300 a month to go with the Phillips Oilers in the Industrial League, so $17,500 looked a lot better than that.

I was not very good the first half of the season. The team wasn't organized and as a result I had to rely more on one-on-one play, and I wasn't really equipped to handle it. I was playing the pivot, but we weren't too smart a ball club.

But I did learn a lot of things, like how to drink, if I'd wanted to. And toward the end of that first year I finally figured out that if you're gonna make it in pro ball you gotta score. Passing to your teammates is nice, but if you've got a bad ball club and you can score better than they can then you're not helping the club by passing the ball. I was getting stronger, and the last thirty-five to forty percent of the season I started to look for my shots.

We were playing in Toledo against the Chicago Stags—

why in Toledo, I'll never know, but that's the way the league was in those days—and I made up my mind that I was going to get the ball. I would yell for the ball and I got angry. I guess it had some effect, because they got it to me and I got 30 points in the first half. And I guess that was the start, as far as I was concerned, of becoming a pretty good professional basketball player.

The last third of that season I probably averaged 18 to 20 points a game. I became the man everybody had to stop to beat the Bombers, and they did, so it didn't make much difference. But it convinced me that to play pro ball you gotta be a shooter, a scorer, you gotta want the ball.

We were playing against people like George Mikan, 250, six-ten, and I was six-eight, 190 to 195, so I had to rely on my speed and skill. I went to the free-throw line a lot because I'd get the ball in deep and fake. We had the six-foot lane, which I thought was wonderful. Of course, the other big guys thought it was wonderful, too, because they'd beat my brains out when I was playing defense against them. But I shot a lot of free throws, and got a lot of lay-ups.

I couldn't stop Mikan and he couldn't stop me. The only way I could stop him was to get him out of the game. There were many times when I would fake, drive, get inside him for a lay-up, and actually stop and wait for him to get close enough to me so he would foul me. If I could get three fouls on him in the first quarter or half, he'd have to go to the bench and then it was a lot easier for me and my team to operate.

The first team I played on had some good players, like the backcourt man, Johnny Logan, who had a great set shot. Red Rocha, who later played excellent ball for the Syracuse Nats and coached the Detroit Pistons. But we weren't great rebounders or great shooters. We were just a bad ball club.

Everyplace we went, we went by train. It took us twenty-two hours to get from St. Louis to New York. The guys would get on the train and bring two cases of beer. They'd go back in the bath area—if you've never ridden a sleeper you wouldn't know what I'm talking about, but they had a bigger area with washstands and benches, and the guys would go back there and drink till two or three in the morning, get to a town the next day, and play that night. One night we played in Baltimore and my roommate, a fellow I played with in college, D. C. Wilcutt, and I went to dinner and a movie. We got back to the hotel about ten-thirty because we had a game the next night against the Bullets. When we got there two of our best players were just getting dressed. We said, "Where the hell are you going?" I was pretty young and innocent at the time. They said, "We're going out to have a great time, see you in the morning." And they had a hell of a time and we lost the ball game.

We stayed in fair hotels, not the best, but not flophouses, either. We got $5 or $6 a day meal money. It doesn't sound like much now, but it was adequate, since we could eat on it. Seventy-five cents for breakfast, $1.25 for lunch, maybe $2.50, $3 for dinner and a couple of beers. So it was all right.

Our ball club wasn't a wild ball club, you know. Some of the guys ran around a bit, but nothing serious. We didn't drink a lot. Some of the guys played bridge, which was, I guess, a little sophisticated for some ball clubs, or we'd play hearts or poker. Our ball club didn't gamble a lot. Some, like the Knicks and, I think, Rochester, you know, guys would lose $50, maybe $100 a night, and that was a lot of money in those days.

There were great ballplayers in the league at that time. Alex Groza and Ralph Beard were over in Indianapolis before they got suspended. There was Max Zaslofsky at Chicago. George Kaftan was playing for the Celtics. Dick McGuire was with the Knicks. Dolph Schayes with the Nats, Bones McKinney and Bob Feerick at Washington, Mike Todorovich at Tri-Cities, Mikan, Pollard, and Slater Martin at Minneapolis, Bobby Davies at Rochester. Great players.

After my first year the Bombers folded, but before the year

ended Ned Irish [of the Knicks] tried to buy the whole club just to get me. Maurice Podoloff, the commissioner, said you can't do that. So the Bombers folded and we all went into a pool. I was picked by the Boston Celtics. At the time there was another league, the American League, and I got an offer from them to play in St. Paul, Minnesota. I didn't know anybody in Boston. I didn't know Walter Brown [the owner]. Later they signed Red Auerbach and drafted Bob Cousy, but at the time I was negotiating with Boston and I had a $10,000 contract. I indicated to them I signed with the Bombers, that was my hometown where I lived all my life, where I was planning to live, and I really didn't have any desire to go to Boston and that I was seriously looking to go to the other league.

I went to Boston and talked to Walter Brown about the contract. He said, "Well, you got a seventy-five-hundred-dollar bonus for signing and a ten-thousand-dollar salary, so why don't I just do this. Why don't I pay you seventeen thousand, five hundred dollars for this season." We talked about it. While we were having our discussion, Maurice Podoloff, the commissioner, called Walter, who told him we were talking about it just then. He said, put Macauley on the phone. He said to me, "If you so much as think of going to the other league you'll be sued, you'll be out of basketball, and your career will come to an end." Well, Walter and I were getting along fine and I was really aggravated that Podoloff came in with that kind of language. So I said, "Mr. Podoloff, do me a favor. You sue me. Let's go to court. Let's find out whether such things as the reserve clause are legal," and I hung up.

At the salary we discussed, I wanted to play in Boston anyway. I didn't want to play in the other league. I wanted to play in the NBA. So we got together and I spent six fabulous years in Boston with the Celtics.

Couse and I came the first year. We were later joined by Bill Sharman, Bob Brannum, Bob Harris, and Jack Nichols. It was the start of the Celtics dynasty.

We didn't have a rebounder. I wasn't big enough. I could

score, run, shoot, pass, play defense, but I wasn't a great rebounder. And we really didn't have a big ball club, and that's what cost us championships. Never did win the division championship or the NBA championship while I was there. But we started something, I think, and I'm still considered part of the Celtic tradition, at least I feel that way every time I go back. For a man who never played on a championship team in Boston, it's very gratifying to be introduced as one of the Celtics that helped form that tradition they have, and I'm very proud of that.

During my years with the Celtics we played against some great players like Dick McGuire, Carl Braun, and Sweetwater Clifton of the Knicks. Sweetwater Clifton was a great ballplayer and a quiet guy. As we found out later, he was quiet because he was somewhat afraid of his own strength. We got in a fight with the Knicks one night in the Garden, and Harris and Sweetwater got into a battle. Clifton was awesome. He doubled up his fists and used them like hammers. He didn't box, he just came in. We didn't want any part of Sweetwater Clifton. He was a nice guy and we were very nice to him.

Charlie Cooper was on our ball club. He was the first black to play in the NBA. I'll never forget, we were in training camp in Boston, and Charlie and John Mahnken, who played with the Washington Caps, and I went over to a little restaurant to get some carryout. We got one carton of baked beans with one spoon and we asked Charlie if he wanted some. He said, "Yeah, just put 'em in my hand and I'll eat 'em." That was the first time I was ever with a black ballplayer where I was conscious of the fact that black people were somewhat different. What Charlie was saying was, "Look, I'm black and you probably don't want me eating out of the same cup you're eating out of, so just put 'em in my hand." So John and I looked at him and said, "What's wrong with you? Eat 'em with the spoon." I think Charlie appreciated that, because he kind of smiled.

He never had any problem with that ball club as far as race was concerned. There were some times during the season when guys would call Charlie a nigger, and there were a couple of fights, as I recall, but Charlie was a great guy. I can't remember any of us feeling, well, Charlie, you're black. Charlie may have stayed at a separate hotel on exhibition trips or something, but it wasn't really a factor as far as were concerned.

Later, in my third or fourth year, Don Barksdale [also a black man] joined the ball club. He played at UCLA and was a great AAU player. He had a tough adjustment to make in the NBA because he wasn't that good individually as far as his moves and his dribbling. He was a good rebounder, but he wasn't a great shooter.

One time, we were playing in New York and Clifton really killed us. We were riding the train back, playing cards, and we got to talking about the ball game, how Clifton was so important as far as our loss was concerned. Bob Brannum said something like, "Oh, that black son of a bitch killed us tonight." He didn't think about it. It didn't occur to him that Don Barksdale was in the crew. It really didn't. But as soon as he said it, everybody just went, "Oh, God." It wasn't a split second and Barks looked around and said, "Yeah, that big jig was really tough tonight." Really broke the tension, as if to say, "Don't worry about it. Don't think a comment like that is going to upset me."

Syracuse was always tough. Al Cervi was the coach. They had Dolph Schayes, Paul Seymour, Red Kerr, Red Rocha. Rochester was really tough, too, with Arnie Risen, Bobby Davies, Bobby Wanzer. Usually they were second to Minneapolis, who had Mikan, Pollard, Slater Martin. Most of the time I was in Boston, Minneapolis won the title. Bud Grant, who later coached the Minnesota Vikings, was on the club. Fort Wayne and Baltimore were also in the league. Philadelphia started to get tough when Paul Arizin joined them.

*　　*　　*

Red Auerbach was a good coach. Red's greatest attribute he's had over the years is his ability to get talent. He sent Charlie Share to Fort Wayne and got Sharman, which was a great addition. But he just didn't have the horses, the size he needed to win, when I was with him.

People say Red was a tough coach, but I never thought so and I don't think the guys who played for him did either. His public image is a lot different from his private image. People see him as a tyrant. They see him agitating referees. They think his ballplayers are afraid of him. Actually, the only time he got obnoxious was when we'd win five or six in a row. Couse and I would say, "Red, you're really getting out of line. All we have to do is lose three or four and you'll be back to a normal human being. So settle down."

Red used to give us a lot of trouble as far as money was concerned. We got $5 a day meal money. Bob Brannum used to have trouble with Red. We'd go on a trip and Red wouldn't give you the meal money for three or four days. That's $20, but some of the guys needed the money to eat on, because they didn't make as much as I did. Brannum would say, "Where's the meal money?" And Red would say, "The way you guys play you shouldn't get any meal money." I said to Brannum, "The next time Red does that, say, 'Okay, Red, if it's that important to you, keep the money.' " So Brannum tried that. Well, Red couldn't get the money out of his pocket fast enough. As soon as you said to Red, "I don't need it," then Red was altogether different. He couldn't be nicer. In all the years I've known Red, anytime I call him for a favor I go through about sixty seconds of guff or a tirade. Then he says, "What can I do for you?" Anything I've ever asked him, reasonably, he's said, "Sure." Sometimes you don't like to call him because you don't want to go through that sixty seconds. But really he's not nearly as tough, as aggravating, as people think he is.

*   *   *

In those days the toughest team in the league was the Minneapolis Lakers. They had Mikan, who was the best player of the first half century. A real superstar. They also had Jim Pollard, who, had he not played with Mikan, would have been even better than he was, and he was tremendous. Vern Mikkelson, Slater Martin, Whitey Skoog; in the backcourt, Bobby Harrison. They had the best all-around team, and they were very difficult to beat. Mikan was the toughest player I played against.

Bob Pettit was awfully tough to play against when I was with Boston and he was with St. Louis. Pettit was leading the league in scoring with a 24-point average. The night before we were to play them, he went into Fort Wayne and had only 4 points against Mel Hutchins, his low of the season. Mel Hutchins was a great defensive player. The next night I played Pettit and he got 44 points. He was averaging 24 points. Take the 4 points he made against Fort Wayne and add the 44 points he made against me, and you have 48, which made his average. And I said to the guys in the locker room after the game, "This is a hell of a way to get your average, isn't it?" He was a great ballplayer, very difficult to play. Good on the boards, good shooter, very strong.

You know, ballplayers are funny. If someone on the other team is scoring and if you happen to be playing defense against him, your players don't say anything but you can feel they're not too happy with you because your man is scoring so much. Doesn't make any difference if your man is Elgin Baylor or whoever, they just get upset with you.

We were playing Philadelphia in New Haven when I was with the Celtics. We played games in different places, because most of the teams weren't drawing that well at home and if you could get a good gate on the road you'd take if for the guarantee. Anyway, I started playing against Paul Arizin that night. The first quarter he got 11 points. Auerbach takes me out and says, "Bob Harris, you guard Arizin." In the next quarter he gets 8 or 9 points. Twenty points at halftime. Third quarter, we're a little upset, because we're close. If we hold Arizin we'd have the lead. Arizin is really giving us problems. He's the type of player when you play him outside he's tough for a big man, because he can drive and shoot from the outside. So, after the second half started, he got a couple more baskets. There's a time out. Bill Sharman says, "For Christ's sake, let me take Arizin." He was upset because Arizin was scoring. So Billy took him. Paul took him right into the pivot. Inside of about three minutes he had three more baskets, about 28 points by this time, and we're going into the final quarter. We're in the huddle and Red looks kind of sheepishly at me and says, "Mac, why don't you take Arizin again?" I just paused, looked around, and said, "Does anybody else want to guard him?" Absolute silence. Nobody wanted any part of him. He had just ripped us to shreds that night. When the guy got hot, nobody could really stop him. You tried, but you just weren't very effective.

The best night of my career happened when we were playing against the Lakers in Boston. I got 46 points. The night before, playing against the Knicks, I was guarding Harry Gallatin, another great ballplayer. He was dribbling, I reached in and knocked the ball away from him, but dislocated the ring finger on my right hand. I didn't know it at the time. It popped out and I popped it back in. It started to swell, and the swelling pressure kept the two joints together.

The next night, I taped my middle finger and right ring finger together on my shooting hand and went out and had the best night of my career. I missed a couple of free throws, or I could have had 50, which really aggravated me.

I got back in the locker room and everybody was taping their fingers together.

My years with Boston were good and my association with

Walter Brown was unique. We really admired each other. His younger daughter became a fan of mine, and that always helps. We were both Catholic, had the same kind of education. We admired and respected each other. It was always difficult to do business with Walter because I really respected him and he wasn't making money in those days. I had a contract with him which paid me $15,000 and another $2,500 if I had a good year. We didn't even define what a good year was. But I made All-NBA and the All-Star team, so there was no problem, he paid me the bonus.

The next year we signed a contract but there was no bonus clause in it. At the end of the season Walter, who thought there was a bonus clause in the contract, said, "Ed, we're a little short of money and we can't pay you the bonus now. But I will as soon as I can." I didn't say anything. I said to myself, I don't think there's a bonus clause in that contract. We didn't carry our contracts around, so when I got back to St. Louis I checked and there was no bonus clause. I wrote him, "Hey, boss, thanks a lot, but you don't owe me a bonus. There's nothing in the contract." But to this day, if I had not said that to him he would eventually have paid me the $2,500. He was that kind of guy.

Another time Jack Nichols, who played for the Celtics, was going to dental school and as a result he couldn't make all the games. But he was very important to the ball club. So Auerbach and Nichols were talking contracts and Red was really trying to chisel Jack because he couldn't play all the games. They went round and round. That was Red's style. I never talked contract with him. I always dealt with Walter Brown. So Red and Nichols are battling. Red leaves the office for some reason and Walter walks in. He says, "How's it going?" Nichols says, "I'm having a lot of trouble." Walter said, "What are you asking for, Jack?" He told him a figure and Walter said, "That sounds reasonable. I'll pay you that." Auerbach walks in again and says, "Damnit, Nichols, we can't give you that kind of money." Brown says, "Hell, Auerbach, we got that all settled. Pay him the contract." That's the kind of guy he was. Super.

* * *

Probably one of the most interesting stories in all of basketball concerns the trade that sent Bill Russell to Boston in exchange for me and Cliff Hagan. Not many people know the real story, but it could have changed the course of professional basketball, in that I don't think the Celtics would have won ten out of eleven or eleven out of twelve championships without Russell. If he'd stayed in St. Louis, I don't know that St. Louis would have either. But I don't think Boston would have because Russell was absolutely perfect for that ball club. Cousy, Sharman out there in the backcourt stealing balls with Russell behind them, stopping everybody. Heinsohn, Loscutoff. They didn't have a great defensive club, but with Russell back there you didn't need one because no one could get closer than fifteen feet. We played them a couple of times when Russell wasn't in the lineup, and they were just an ordinary ball club. With him, they were just superb.

But getting back to the trade, that March, just before the play-offs started, my son, Patrick, who was just under one year old, had a cold. He'd had problems with his kidneys when he was born, had taken a lot of penicillin, and we thought we'd lose him. Anyway, the doctor said, "He has a cold, but I don't want to give him penicillin because he's had so much." We took him home, and half an hour later he was in convulsions. We took him to the hospital and were told that he had spinal meningitis. He had a very high fever and wound up with his brain completely destroyed. He was cerebral palsy, never could talk, walk, or think. He spent the rest of his life in a crib, wearing diapers, he could only roll over [Patrick died at the age of fourteen].

So now the season is over and I've really got a problem. My wife, Jackie, and I are back in St. Louis and the draft meeting is in April or May. Walter Brown called me and said, "I'm at the draft meeting and Red wants to make a deal to send you and Cliff Hagan to St. Louis in exchange for Bill Russell, but I don't want to make the deal. I can't

93

imagine the Celtics without you."

To this day, I'm thoroughly convinced that if I'd said "I can't imagine not playing with the Celtics," there never would have been a deal. But I said to Walter, "I've got a problem. We don't know if our son will recover. I'd love to stay with the Celtics and if you were trading me to any other club, I'd say no. But I was born and raised in St. Louis, my wife is from there, we've got a problem with Patrick, and if you made the deal with St. Louis you'd really be doing me a favor." He said, "Okay. I just wanted to check, because if you didn't want to go we wouldn't make the deal." And that's how the deal was made.

I think Bill Russell was a fantastic player. I disagree with some of his philosophies. He doesn't sign autographs. He didn't go back to the Hall of Fame to accept the honor of being inducted. I think that's bush league. But I'll say this, he was the most dominant player to ever play the game. There have been a lot of ballplayers who are better, individually, better shooters, dribblers, rebounders. But no one individual who could put it all together was as important to a particular team as Bill Russell was.

In 1957, the Celtics won their first championship. That was my first year with the Hawks. We played them in the finals. The Celtics won in seven games by one point, I guess, or maybe it was in overtime. The next year the Hawks won the championship against the Celtics because, I think, we had a better ball club, had more desire, were better coached— and because Bill Russell sprained his ankle in the third game and couldn't play. If Russell had not sprained his ankle and had been in the lineup—and I don't mean to take anything away from our ball club—I really don't think we would have won the title. The guy was that important.

*   *   *

94

In St. Louis I played for Ben Kerner and we had a good ball club. Hagan, Charlie Share, Pettit, Slater Martin, Jack McMahon, great names. Jack Coleman came off the bench. Alex Hannum was our coach. He and Ben Kerner didn't get along too well. Alex was a great coach, but the worst poker player in the world. He and Kerner did not see eye to eye on what Alex's salary should be the year after we won the NBA championship. Red Holzman had been coaching my first year there and after twenty-five games Kerner fired Red and turned it over to Dugie [Slater] Martin for about a week, but he said, "I can't coach and play." So Kerner hired Alex, even though he didn't really want to hire him. But Alex turned out to be a great coach.

After that first season they couldn't get together on a contract. They're talking on the phone and Alex says, "Unless I get this figure, I can't coach your team." Alex was bluffing, and Kerner said, "You mean you're retiring, because I can't pay you that much." Alex says, "I guess that's right," and he hung up the phone, thoroughly convinced that he'd get a call the next day from Kerner saying, Let's talk some more. That didn't happen. Kerner told his publicity man, Marty Blake, to prepare a news release that Alex had retired as coach. Alex was out in California when it went out and I can just see the look on his face.

So Alex didn't come back and Ben asked me if I wanted the job. I said, No way, you're not going to get me in that trap. Kerner hired and fired coaches regularly.

So he hired Andy Phillip, who lasted about seven games. Kerner called me in and said, "I'm going to replace Andy Phillip. I've got three options for you, Ed. First of all, you're not playing that well now, and I think you ought to consider retiring." I said I didn't think I was playing that badly. "The second option is a deal sending you to the Philadelphia Warriors. The third option is for you to coach my ball club." I laughed and said, "You're a hell of a negotiator, Ben." It was like playing Russian roulette with six bullets in the cylinder. "First you want me to retire, next you want me traded to Philadelphia, or you'd like me to coach your club." He says,

"Yes, you'd do a good job." And I agreed to coach.

It worked out fine. I coached for two years. We won the Western Division my first year and got knocked out of the play-offs by Minneapolis. Then we won the Western Division title my second year and went to the finals against Boston.

The series was tied two games apiece. We lost a heartbreaker in St. Louis by one point. Now we're trailing 3 to 2. This is Tuesday and we're traveling to Minneapolis for a Thursday game. Obviously, Minneapolis is favored. They have Elgin Baylor and a good club. Now remember, Kerner has a propensity for firing coaches. I'd lasted as long or longer than any coach he'd had, maybe ten games shy of being with him for two years. Our problem was, we didn't have any veteran substitutes in the front court. We had rookies Bob Ferry, Cal Ramsey, and Dave Gambee, nobody behind Pettit, Hagan, and Lovellette. I knew what would happen if we lost, I knew if we didn't win that first round of play-offs, I was going to go to Kerner and say I couldn't win the championship for you so you'd probably be better looking for another coach.

On Tuesday, we lost to Minneapolis. On Wednesday, on the way to Minneapolis, Kerner stopped in Chicago, met with Paul Seymour, then the head coach of the Syracuse Nationals, and secretly hired him as coach of the Hawks. Remember, we're still in the play-offs but we haven't been beaten and nobody knows Kerner has hired Seymour.

In Minneapolis, I walked into the locker room prior to the game, and it was an eerie feeling. I couldn't read the team at all. Everybody was quiet. It could have meant they were thinking about what they had to do, or they could have already given up. Anyway, we beat the Lakers by 16, 18 points that night. We whacked them. I'll never forget it. I didn't get to the locker room for three or four minutes, but when I walked in, the guys were all there. Pettit and Hagan walked up to me and said, "Ed, that one was for you." I really felt gratified.

So now the series is tied 3 to 3. Kerner had two basketball coaches, and nobody in the country knew that Seymour had been hired. It's a well-guarded secret between the two of them. We win that seventh game on national TV and now we're going into the finals against Boston, and still nobody knows that Kerner has two coaches for the next year.

Now we're going into the finals against Boston, with Sam [Jones], K. C. Jones, Cousy, Sharman, and the whole roster they've been beating everybody with. After that seventh game against the Lakers they asked me on national TV how I thought we'd do against the Celtics. I said, "I think we're going to do great. They ended their series in four games, we went seven. We're sharp and ready to go. They're sitting around, fat, sloppy, and lazy. I think we're going to win the series."

When I got home my wife, Jackie, who'd been watching, said, "Do you really think you're going to beat the Celtics!" And I said, "Are you out of your mind? If we win one game we'll be lucky. When you're on television you don't tell people your real feelings." I didn't think we had a chance because we didn't have any firepower in the backcourt. But we wound up going seven games, losing the last by 10 points or so.

After the game Kerner and I went down to New York for the draft meetings. I went to Mass at St. Pat's and there was a note in my box when I got back asking me to see Mr. Kerner. He started out rather sheepishly. "Ed, you've done a great job as my coach and I want you to be my coach next year, but here's the situation. . . ." And he told me he'd already signed Paul Seymour.

Now Kerner was a nice guy, but he had this penchant for getting rid of coaches rather quickly. If I were coaching I wouldn't mind being told at the end of a game I was relieved of my position, but with the volatile personality he had, if we got off to a bad start next year, I could just visualize Ben, with another coach in the wings, firing me at halftime. I would have liked coaching in St. Louis for three, four, five more years, but I didn't have ambitions of being a professional NBA coach for the rest of my life. So I told Ben, "I can understand your hiring Seymour because you thought he would be the

97

coach you wanted for next year. I don't necessarily agree with it, but if you made that decision I think you're much better off having him."

He offered me the job as general manager. The next season I was going to do telecasts of the game, but he hired Dugie Martin without letting me know, and I could see the writing on the wall. So I said, "Ben, we've had a good time together, but it's best we go our separate ways." He paid me for the final year on my contract, and was very good about it.

It's amazing some of the things that go on in the NBA, and everywhere, and nobody ever knows about it. I thought I was a pretty good coach there, but amazingly I never had an offer to coach in the NBA after that. I spent the next twenty-five years in radio and TV.

The best ballplayers I've played with were Cousy, Sharman, Pettit, and Hagan. Cousy was a phenomenal passer. One of the first practices in Boston, Couse saw me cutting through the middle. I didn't think I was open but he hit me, literally, in the back of the head with the ball. I said, "If he can pass like that I'm not going to take my eyes off him. We played well together. I was quick, fast, got down the floor in a fast break, and could usually get down faster than my defensive pivot man, so I followed him all over the floor, was behind him a lot of times when he'd come down the middle in a fast break. We'd have a 4 on 3, line up a shot a little bit back of the free-throw line. I shot the one-handed jump shot. For a pivot man I had a pretty good shot from the outside.

In his early days, Cousy had a tendency to try to dominate play at the end of the game. He changed his game as we went along. He developed an outside shot. He had a great running hook shot. He was good on the lay-up, but he never did develop the jump shot. But he was a phenomenal scorer who made things happen.

Sharman was just an incredible shooter with great concentration, great practice habits. He was a very good defensive player, and people didn't give him credit for that. He was a tough player, who didn't lose many fights. He got in a fight one time with Nobel Jorgensen of the Nats, who was six-eight, 230, and it was one punch and Willie landed it. Got in a fight one time with Andy Phillip. They guarded each other for five, six minutes—with a lot of pushing and shoving. Then, all of a sudden, one punch, and Willie won. Willie didn't talk. When he'd had enough, you knew it.

For a man his size, Cliff Hagan was very difficult to stop. He had the hook shot, he was a good rebounder, much better than he should have been for his size. He had a beautiful body.

But I guess the best one I ever played with was Bob Pettit. He was probably the most dedicated ballplayer. He just did the job. He had a lot of fun. He was a great poker player, he liked the girls, and he didn't drink much. He knew what he could do, and when he went out on the court, he did it. An excellent offensive and defensive rebounder. Strong upper body, a good shooter, but horrible as far as handling the ball. He really couldn't put the ball on the floor for more than one bounce, but he learned to be effective with that one bounce, to get past his man and go up for the jump shot. He was just a delight to coach. Never had any problems with Bobby. All you had to say was, "We play tonight at Madison Square Garden, see you there." And you knew he'd be there, give you one hundred percent. You knew what you were going to get out of him every night. I believe he made the All-NBA team every year he played in the league, and he deserved it.

He was the best ballplayer I ever played with, but don't get me wrong, there have been players with more natural ability. But I don't think it's fair to compare a Bob Pettit with a Larry Bird, or a Bob Cousy with a Jerry West. West and Robertson learned from Cousy. Larry Bird maybe learned from Bob Pettit. The whole physical structure of the game as time goes on gets better. If I were playing today, I'd be dribbling behind my back, might even be playing in the backcourt with Magic Johnson. The kids today are more physical, better developed. They've had the opportunity to see other players do something and they take it for granted that it can be done and they go from there. But Cousy and Bobby Davies didn't have anybody to model themselves after. They didn't know whether it could be done. They were pioneers.

Other guys I played against who were really tough were Elgin Baylor and Paul Arizin. I didn't have any trouble with Arizin before he went into the Marines, but he must have done nothing but played ball there for two years because when he came back, oh, was he tough. He could put the ball on top of his head in the corner and shoot it. I couldn't play him. Before he went into the service I used to stay away from him. He couldn't shoot the outside shot, and I'd give him two or three steps. But later, when he started hitting the set shot, I had to go up on him and he was quick and could go by me.

Dolph Schayes was really tough, too. He shot the two-handed set shot, came across, shot the little one-hander. Never did shoot a jump shot, either. He was a great rebounder. He used his body under boards and he was tough.

For his size, Slater Martin was really unbelievable. He and Couse put on some great exhibitions against each other. Sometimes he and Sharman would go at it, too.

Looking back over my career, I'm really proud of what I was able to accomplish. When I started, I had no idea I'd play professional. There was no Hall of Fame, so I had no ambitions to get into it. I just wanted to be as good as I possibly could. I had my own criteria, and I guess my expectations were pretty high. I'm proud of what I did.

I wasn't the greatest basketball player that ever lived, but if you're the first to do something, nobody can ever duplicate that. I was the first in college basketball history to have a shooting percentage for the year of over fifty percent. I was the first Celtic ever to have his jersey retired and hoisted to the top of the Boston Garden. I was the MVP in the first

All-Star game. That's something I'm really proud of. I think I was the youngest to be inducted into the Hall of Fame. It's nothing you can brag about—you don't go around saying to people, "I'm in the Hall of Fame." But it's something that quietly means a lot to ballplayers.

Basketball has meant a lot to me in my life. While at St. Louis University, I met my wife, Jackie. If I hadn't gone there on a basketball scholarship I never would have met her. Together we had seven great children and now have nine wonderful grandchildren.

I made a few bucks and met a lot of real professionals. As you play against opponents you learn to hate them. But once the game is over, you enjoy being with them. Now, as we see each other at golf tournaments or at the Hall of Fame, the stories get better and better. As we talk about what happened thirty years ago everyone scores more points, we play better defense, and never talk about the losses, only the victories.

I've had the pleasure of teaching hundreds of young men the game at our basketball camps. Our most illustrious student, Senator Bill Bradley, was with us for five years. I've traveled to England, Ireland, the Philippines, Uruguay, and Mexico, teaching young men and women this wonderful game. It's been a lot of fun, but I never dreamed it would happen to me.

Dolph Schayes. (Courtesy Basketball Hall of Fame)

Dolph Schayes

When Dolph Schayes graduated from New York University in 1948, there were two professional basketball leagues, the National Basketball League and the Basketball Association of America. Sought after by the Knicks of the BAA, Schayes chose instead to sign with the Syracuse Nationals of the NBL. In 1949, when the leagues merged, Schayes, still with the Nats, emerged as one of the dominant players in the new NBA. Although he was six feet, eight inches, he was best known for his uncannily accurate two-handed, over-the head, outside set shot, his passing ability, and his rebounding. Some have even referred to him as the prototype for Larry Bird, in that he was skilled in all aspects of the game. He was consistently in the NBA's top ten scorers and rebounders and a perennial All-Star selection. At one time, he held the Iron Man record until it was surpassed by his teammate, Johnny "Big Red" Kerr. After retiring in 1964, Schayes was named coach of the team which, by that time, had been sold and moved to Philadelphia. Today he lives in Syracuse and is in the real estate business. He has four children—two daughters and two sons—one of whom, Danny, now plays in the NBA for the Denver Nuggets.

I started playing basketball in the Bronx in the schoolyards of P.S. 91. I wasn't a gym rat, I was a schoolyard rat and I just played every chance I got, even in the summer. I was very tall and I was always playing with older, better players. We'd play in that schoolyard and in order to keep playing you had to win. Luckily, I was taller than everybody else, and so if somebody had to be picked from the losing team, it was always me.

In those days every neighborhood, every block, really, had a club. Ours was called the Amerks, probably short for Americans. We formed a team for the Community Center and played in a league there. We played at night in a gym with a very low ceiling and the competition was strong. That was my first taste of organized play.

I played in junior high school and then from there went first to a prep school, which folded after a year, and then on to De Witt Clinton High School, where I joined the team in midseason. At that time, I was also still playing ball for the Amerks, whose season was even longer than the high school season. So we played a tremendous amount of basketball in the fall, winter, and spring. The only time we didn't play was during the summer, since most of the kids in the neighborhood either went away to camp or up to the country.

I always practiced playing the whole game. I think what aided my play most of all was not trying to take advantage of my size. I realized I was much taller than everybody else, but I wanted to be just an outside player and learn the game from the guard's position. So, basically, I learned the schoolyard game, which was the purest form of basketball.

In those days I was six-six or six-seven, and there weren't as many tall guys then as there are now. The other players would say, "Get inside, get inside," but I just naturally gravitated to the entire game. Of course, this helped me tremendously when I got into professional basketball because I was able to bring the taller centers out, be a forward, and play the passing game, which was all very effective for the team. Actually, I felt like I was cheating if I scored from a foot or even two or three feet away. Or maybe I just didn't like the body contact inside, because in those days you had the six-foot

104

lane. The lane was so small a big guy could really dominate, just plant himself inside, get the ball, and then lay it in. When Mikan played in those early years of pro ball, that's exactly what he did, and they had to change the rule because of him.

My high school career ended in January 1945. The war was still going and sports was in a depressed, ersatz state. Most athletes never did go outside of New York in those days. Frank McGuire hadn't yet started his pipeline to North Carolina.

Our whole high school team got a blanket scholarship offer to Purdue, of all places, and we almost took that. Then we all decided that we wanted to go to City College, because we felt that Nat Holman was the greatest coach going. He found out about us, liked us, and, as a team, we went to his camp as waiters. Nat's a wonderful person, but he made a terrible mistake in judgment with us. Before the camp season opened he got all his waiters together and explained what we would do. His explanation treated us like second-class citizens. "You guys are going to live in a tent," he said. "You can't go swimming. You can't do this. You can't do that." And this was a guy who was trying to recruit us and probably would have had the greatest team of all time because we'd had such a terrific high school team. But he turned us all off. We didn't go to CCNY and, of course, he was very angry. He even threatened to blackball us at every college in New York.

New York University offered me a scholarship. I lived very close to the Heights, which was their uptown campus, and I'd seen the team practice often. Actually, our high school team had even scrimmaged the NYU team and beat them for a while. They kept the scrimmage going until they got ahead, then stopped it.

There were other schools I could have gone to, like St. John's or Columbia, though I think with Columbia it was one of those deals where I would have had to pay since it was an Ivy League school and they didn't offer athletic scholarships. Of course, it was a prestige thing for a lower-middle-class, first-generation kid to go to a school like NYU, so when they offered me a scholarship I took it. But I think the main reason

I chose NYU was because it was within walking distance of my home.

It was too bad about CCNY, because Nat is really a wonderful person. I wanted to go there because I loved the game and the way they played it at City. As it turned out, though, NYU did play the same way. I think it was a matter of the NYU coach realizing that that was the best way to handle the type of ballplayer he got. So, rather than impose his will or style, he just said, "Play." I don't ever remember getting a play or a defensive set. We just played ball.

It turned out to be a good situation for me because when I came to NYU they were kind of weak at center and I was able to move right in. But I was always much younger [because others had been in the service before college] than everybody else by a couple of years and I wasn't that strong. However, I did complement the other players and we had a very strong team.

I would say that the era I played in, 1945–1948, was probably the zenith of college basketball in New York City history. It was just a window that occurred due to circumstances. The war had ended, everybody was working, there was a euphoria in the air, sports were becoming preeminent again, and basketball was a New York game. It was just one of those freaks of time. So it was a pretty heady experience for a sixteen-year-old to go into Madison Square Garden, where we played for three and a half years, to sellout crowds every game.

In those years there must have been twenty newspapers covering sports and every one of them played up the game. There was a lot of excitement. Everyone wanted to come play in New York because that's where they would be seen.

I was only a fair player. I was overshadowed by Sidney Tannenbaum [Sid Tannenbaum, who played for the Knicks for one season, was knifed to death in his Brooklyn machine shop in 1986.], who was a great talent, and Don Foreman. At that time basketball was a game where each side would only score 40 to 50 points, but we'd score up in the seventies and eighties, because that's the kind of team we were. We'd run, and that was new and exciting.

I had a bit of a knee problem in my second or third year, which meant that I hobbled along a lot of the time. Still, I did okay. Then, all of a sudden, I must have gotten stronger or smarter or whatever, but that final year I seemed to gain a lot more confidence. Tannenbaum had graduated and we weren't supposed to be a good team, but it turned out we had a wonderful year. We won nineteen games in a row. But I was really nothing sensational. If I made All-America, it was only the third team.

I went to school, got grades, and, being young, I didn't think I was different from anybody else. I just loved to play basketball and I was good at it, so, when the time came, I said, "Pro basketball sounds like it would be fun." I was excited about the prospect of playing pro ball. I really didn't have ambitions about becoming a doctor or a lawyer. I didn't have any father's business to go into. I was really kind of floundering around as to a career. I remember one day the School of Engineering, which I attended, had an assembly orientation. Some fellow got up and said, "Four years from now I don't know where you guys will be," and he went through percentages of the past years of how other classes had graduated and where people had ended up. I think he said ten percent would be engineers and eighty percent would wind up in their father's business. Because I didn't particularly want to be an engineer and because I didn't have a business to go into, I had dreams of becoming a professional basketball player.

In those years there were two leagues, the Basketball Association of America, made up of the arena owners, the hockey guys who wanted to have another sport to keep their arenas going, and the National Basketball League, which was an outgrowth, after the war, of the midwestern league, in which Fort Wayne dominated. There was a team from Indianapolis, one from Minneapolis, and others from Sheboygan, Rochester, and Oshkosh.

When I got out of college, it just so happened that the BAA needed some teams and so they went to the strongest teams in the National Basketball League, which were Rochester, Minneapolis, and Indianapolis, I believe. These teams decided to leave the NBL and join the BAA. I can remember that summer being drafted by both the Knicks in the BAA and Syracuse in the NBL. The BAA felt that they were in a very strong position with their player personnel and they didn't want their salaries to go crazy, so Ned Irish, who was a businessman and owner of the Knicks, established a limit for their first-round choices of, I believe, $5,000, which was to be top dollar. They were able to do this because they believed that the NBL would fold.

Syracuse then called me up and said, "We'll give you seventy-five hundred dollars." I went back to the Knicks and they said, "We can't go any higher than five thousand dollars." For that reason, I decided to go to Syracuse, even though I'd never been out of New York City in my whole life other than to play games in North Carolina and Rochester.

The NBL was made up of some weird-sounding teams. Syracuse was the only team in the East. We had to travel to Waterloo, Iowa; Sheboygan, Oshkosh, [Wisc.]; Hammond, Indiana; and Fort Wayne. And then there was the Anderson Packers, a team owned by a very wealthy man named Duffy. So that was the league.

When the season ended, the Indianapolis club folded. That was the team made up of the entire University of Kentucky team with Groza and Beard, one of the greatest college teams of all time. They wanted a franchise of their own and took Indianapolis. Later they were accused of being involved in a scandal which occurred at Kentucky before they got into pro ball.

In 1949, the BAA decided to take in more NBL teams, and that season, 1949/50, was the first year of the NBA, with an unwieldy league of seventeen teams. Many NBL people have said that without them the NBA wouldn't be alive today, that they helped save a lot of floundering franchises. And the truth is, the BAA was very weak. I think the Rochester, Minneapolis, Syracuse, and Fort Wayne group really did save the

NBA because they were very strong franchises that brought in a lot of life to the league.

In 1951 there was a falling out, a watering down, so to speak. I think it was Ned Irish who spoke about an incident where there was an eight-o'clock game in Madison Square Garden between the Knicks and Sheboygan which was advertised on the marquee. At five minutes to eight this long station wagon drives up and all the Sheboygan players come out after they had driven for something like ten straight hours to play the game. Irish supposedly said, "This is kind of bush-league." So the Sheboygans and Oshkoshes went down the tube.

That 1949/50 team that I played on had Al Cervi as coach. He was one of those few fellows who made it in professional basketball without ever having gone to college. He was a schoolyard-type player who made it because he was a great competitor. He was a legend in that league. He was probably thirty years old at that time, which was quite old for basketball, especially in those days. He was a battler, very defense-minded. His teams always played excellent defense. He was also a very difficult person to get along with because he was insulting. He'd belittle just about everybody. Nobody could measure up to him. He'd say things like, "You couldn't guard your grandmother." Although he was a fine coach and player, he missed the mark because, as a psychologist, he just didn't have it. He treated everybody the same way. He was monolithic in that he used only one strategy, which was to insult the hell out of everybody. In my case, even though I didn't like him, it worked. I'd never had that type of coach before, the kind that tried to make me more aggressive. In fact, he actually had a lot to do with my becoming more aggressive, because that's the way he was. When he played he was fire. He played with all his heart and soul. He'd fight and push and shove and it kind of rubbed off.

Pro ball was the answer to my prayers in that I was able to just play basketball all the time. Whether I realized it at the time or not, I loved the game. I loved to just get there and practice and play. I was able to hone my skills. I was fortunate because of my size. I started out inside as a center, but I just couldn't cope with the Mikans and another seven-footer named Don Otten. I couldn't guard in that three-foot lane. So I just gravitated toward becoming a forward.

Luckily, in those days I wasn't really supposed to play defense. The teams back then were categorized in certain ways. There was a center, a passing guard, a shooting guard, a scoring forward, and a defensive forward. I happened to be the offensive forward, so I would always play against the defensive forward and he couldn't score. So I was able to kind of free-lance. I was very fortunate in that respect because it really helped my rebounding a great deal. I never boxed out. I don't teach it now because I never did it. So I would play the defensive forward, he would never get the ball, always passing off to the offensive forward, who would do the scoring. So I was always able to leave him and help rebound. That gave me a lot of freedom, which helped my overall game.

In those rare instances where I had to play defense, I really didn't do a very good job. I'd hold my man to 30 points a game, which of course made Cervi very angry. It also didn't help that I was getting a lot of press, which would often promote jealousy. Cervi wanted me to play more defense. I'd say, "Look, Al, the guy I'm playing isn't scoring because he never shoots the ball. They never give it to him."

So that helped my game a great deal, especially my rebounding. It also helped build my confidence. I led the league in rebounding and here I could hardly jump off the floor more than two or three feet. But because of the freedom I had, I was able to bound in from the outside, time the ball, and get to it before anybody got there, even though there were better jumpers than I was.

This also simplified my offense, not that I realized that at the time. I had a great shot from the outside and if they let me shoot it, I'd make it, and if they came up on me, I'd just go to the basket. It was quite simple.

So the pro game was something I grew into as well as the

aggressiveness, which came about as a result of playing with this gashouselike, alley-cat type of team. We were all battlers and it rubbed off. You begin to think that way and your whole personality changes. For me, I became more of a battler.

This attitude was also reflected in the fans. If somebody had done a study, and it probably would have been a good doctoral thesis on a Phys. Ed. level, they would have found something I'd call the Syracuse Syndrome. We were like the Green Bay of the NBA. It was something like a small-town inferiority complex. It was us against the big-city guys and we were gonna show them. Even in politics, upstaters don't particularly like folks from New York City and everything the City stands for. Upstate politics are Republican, while New York City is all Democratic. That feeling of the small town of David versus the Goliath of Boston and New York pervaded. There was great pride in Syracuse about their town playing against the big league. It was amazing, tiny Syracuse playing against those major cities.

Then add to that the weather up here, which was an uncanny aid to us. In those days, you either flew in by DC-3 or took the train. Because teams were always trying to save money, they came in either the day of the game or the night before. Many times there would be terrible storms, with cold and icy conditions. And then we also had a very good team.

Now the mind is like a computer and it got conditioned so that the opposing players knew that when they came to Syracuse to play they were going to have to face a great team, hostile fans, and that goddamn cold and ice. I think that whole syndrome helped us win. It must have added at least a couple of points to our score, because we were almost invincible at home.

Syracuse was always a great labor town. It probably still is. There were lots of steel factories and industrial mills, and the type of people who lived up here really liked to let loose at a basketball game. The fans were always feeling their oats and I honestly think that the policemen who were brought in to control the crowds also weren't too happy with the Bostons, Philadelphias, and New Yorks.

In those days some of the other coaches in the league were very colorful, guys like Eddie Gottlieb and Red Auerbach. Philadelphia, Boston, and New York were especially big rivals of ours. And in those days we played those teams nine or ten times a year. If you yelled at a guy like Eddie Gottlieb, he'd just yell back at you. There would be these verbal exchanges, especially with Boston, and then the players would get into it. Then we'd battle, and in those days there were a lot of guys who would really get into it. Bill Sharman was one. He was a tough guy. He'd just pound on your back. And so, before you knew it, there'd be a fight. We must have had a dozen fights a year.

I got into a lot of pushing and shoving matches because I was always played by the defensive forward, who was more like a cop on the beat, or a hatchet man. I got into it with Tommy Heinsohn a few times, because he had a tendency to punch. Boston was a very physical team because that was Auerbach's way of testing your manhood. It was like, "Let's see how much he'll take. If you punch him, will he quit?"

Anyway, this whole aura, this mystique, kept building up around our team. It was just a negative experience for the other teams to come up to Syracuse to play us. As far as I was concerned, though, I was just tuned in to play. I didn't know what was going on a lot of the time, but I do know that there was this big, three-hundred-pound, bald-headed guy they called "the Strangler." He always managed to be near where the players walked in and out, and I guess he grabbed a few referees in his day.

I think one of the toughest guys I had to play against was Paul Arizin. He was an amazing shooter. He was six-four or six-five, and he shot the ball on a line drive. I probably admired him in the early days as much as anybody. In the later days it was Bob Pettit, though I never played against him, man to man. It was rare, in fact, that I'd be pitted against Arizin, either. Both of those guys would have killed me. I admired Arizin because he seemed to be so frail. He had an allergy or something which caused him to almost throw up every time-out. Then he'd just come back out on the court and kill you.

I always had the best defensive man playing me, but after you get a reputation you get what they call a license. Consequently, referees would, on any close call, usually give the offense the better of it. So the defensive guy was always in a bad situation, in foul trouble, and the other guy would have to come in as a substitute and you'd usually do great against him.

I think that any player, if he plays a lot and has the ball often enough, has to score at least 15 points a game. In later years, Red Auerbach realized that you could nullify a player's offensive output a bit if you made him work harder at the other end of the court. So he did that with Frank Ramsey, who would give me a lot of trouble. I was much taller than he was but I was basically an inside player, so Ramsey would make it difficult for me to guard him at the other end of the court, what with all the switches I'd have to make. The advent of that theory, of making an offensive player work harder, bothered my game quite a bit.

I think that Mel Hutchins of Fort Wayne probably gave me as much trouble as anybody. He had great natural ability as a defensive ace. He didn't have the incentive or drive to be super-great. He certainly had the body, but he never quite reached the heights of the real greats, although he certainly had the potential.

As far as I was concerned the introduction of the 24-second clock was terrific because I was able to play more basketball. The game became forty-eight-minute basketball rather than thirty-five-minute basketball because, in the last quarter, without the shot clock, teams would hold the ball until they were fouled. The entire final quarter consisted of one team fouling the other. The team that was ahead would naturally give up a foul, so they could get the ball back. It was really a disaster. Without the clock I think the pro game definitely would have disappeared. I'm sure it helped every shooter, because it gave more opportunities to put the ball up. There's no real defense against a good offensive player one-on-one. There really isn't, because he knows what he's going to do and there's just no way the defensive player can react fast enough, especially if the shooter keeps getting the ball.

I think the year Johnny Kerr joined the team was the year we won the Championship. Mikan had retired a year or two before, which was fine since with him on the Lakers we were always fighting with Minneapolis for first or second place. Johnny Kerr was probably the person who helped us the most, because prior to his arrival we never really had a great center and he fit in perfectly with our style of play because he was a passing center. He always used to say that he was going to write a book, *Twenty Years in the NBA Without the Ball*, because when we did give it to him he'd always pass it off. But he would certainly liven things up quite a bit. He was one of those players who was never really serious about the game, or at least that's the way it appeared. He was not the kind of player that either Al Cervi or I would have liked, but he produced. He helped us greatly with his high jinks on and off the court.

That year was a great experience. We had always been very successful, but that year we happened to play Fort Wayne in the finals. We won all four games at home because Fort Wayne could never beat us there. In fact, I think it took them ten years before they won a game in Syracuse. We won that Championship, as I remember, on Easter Sunday in a very close game, and the result was euphoria. And it wasn't the money, because the money wasn't there. It was just that we had come so close before and, after five or six years of being in professional ball, I'd finally been part of a Championship team. It's hard to describe the feeling of saying you're the world's champ.

While I was playing I never felt any anti-Semitism and I don't think there was any. If there was anything in the early days,

I think there might have been some antiblack sentiment. The owners of the teams, even though they were very liberal, were afraid that they would lose patrons and I honestly believe that unless a guy was a sensational player they really didn't care to have a black man on the team.

We had a black man on our team, Earl Lloyd, who was one of the first in the league, along with Sweetwater Clifton and Chuck Cooper. I think he always got the poor end of the stick as far as playing was concerned. He was always doing the dirty work, fouling out of the game. Actually, he helped me a great deal because with him in there I was free to rebound and get a lot of glory, since his man was usually the other team's offensive ace. Earl and I were roommates most of the time, and I don't really recall any problems he had on the road. Of course, we never went to southern cities.

Don Barksdale was another early black player. He was supposedly going to be the first black superstar, but he never quite developed. He played for Boston and he was a very good person, and I think he was accepted by the fans.

I think there probably was a quota in those early days, but it was certainly unannounced. There never were more than one or two black players on a team. Boston broke that mold later on, in the late fifties, and, as it turned out, the idea of limiting blacks on a team because the fans might not accept them meant nothing. I don't think it hurt or enhanced attendance one bit. Even today you have your great debates as to how important it is. Does New York need white players? I think if they could play it might help, but if they won games without them it wouldn't really matter. But if you lose and have an all-black team, I think immediately they'll say that that's the reason you're not drawing. But as far as I can see, the reason is that the team just isn't winning.

I was very proud of the Iron Man record. It ended because of an errant elbow. I broke a cheekbone and I just couldn't play anymore. I had to have an operation and it would have been very dangerous to continue to play unless I wore a mask, which I eventually did. I was aware that I'd broken the previous record, held by Harry Gallatin of the Knicks. All I wanted to do was keep going and play forever. You always feel you can play forever, that it'll never end. But it does.

I recall I did break my right wrist in a game and then continued to play after they put a lightweight, rubberized cast on it. I remember when I broke it I tried to come out and play right away. We took five time-outs to see if I could come out and shoot the fouls, because in those days there was a rule that said if you were shooting a foul and came out and had somebody else shoot it for you, then you were out of the game. It happened in the first quarter when I got submarined and fell on my face and hand. They didn't know whether I could still shoot so they sent me out there to try and I found I couldn't do it. But after they set it and put a cast on it, I was able to play.

I had a short fuse with referees, even though they put me on the line a great deal. I would average almost ten foul shots a game. Still, I would make snide remarks, wisecracks, and I guess I was really a son of a bitch when it came to referees. I really don't know why that was, but I suppose I must have been following the lead of our coach, Al Cervi, who was like that. I got thrown out of a few games, but it wasn't because of yelling at referees. I can recall one time I had five fouls and disagreed with the call of a referee. As captain of the team, I was allowed to talk to him and so I said, "Do I have one talk coming?" He said, "Yes." I said, "You're a homer," or something like that, and then he threw me out of the game.

Travel was boring. The times between games and waiting for the game to begin was really the pits. In order to keep busy, I would do a lot of reading. There was also the usual card playing. We had to do something to keep busy on train trips that were sometimes eighteen to twenty hours.

As far as contracts were concerned, the feeling between myself and the owner, Danny Biasone, was more like a father-son relationship. He was a really unique individual in that he was a very nice person. You always had the feeling that he wasn't trying to take advantage of you, that what he told you was the truth. That might have been a naïve way of looking at things, but if he told me something, I believed him. All the negotiating was done by yourself. A couple of times I felt I wasn't being treated well, but Danny said, "We lost money last year, so we have to do it this way," and I went along with him because I loved to play. I think that today, if the sports attorneys weren't involved, the players would probably play for much less just because they want to play. To play ball and get paid for it is the best of all worlds.

I never really got into any negotiating hassles. I might have held out for a time, but as soon as training camp would start, I'd come in and sign. I just wasn't a negotiator. The stakes weren't high enough in those days. Although I must say that an interesting thing happened when George Yardley came to Syracuse. He was the highest-paid player in the league in those days. I think he was being paid $25,000 by Detroit and I was making $15,000. He was traded to Syracuse because Fred Zollner didn't want him anymore. When he came to Syracuse, Danny Biasone told Zollner, "I can't pay him $25,000. I can pay him $17,000." And so Detroit paid him $8,000. Then, when he came here, Biasone came to me and said, "Yardley is making $17,000. Since you're the number-one guy you've got to make more." So that raised my salary immediately, which was one of the reasons I liked George Yardley so much. But then, of course, I started to reason that I could have been paid much more money all along. So it was obvious to me that the ploy of being a nice, non-negotiating person really didn't pay off.

Before the opening of the 1963/64 season, we were sold and moved to Philadelphia. Alex Hannum, who played with us in the late forties, I think—a marginal player at best, and I think Alex would tell you that—was the Syracuse coach. He loved Syracuse because of Danny Biasone and didn't want to go to Philadelphia. So they were looking for a coach in Philly. I didn't have a particularly good year in '62/'63. My knee was

117

giving me some problems. I'd had an operation on it and I wasn't sure how it was going to come out. So I got talked into coaching, and I really didn't have my heart in it. To this day I rue that decision, because I really think I had some good years left in me. As it turned out, sometimes when you have an operation you're better off. My knee turned out much better than it had been. The doctor did a terrific job.

That year I did play a little. I was almost like a player-coach, but I couldn't concentrate on my game and coach at the same time. Some guys can do it, I couldn't. So the decision to coach was the worst decision of my life, because I loved the game and foolishly I didn't say, after I realized my knee was okay, "Hey, I want to play. I don't want to coach." I should have done that, but I was a loyal person. I'd said I'd coach, so that's what I did.

I coached for three or four years. It was a job, that's the way I looked at it. I had started to lose my love for playing, what with the injuries and everything and not being as effective as I would have liked. Then, when I realized that I got my zest for playing back, it was too late.

I was never able to make the division between management and players. I was coaching my buddies, like Johnny Kerr. When you're coaching you have to be a completely different person with a different personality. As a result, I had a difficult time the first couple of years. It wasn't until then that I really got down to coaching, and I think my best year was the year I got fired. I thought I was just beginning to become a good coach at that point. That was 1965/66. Wilt Chamberlain was on the team and we never really saw eye to eye. I think that was because I was an old-school-type player who really broke his back for the few bucks I earned. I obeyed the rules and now here was this completely new type of player coming in, getting paid well over $100,000, and to be honest, I didn't think he was that much of a pure talent. In other words, even though I was his coach, I didn't particularly go for his type of play, and that was a mistake. I should have lived with it and made the best of the situation. But I wasn't the only coach to have that kind of problem. I think Butch

Van Breda Kolff also had that problem with Chamberlain. He also came from the pure New York–style play and here comes this guy who was very egotistical, who dominated everything, who didn't obey the rules. I think Larry Costello ran into that same problem when he was coaching Wilt in his later years.

Things were changing. The star system came into play. Of course, when there's a superstar around, you have to treat him a little differently. Eventually, I got to like Wilt as a person and understand his talent. I could never really do things that way, just get up close to the basket and dunk the ball in. It just seemed too easy. To me, it wasn't pure basketball. It was winning basketball because he put the ball in the basket, but it didn't seem very skillful to me. Of course, it was just a different type of player, one who was difficult for me to adjust to—but eventually I did.

After I left coaching I got into the league office. All those referees I was screaming at, now I became their friend. That was okay for a while, but it wasn't really a very happy time for me. If I were to do it again, I probably would have made the break, just gotten out of basketball immediately. But it was in my system, in my blood, and I just wanted to be around it.

The final break came after I got into coaching again in Buffalo with an expansion team. I got fired from that job early on and I felt I'd better spend time with my family, because your family really suffers when you're a professional sports person. You're just never, never home.

It's funny, but one thing that does happen when you're a sports star is that you get lionized your whole life and you begin to believe you're some kind of a special person. When you finally quit, it's an adjustment you really have to make. You have to say, "Hey, I'm just like everybody else." People make a fuss over you, so what? Your basic personality should never change. It was difficult for me because professionally I think I got very spoiled by all the attention I got and I never really managed to cope with it, and I do think it affected me.

Looking back, I think one of the biggest changes in the game was the advent of the sixth man. The small forward was also a big change, as is the quickness of the game and the players. Eventually, I think they'll have to do something to keep the quick players from bunching up inside. Maybe the 3-point rule will help widen it out a bit.

I think the advent of the black athlete has also made quite a bit of difference. They have a greater desire to excel because they have to get out of the ghetto and so they're willing to dedicate themselves to playing that much more.

I watch the game closely because my son, Danny, is involved in it as a center for the Denver Nuggets. He's got to guard people like Jabbar, Moses Malone, and Artis Gilmore. The most important part of his job is physically to keep them from being too close to the basket. There's pushing and shoving all the time. We had a little bit of that, but I think it's a more physical game today. I think the players are stronger. I don't think it can be cleaned up because there's just no way of doing it. Referees understand that the defensive player cannot allow the offensive player to get too close, so he's got to be a little lenient in that tug-of-war that goes on.

I admire most of the players today. I especially admire those players who play a team game and excel. The players who score, the Michael Jordans and the Dominique Wilkinses, they're great talents, but I'd rather admire a player who can be more of a team player. Obviously, someone like Larry Bird comes to mind, as does James Worthy.

You see the faults in his play, his slowness, his lack of judgment, but my son shows that he's a great team player, probably too much so. He doesn't have the ability that some of these guys have, but he's got team-mindedness and that, I think, is important.

For a while, years ago, I was affiliated with a summer camp. Then I started a basketball camp of my own, which was probably the second one in the whole country. Kids could go there to learn basketball. I still have it, but it's very minimal now because of the tremendous influx of other sports camps.

Today I'm in real estate. I build and manage apartments. Not that I particularly enjoy it, but it's turned out to be a very good way of earning a living. Especially in these times. It's probably the number-one maker of fortunes. Not that I'm a big operator, but it is very comfortable.

Nat "Sweetwater" Clifton. Knicks versus Baltimore, January 8, 1954; Clifton is number eight. (N.Y. Daily News Photo)

Nat "Sweetwater" Clifton

In the 1950/51 NBA season, Nat Clifton and Chuck Coo-
per became the first two black men to play in the league.
Clifton, who came from the Harlem Globetrotters, played
first with the New York Knickerbockers and then with
the Detroit Pistons, where he ended his NBA career after
the 1957/58 season. Today Nat Clifton lives in his home-
town Chicago, on the South Side, just a few blocks from
his ailing mother, whom he cares for. Best known as
"Sweetwater," the self-described "biggest and most fa-
mous cab driver in Chicago" explains how he got the
name: "You see, I never did drink or smoke or anything
like that, and whenever they asked me what I wanted
when we went out, I'd say, 'Bring me a pop.' So that's
how it started. I never drank much other than soft
drinks."

I was born in Little Rock, Arkansas, but I was raised in Chicago and I been here since I was six years old. I started
playing basketball when I was a freshman in high school. By
the time I was a sophomore I was sort of like a star. You know,
I was considered a big man back then. I was already six-five

when I was in high school and I only growed one more inch by the time I got to be a man.

When I was growing up in Chicago there wasn't but two black schools in the city and you had the choice of going to either one, so I chose the one closest to my neighborhood. When I finished with high school, I went to Xavier University down in New Orleans, which was in the Southern Conference. Lots of people get that Xavier mixed up with the college in Ohio, but at that time blacks wasn't going to Big Ten schools or places like that. I had a scholarship to five or six black schools like Tuskegee, Morris Brown, and Clark, but I chose Xavier because that's where the team I played with in high school went after they graduated and I wanted to keep playing with them. So that was my reason for going down there. One year, 1943, I think it was, we won the Southern Conference championship and I was voted the Most Valuable Player in the league. I was playing center, you know, but when I came along there weren't that many big guys that could do everything like I could. I was a big guy who could do a lot of things. I was taught not to do just one thing. I was taught to play guard, forward, center, anywhere they put me.

After college, I went into the Army for three years and I played basketball with the 369th Battalion. I remember we had this big tournament in Florence, Italy, and the Bulldozers of the Third Armory won it. They had real little guys and they were fast and they just outrun everybody and so they won that tournament. But that year I was voted on the All-League team as center. But the unit I was in was real small and they didn't have too many good athletes, just a few. I remember we had a guy named Lieutenant Lowry, he was good. And another boy out of New York named Reggie Johnson, and he was good, too.

When I got out of the service and came home—it was '47—I started playing with a team called the Dayton Metropolitans. We had a bunch of college ballplayers on that team who came from Ohio State, Michigan, Purdue, Wisconsin, and schools like that. We had a good, small, semipro team. It was a mixed team, with three blacks and nine whites, a team

124

with some good stars. We were pretty good and we beat some teams like the Lakers and the Rochester Royals when they had Bob Davies and that bunch.

After that, I left and went to New York to play for the Rens for a while. They were located on Seventh Avenue, up near Small's Paradise, right across the street from a place called the Renaissance. We used to play upstairs. I played there about half a year and then I got with the Harlem Globetrotters. Abe Saperstein signed me to a contract. He'd heard about me, but it was kinda hard for him to catch up with me 'cause everybody had me going all the time. I played with them for two seasons—1947/48 and 1948/49—along with Goose Tatum and Marcus Haynes. We used to go around the country playing local teams and we'd beat them all the time. We were good enough to play with anybody. We played the Lakers when they had George Mikan, Vern Mikkelson, and that bunch, and they were the only team that could possibly beat us. We also used to play the College All-Stars, with Bob Cousy, Bill Sharman, and that kid from Philadelphia, Paul Arizin. I think that was 1949 when we played them. We played all the big cities in the U.S. Played something like twenty-five games against the All-Stars, and we won something like seventeen and they won the rest.

One of my greatest thrills was playing down in Brazil, in the Cyprus stadium. The seating capacity was something like two hundred thousand people and they had something like a big drainage ditch to keep the fans away from the field because they had a lot of riots down there. We played their Olympic team down in that stadium and we beat them, though we thought they were gonna kill us after we did. There was a lot of publicity about the game, in the local papers and all, and they were always talking about how they was gonna beat us. But we beat them and that was a thrill. Another time we played in Berlin, Jesse Owens came over with us, in front of seventy-five thousand people.

Now in 1950, me and Abe Saperstein had a little dispute about something. In my opinion, he was paying the All-Stars more money than he was paying the Globetrotters and I happened to find out about it. So I became a little peeved with him and I decided I was going to go someplace else. When he found that out, he tried to sell me off. Quite naturally, he wanted to get something for me, you understand. So Abe sold me to the New York Knickerbockers. Now he gave me some money. He told me he sold me for $5,000. So he got $2,500 and he gave me $2,500. Being a kid—I wasn't too old then—well, I was old enough, but I hadn't had any experience or anything like that—at that time I believed him because I thought everybody was honest. That's the way I was raised, to take a person by their word. But later I came to find out that it was something like $20,000 he got, you understand what I mean? But you know, you got to take the bitter with the sweet. You can't be angry about things like that. If you're not up on things you just have to bounce the way the ball bounces.

So I got with the Knickerbockers. At the time I signed with the Knicks I was getting something like $7,500. At that time the top player in the league wasn't getting any more than $10,000, you understand. Now as I recall, the minimum they could pay you was $7,500. That was the standard. Like today, the lowest they can pay you is around $85,000, you understand. Back then certain guys got certain deals, but the deals you made were on your own. You didn't have an agent like they do today. Now these guys today, when they sign a contract, they got an agent and two or three other people that advise them. We had no one. We were just on the ground floor ourselves. So I negotiated my contract with the Knicks myself. Before I left I got up to $10,000—that was my limit. In those days, if you played good they'd give you a raise. I was raised every year, from that $7,500 all the way up to $10,000, so I couldn't complain, you understand. At the time there wasn't that kind of money in the game. Well, it was there, but the owners were getting it, the players weren't getting it. The owners was lickin' their chops, to put it that way, and we were taking the crumbs. I imagine the money we were getting then would now be only meal money for the guys today.

Now when I got into the league there was only two blacks—me and Chuck Cooper. Earl Lloyd came in a little bit later on. Chuck was with the Boston Celtics and I was with the Knicks. The reason why Chuck is said to be the first black player in the NBA is because their season started on a Monday and our season started on a Tuesday. That's how close it was. Actually, I was the first to sign a contract because I was sold before the season even started. Now really, to be fair— I like Chuck and by his being dead I won't say anything—we both should have been considered together as the first black players in the league.

When I got to the Knicks they had Vince Boryla, Harry Gallatin, Connie Simmons, Dick McGuire, Max Zaslofsky, and Ernie Vandeweghe. I have a picture at home with all those guys. Most every year we won that Eastern Division, until Boston got Russell. The reason we didn't win the championship was because we didn't have a center, 'cause I wasn't big enough and Harry wasn't big enough. Connie was big enough and he could shoot, but he couldn't rebound and he wouldn't guard. So that was our downfall. One year, I think it was 1952, we were supposed to get this guy named White, I think, in the draft, but he was involved in the New York City scandals. If we'd've gotten White it woulda been like having Bill Russell.

We had a running team. I could run, we all could run. We'd get the ball and we were gone. That's the way we'd do it. We beat a lot of teams in that league, but we couldn't go all the way without a center.

My game? I was a rebounder and a passer. My assist record, if you check it out, was good for a big man. I would feed a lot. The guys would run to me and I'd give them the ball. I'd give it to Harry or whoever else was there. I thought I was pretty slick as a passer.

When I first came with the Knicks I found I had to change over, you know, play in their style. They didn't want me to be fancy, or do anything like that. What I was supposed to do is rebound and play defense. Some of the men I guarded were Bob Pettit, George Mikan, Arnie Risen, and Dolph Schayes. Schayes used to run me until sweat was coming down me.

127

That's all he did was run. And he was a gunner, too. He'd
shoot all the time, you understand. Those were the men I was
guarding, so you know I was pretty much kept busy all the
time. Those were the stars on the other team, and to keep up
with them I had to be pretty good. On offense, I averaged
about 12, 13 points a game, but I never did shoot too much
because in those days you wouldn't want to be known as a
gunner. That's what they called it. If you shot the ball ten
times you were supposed to make at least six baskets. So I
would never shoot unless I was hot. I would never say to
myself, "I'm gonna set myself a limit." I just wanted to help
the team win. Now today, a lot of these guys got no princi-
ples. They just shoot whenever they want to. But you know,
it would be nice to play today.

Later on we got some other guys like Carl Braun and
Richie Guerin and Kenny Sears from L.A., and we had a
pretty good team. But they broke us up. They sent Harry
[Gallatin] and Dick [McGuire] and me to Detroit. I would
have liked to stay with the Knicks and play with the guys they
had, but I guess they decided to send all three of us together,
since we were sort of like a team, Harry, Dick, and me. I
would have been happy playing with the Knicks, but the
thing is all the time I played there they never did get another
good black ballplayer to play with me, somebody who knew
what I was doing, you understand. And that kinda held me
back, 'cause you can't do something with the other guys because they played the straight way. I felt like I was sacrificing
myself for some guy and I don't think other guys would have
done that. I'll put it this way: at that time they weren't making
any black stars. You already had to be made. It was frustrating, but here's the way I played it: I played the way the guys
wanted me to play. I played by the rules that they'd set up,
and I tried to do whatever they wanted me to do. I didn't have
any self-respect in those days, you know. I have it now but I
didn't have it then. What I should have done is this, what I
should have done is that. That's the way I feel now, but now
it's too late.

In other words, being the first in something, you don't

want to do anything that'll mess it up for somebody else. Maybe if I'd have screwed up some way there wouldn't be any blacks in the NBA today. There was pressure on me, but the thing that made it okay was that the fans, especially the kids, really liked me. I really appreciated that. I think that maybe that was the biggest thrill I had.

The only thing is, I'm sorry today that I couldn't have done much more. I could have if I'd had someone behind me, pushing me in the right direction. What I had was Joe Lapchick. He was a good coach but he didn't have the imagination, you know. He wasn't really up to what the modern-day game was. He had that old-fashioned style that the Celtics had earlier.

But I'll tell you, the Knick fans were something else. You know, we had a tremendous following. We played in that little Madison Square Garden, which brings to mind something I wanted to say. The reason why I think we never did win a championship was because when I was there every time we'd get ready to play in the play-offs they would switch us from the Garden to the Armory. It was because the circus or the rodeo came to town. I think they had some kind of contract with the Garden. I think we'd have won the championship a lot of times, maybe three, if they'd kept us in the Garden, because that was our floor and there we were fast and we were good.

The reason I believe the New York crowds accepted me was that I was a Globetrotter and they'd seen me play before. They knew just what I could do. But they didn't know that when I got with the Knicks I was held back because I couldn't do everything I'd done with the Globetrotters. The Knicks had a style and a plan, and I had to go along with their style.

When we traveled, there were a few places I couldn't stay. In St. Louis, I couldn't stay there. But I tell you what, I believe I coulda stayed in any of those hotels but I had to eat my meals in the room. That was my understanding. But by my being a Globetrotter, I knew the hotels. And somehow I was glad to get away because when you play with the Globetrotters you make friends in a town and those friends got to be like family. And any time I played there, those guys would come around. I'm glad there wasn't those type of guys they have today, though, going around feeding these kids dope and stuff like that. These were clean fellows. They liked sports and they liked what I was doing and they tried to keep me clean. They didn't give me any of that coke business and smoking reefer. I'm really sorry that happens these days. I think these kids have a better opportunity than I had; at least they can make some money.

And another thing, when we'd go to certain places and finish the game, I'd go right back to New York, or else on to the next town where we were gonna play the next game. I kinda liked being on my own. I was on my own anyway, so what was the problem, you know? I never was a hang-out guy.

I did have one incident with another player. It was during an exhibition game. I had a little trouble with a guy from Oklahoma named Bob Harris. I did a little Globetrotter stuff to him and he said where he came from people didn't do him like that. I'm not gonna say exactly what he said but it kinda made me angry. He looked like he was gonna hit me, so I hit him first and knocked him out. He was six-ten and you know, you don't realize how strong you are till you do things. But after that I didn't have any more trouble with anybody.

The truth is, I've had a lot of guys trying to stop me from doing things. The other teams would always get the toughest and roughest guy to put on me. I knew that, but it would keep him from playing his best, too, so I never worried about it. Several big guys used to guard me, like Vern Mikkelson [of the Lakers] and Bob Brannum of the Celtics. But that was part of my life.

I'm gonna tell you something, in my day the fans in other cities never gave me any problems. They knew what I was there for, that I came to play, that I didn't go out there to change anything. They knew the kind of ballplayer I was, and I didn't come out looking for trouble. And when people said something to me, it was always nice. I never had anybody say, "We don't want you here." They always accepted me.

I think 1954 was my best year with the Knicks. We almost won the championship that year. We had the Lakers down 3 to 2, and in that sixth game I rebounded the ball and gave it to Al McGuire and he went down the floor and made a lay-up. But they said it was no good and we lost the championship.

When the Knicks traded me to Detroit I stayed there one year. When you feel you're not wanted, that you're not appreciated, you get out. That's the way I am. I don't care what I'm doing. I moved out when I thought I was of no use to them and they was no use to me.

But that Detroit team I went with was a good one. They had George Yardley and Gene Shue, Walter Dukes, Dick McGuire, Harry Gallatin, and myself, and Red Rocha was the coach. We went to the play-offs that year. I hardly ever played with a team that did not go to the play-offs.

I would have to say that Bill Russell was the most difficult player to play against. At that time we didn't understand Russell because he brought something into the league that we wasn't used to. He was a guy with perfect timing. He'd wait until you released the ball. See, all Russell did was stand back under the basket, you understand, and wait for the player to come to him. And then when you were ready to shoot he would come up and hit the ball some kind of way. I don't think he could handle some of the big guys in the league now, but he did then. I was six-six and he could block my shot.

I think Chamberlain was the biggest, strongest guy I ever played against. But they got some good big guys around now, like the guy from Houston, he's gonna be great. I think Samson has to work on his manhood. He's like a little kid. He don't wanna play. He plays when he wants to. You can't do that. You have to play all the time. The only guy I see around now that I like is Michael Jordan, who plays with the Bulls. I think he's about the greatest thing I ever seen for a little guy. Here's a six-six guy that can do everything. He kinda reminds me of me but he's a lot better.

I think today it's the greatest game ever played. It's better than it was when I was playing. But the thing that they do too much of today is throw the ball away. Now if they could keep the ball, control it better, it would be the greatest game ever played. They can do everything today. They have bigger men than we did. They can do more things than we did. They jam the ball. They dunk the ball. I was probably one of the few men dunking the ball back in my day. I didn't stuff it, but I would dunk. That was part of my game, too. I'd go around a guy, jump up and *boom!* The fans liked it. They always like excitement.

So guys today are better than we ever were, but they're playing a different kind of game than we did. We played more ball control. We didn't throw the ball away, you understand. These guys come down the court and throw the ball away seventeen, eighteen times. But we didn't do that. We held that ball and got what we wanted out of it. It was very seldom that we threw it away. We had better ball handlers, I'll say that. It was quicker when I was playing, but I wouldn't say it was faster, because the guys today are fast.

I stayed with the Detroit team for one year, then I got out and went with the Harlem Magicians, with Goose and Marcus, who'd quit Abe in 1954 and started their own team. Abe just didn't want to pay any of us any money. I can't understand that. He could have kept the whole team going and still made his money and everybody would have been happy.

I stayed with Marcus and Goose for three or four years and then I went back to Abe. I played two years with him and then, in 1965, I finished. I got my knee hurt. When I got hurt, I said I'm gonna drive a cab for a while. I had bought my home and everything, so I didn't have no problems. You know, you didn't need much money then, not like you do today.

The thing about driving a cab is that I'm out there. I can be alone, have time to think, and I can do some good things. It doesn't make me uptight or anythir.g. I just enjoy doing it. I had a good job offer from Gulf & Western in 1978, with an expense account and all like that, but I refused it because I didn't want an eight-hour job. I've got a mother, she's an invalid, and I have to be around her. I'm the only child. Nobody but me.

You know, it's a good life. It's not really bad. Everything I ever did was good, except I didn't make no money. The guys I negotiated with when I was with the Knicks were nice guys. They gave me whatever I asked for, I just didn't ask for enough.

Another thing, I been all over the world. I been to France, Hong Kong, Singapore, Manila, Australia, been to Italy, Belgium, Holland, Switzerland, Germany, been to South America, Rio, Lima, Buenos Aires, even Cuba. We was there before they put the iron curtain up. I've had a great life. I can't complain. The only complaint I got is that I would like to have just one year made big dollars, you understand?

Bill Sharman. Knicks versus Celtics, January 9, 1957; Sharman, number twenty-one, is fighting Richie Garron. (N.Y. Daily News Photo)

Bill Sharman

Bill Sharman joined the Boston Celtics for the 1951/52 NBA season and retired ten years later, in 1961. During his playing career, he earned the reputation as a fearless competitor and consummate shooter. He won the free-shooting title seven times; he was the first player to make over 50 free throws in a row in 1953; he is the only player ever to have three separate streaks of making 50 or more free throws; and his 56 straight free throws made in the 1959 play-offs against the Minneapolis Lakers still stand as a league play-off record. After retiring as an active player, Sharman coached the Cleveland Pipers in the ABL (1962), the Utah Stars in the ABA (1971), and the Los Angeles Lakers in the NBA (1972). In 1980, he was named general manager of the Lakers and became president of the team in 1985. He was elected to the Hall of Fame in 1974 and is the only person to hold ten championship basketball rings in three different leagues and in four different positions. Because of a problem with his throat, he is unable to grant interviews, but he agreed to provide written answers to questions about his career in the NBA.

Actually, I started getting interested in playing basketball when I was eleven years old, when my father put up a basket on our barn in the backyard. My first organized basketball began in the seventh grade, when one of the coaches started a lunch basketball league in junior high school. From there, I played three years of high school ball at Porterville, California, and we were lucky enough to win the championship each year.

During my high school years, I participated in almost all of the athletic events available, and my senior year I earned a varsity letter in five different sports: football, basketball, track, baseball, and tennis. I remember that on one Saturday, I played a tennis match in the morning, which I won; participated in a track meet, in which I won the discus and shot put, and finished third in the high hurdles; and then pitched for our winning baseball team in the afternoon. It was a long day!

Since professional basketball was not very well known or recognized in the early forties, baseball was always my favorite sport. So, at that time, I was always hoping I could develop enough to become a major-league baseball player.

After I graduated from high school in 1944, I enlisted in the U.S. Navy for two years. After I was discharged, I enrolled at the University of Southern California, in 1946. There I played basketball and baseball and was selected as an All-American on most teams during my last two years of basketball. I was six-two, 180 pounds, and played forward under a very set (slow-down) system, which made it difficult for me to adjust to once I got into pro ball, when I was immediately switched to the guard position. As such, I was very fortunate later to play with Bob Cousy, who was such a great playmaker and took the burden off my shoulders to be a point guard. This left me more time to concentrate on my shooting, scoring, and defense, which were my main contributions to the Celtics.

In 1950, I signed a bonus contract out of USC with the Brooklyn Dodgers baseball team for $12,000, and at that time I never really expected to ever play professional basketball. However, even though the old Washington Caps pro basketball club knew I wasn't interested, they still drafted me for their team. So, during the next summer when I was playing class-A baseball in Colorado, the Caps kept calling me, until I finally decided to try both sports for a couple of years to see which one I liked best.

The Caps started their negotiations at $4,000, but I eventually agreed to $8,000 plus a $1,000 signing bonus. They told me the $1,000 signing bonus was the biggest they ever offered in the history of their franchise. Today this is probably hard to believe, but it's true.

After finishing the baseball season in Colorado, I reported to Washington, D.C., to start my first season in the NBA. What an experience that was! The first shock was playing so many games compared to the small schedule we were used to in college. Then I find out that our coach, Bones McKinney, would not fly and we had to take trains, buses, and drive cars to our games. We even had to hitchhike to one game when our car broke down. At that time, 1950/1951, there were no NBA teams on the West Coast, and St. Louis and Minneapolis were our two longest trips. Needless to say, we spent most of our time just traveling and trying to get from one game to the next.

Coach McKinney said he wasn't really afraid of flying. However, he had a fatalistic philosophy and told us he didn't mind being in an airplane when his number was up. But, certainly, he didn't want to be up there when one of the other passengers' number was up.

During that first season we had many exciting and hectic experiences that could fill a couple of books. When we drove, we usually had four players in each car and spent most of the long hours playing cards. Our rules were if you lost, that meant you had to drive until the next game was over.

I remember one time we got caught in a snowstorm and we were going to be late getting to our game that night in Philadelphia. So we decided to dress in our game uniforms in the car while we were driving. As you can imagine, with four huge bodies and eight arms and eight legs flying all over the car and out the windows, it was like a circus. It reminded me of the old saying about having a bull in a china shop. We got there just as the game was ready to start. We had to play without any warm-up.

Unfortunately, about halfway through my rookie season, the Caps developed financial problems, and finally folded in December 1951. So Boston eventually wound up with my contract, which started a very exciting career for the next ten years.

In the fall of 1951, I joined the Boston Celtics for the first time, after reporting late from the baseball season. The reason being that I was on the Brooklyn Dodgers' roster for the last month of the baseball season that developed into a tie with the New York Giants for the National League pennant. So I was with the Dodgers during the three-game play-off series, in which Bobby Thompson hit the famous home run in the bottom of the ninth inning that sent the Giants into the World Series and me to the Boston Celtics.

Since I joined the Boston team a few weeks late and their training camp was already in full swing, I really had a great deal to try and catch up on, besides learning a completely new system. Auerbach was always a very tough advocate of hard work and conditioning early in the season. He always felt you could usually steal a few extra games early in the season by having your team in better shape than your opponents'. This edge, naturally, wouldn't be available later on because the schedule was so heavy and every team played so many games. The record shows that this theory proved to be extremely effective, and Auerbach teams usually started out very fast with winning records. He felt this put pressure on other teams and sometimes they would panic and make foolish trades when they got off to a losing start.

One reason Auerbach was able to do this was that there was no league restriction as to when you could start training camp. Today it is an NBA rule that every team has to start on the same day and can only play a maximum of eight preseason exhibition games. At that time, however, there was no limit and Auerbach would always schedule at least twenty exhibition games to get that extra early experience and try to get off to a winning start.

Accordingly, those first few weeks when I joined the Celtics were the toughest training and conditioning period that I ever went through. Later, I learned to run and practice at least a month before we started our regular training camp so I could prepare myself for his vigorous conditioning program. His daily schedule was usually two and a half hours of practice in the mornings, a strategy meeting of plays, system, et cetera, at noon, and a three-hour session of running and scrimmaging in the evenings. Needless to say, it was tough, and I was never so sore or stiff at any time in my whole career as I was that first week in Boston.

When I joined the team, the two main stars were Bob Cousy and "Easy Ed" Macauley. Teaming up with Cousy in the backcourt was a great experience and a very big adjustment for me. As I mentioned before, in high school and college I always played forward, so with Cousy's extraordinary vision and playmaking skills, he handled the ball most of the time. The thing that amazed me the most was his exceptional peripheral vision. It took me a long time to really adjust and learn that if I would run and move enough without the ball to get open, he would usually see me and find a way to get the ball to me—even in heavy traffic when I thought it would be impossible for him to see me and complete the pass. Before I learned this, I had many passes bounce off me because I just wasn't expecting the ball in some tight situations. So when the sportswriters nicknamed him "the Magician," they certainly picked a very appropriate name.

At that time, Ed Macauley was probably the most talented center in the league. He was extremely smooth and a great passer and shooter with outstanding running speed. However, at six-ten and 210 pounds, he lacked the physical strength to bang around with some of the bigger centers in the league such as Charlie Share, who was seven feet, 280 pounds, Larry Foust, six-eleven and 260 pounds, and especially George Mikan, at six-eleven and 240 pounds, who was a super player and an all-time great.

However, our team developed into a very good finesse club and we were probably the best in the league in execution, passing, and scoring baskets. Although we didn't have the size or strength to rebound with some of the bigger and stronger teams in the league, we finished second in our division my first year with a 39–27 record, which was only one game behind Syracuse.

This was pretty much the pattern of our team for the next four years, during which time we finished second each season. Finally, in 1956, we got Bill Russell in a trade with St. Louis for Ed Macauley and Cliff Hagan and, as the old saying goes, "The rest was history." Russell's tremendous skills in rebounding, defense, and shot blocking were exactly what we needed and we started a dynasty that has not been equaled or matched in any other professional sport today. This includes fifteen World Championships and seventeen NBA final series appearances.

I'd also like to mention that Boston drafted Tom Heinsohn and got Frank Ramsey out of the service the same year that Bill Russell joined the team. Both were super players that are now in the Hall of Fame. Plus, we had many other great players on that club, which made us the deepest team in the league.

I actually believe that the 1956/57 championship Celtic club was the beginning of an era that emphasized and stressed the value of the fast break that has come to represent the style of modern-day basketball that has become the most effective system used today. Before Boston developed this technique of pushing the ball up-court and running at every opportunity, the old style was more of a deliberate slow-down, set-up system that would seldom fast-break.

So, with the addition of Bill Russell, who could control the boards, it allowed us the opportunity to take off early and gamble on the running attack, which was responsible for a lot of easy baskets. Therefore, with Auerbach's coaching, Russell's rebounding, and Cousy's playmaking, the first truly complete fast-break system was developed and refined. Accordingly, I believe these three people deserve most of the credit for starting this style that has become the most dynamic offensive system in basketball history.

Along with the increased usage of the fast break and the running game, another topic comes to mind that I would like to comment on. This involves the tremendous difference and improvement in players' shooting percentages through the years compared to the early percentages in the NBA.

For example, in the 1984/85 season, the Los Angeles Lakers shot 54.5 percent as a team for the entire season. The first year the Boston Celtics won the championship, in 1956/57, they shot only 38.3 percent. After checking the record books, I see where Dolph Schayes, the great forward for the old Syracuse Nationals team, who might have been the greatest outside shooter of all time, only had a career shooting percentage of 38 percent. Bob Cousy's career average was only 37 percent. Even George Mikan, who played with the six-foot free-throw lanes and who took most of his shots in close under the basket, only shot 39 percent. Probably the most remarkable stat is the great Hall of Famer Joe Fulks, who was considered the best shooter and scorer in the NBA during his time in the early years of the league, only shot 30 percent for his whole career.

I think that some of the unusual and unrecognized reasons for the lower shooting percentages are as follows:

Most of the basketball buildings and arenas then were very old and run-down, which made it extremely difficult to play in. In Baltimore, we used to play in a roller-skating rink. In Syracuse, we played in an old building at the fairgrounds that had a leaky roof, a warped floor, and very little heat. They had very few basketball arenas as they do today and most of them had poor lighting, all kinds of different, inadequate floors, bad temperatures, et cetera. Many were used for hockey and we would play right over the ice with no insulation except the basketball floor itself. Suffice to say, with cold, stiff hands and fingers, it certainly didn't help the shooting touch and percentages.

Also, the basketballs were not molded until the late fifties and were often lopsided and not even round, which made them more difficult to dribble and shoot with.

Transportation was another problem and certainly a factor in the early years. Especially before they started using the jet airplanes. We often would leave on a lot of road trips by trains, cars, buses, et cetera, and travel all night just to get to the next game on time.

Another thing is that with less running and team movement, the officials used to allow a lot more pushing, shoving, holding, hand-checking, et cetera. I believe that this is why they had so many fights in those early years.

However, like everything else in sports today, with the younger players getting better coaching and exposure at a much earlier age, there is no doubt that today's athletes are bigger and better. But I just wanted to point out some of the reasons that there is definitely not that big a difference in shooting ability between today's players and those in the early years of the NBA, at least as is indicated by their shooting percentages.

After playing professional basketball and baseball for five years continuously, with both seasons overlapping each other, I finally decided I had to make a decision as to one or the other. In addition to the physical wear and tear of both sports, the mental strain was tremendous, with the constant pressure of producing at peak level all year round. In those days, no one had a long-term, guaranteed contract, which usually meant that if you had a bad year or even a bad month it was very likely that you would be cut or traded.

As a result, the main reasons for choosing basketball over baseball were, first, that I was a starter and a key player on a winning team, with the Celtics. I enjoyed living in Boston and really liked the Celtic players and management. Secondly, in baseball I had not established myself in the major leagues, and the Brooklyn Dodgers were a very strong team at that time, with a solid outfield. Accordingly, my chances of moving up and into a starting position didn't look very encouraging at that particular time. Also, I was making more money playing basketball, and by staying with the Celtics I wouldn't have to move my family around the country as much. So it seemed good to be able to settle in one place after moving around for five consecutive years to different cities across the country. Now I could just concentrate on one sport, which improved my production and contributions to the Celtics immediately.

Scoring and defense were my two biggest contributions to our teams as a player. However, I guess I will always be remembered more for my free-throw shooting. Since free throws were something you could do by yourself, I started practicing them at a very early age. Being lucky enough to have some natural ability and receiving some good coaching, I developed the proper fundamentals, and free throws came pretty easy for me. In high school and college, I was always the best shooter on the team and I didn't miss a free throw during our twelve league games when I was a junior at USC. So, with that early success, it encouraged me to practice and concentrate more on them, which carried over into my pro career.

I finally ended my playing career in 1961, after eleven years in the NBA. I was thirty-five years old and, although I felt I could still play and contribute to the team, I didn't want to feel I was just hanging on to receive a paycheck.

Also, that year Abe Saperstein, of the Harlem Globetrotters, started a new pro league, the American Basketball League, and I was offered a long, lucrative contract to coach the new team in Los Angeles.

So, with the opportunity to return home to California, and a chance to coach, I decided it was a good time to retire. It was a very difficult decision, because I thoroughly enjoyed playing, even to the point of enjoying Red Auerbach's extremely tough running and conditioning program and practices. Most players hated it, but I loved it! Even today I still enjoy working out and competing in many sports and activities like golf, tennis, and volleyball.

After I retired as a player, I had several thrills, all connected to basketball. I coached in three different professional basketball leagues and was lucky enough to be the only person to ever win championships in all three leagues. In 1961/62, I coached the championship Cleveland Pipers in the American Basketball League; in 1970/71, I coached the championship Utah Stars in the American Basketball Association; and in 1971/72, I coached the Los Angeles Lakers in the National Basketball Association. That year we set the NBA record of winning thirty-three straight games.

During my first couple of years in the NBA the players that gave me the most trouble offensively were Bob Davies, Ralph Beard, and Bobby Wanzer. Then, a little later, in my middle years, it was players like Carl Braun of the Knicks, Gene Shue of Detroit, and Richie Guerin of the Knicks, that were extremely tough to guard. Then, my last season, 1960/61, it was definitely Jerry West and Oscar Robertson, who were two of the all-time greats.

On defense, the player that gave me the most trouble my first years in the league was Al Cervi, of the old Syracuse team. He was very quick and extremely strong and physical, and he took great pride in his defense. During my middle years it was Slater Martin who gave me fits, as he was very fast and also a very smart player. I could sometimes shoot over him with my jump shot, but hardly ever was I able to drive around him for an easy shot or lay-up.

Then, my last year in the league, it was Jerry West again who was a super defensive player besides being a super offensive player. Although they didn't keep track of the stats as they do today, I would say that Jerry West blocked more shots and had more steals than any guard who ever played in the NBA. He had those long arms and great quickness that was very deceptive until he stole the ball from you a few times. Later on, I was lucky enough to coach him with the Los Angeles Lakers and had a chance to enjoy and appreciate all his magnificent talents, rather than having to play against him. He is one of the very few players that was a true superstar on offense and defense. There are only a couple of other players in the history of the league that you can say that about

144

at both ends of the court. Many are superstars at one end, but not both. Just for fun, try to name any others.

After thirty years of being a professional basketball player, coach, general manager, and president, I feel there are some changes that could be made in order to improve the game.

First, I'd change the rule to avoid having players foul out of the game. I think it is a terrible shame that fans pay good money to see the best players in the world perform, and they are often on the bench due to fouling out when the most exciting part of the game is decided in the last few minutes, or in overtime.

Instead of having a player foul out on the sixth foul, you could give the opponents the free throws plus the possession of the ball out of bounds. This would be severe enough penalty to avoid letting the game get too rough and out of hand.

I would also widen the playing floor two or three feet on each side of the court. Today the players are so big, I believe this little adjustment would really help the game and eliminate a lot of the congestion, pushing, and shoving around the basket. This would allow more player movement and create a much faster and exciting game.

I would also suggest using three officials. Too much goes on for two officials to monitor the game properly. This is especially true of fouls off the ball, goal-tending calls, last-second shots regarding the clock expiring.

And finally, I would try to improve the present eighty-two game schedule. The season is just too long, and there are too many unnecessary and unimportant games.

It might be a good idea to divide the season into two halves and then arrange some kind of play-off setup in the middle of the season as well as at the end.

George "the Bird" Yardley

George "the Bird" Yardley

George Yardley joined the Fort Wayne Pistons for the 1953/54 season. He ended his NBA career with the Syracuse Nationals, retiring after the 1959/60 season. Yardley, the first NBA player to score 2,000 points in a season (2,001 for Fort Wayne in 1957/58), was a prodigious scorer who combined a fine shooting touch with superior leaping ability. He was an extremely graceful athlete who dazzled fans with the "hang time" on his jump shot and with his uncanny knack for using the backboard to make his shots. Today Yardley lives with his wife in Newport Beach, in his home state of California, and makes his living as president of the George Yardley Co., manufacturers' representatives. Despite two bad knees, one of which is a plastic prosthesis, he is still active in sports, especially tennis.

I grew up in Los Angeles. My father put up a backboard when I was seven or eight years old, so I always had a basket around the house. I played ball in grammar school and junior high school, but I never made the team. When I got to high school, my family moved to Newport Beach. I was too small to play varsity ball, so I played class-D, then -C, then finally class-A ball.

When I graduated from high school I was six feet tall and weighed about 135, 140 pounds, and was very, very slow in maturing. I went to Stanford and didn't make the team there as a freshman. As a sophomore, I was twelfth or thirteenth man. Then I grew a bit, although I was still relatively frail and thin. I did play on the team as a junior and I did fine as a senior. Since it's been thirty years, I could say I was All-America at the time, but I wasn't. I was mentioned on a number of All-American teams, though, so there was some promise there.

I graduated with my class in 1950, but stayed on another year to get my master's degree in business. The Korean war was on and they were drafting people, but I felt my talents were better in basketball than in shooting people, so that's another reason I stayed on in school an extra year.

When I left school, I was drafted by two teams, Fort Wayne and Tri-Cities, both in different leagues. My college coach was Everett Dean, who had a lot of friends in the Midwest, and since my publicity wasn't real good they took his word that there was a chance I could play basketball. As a result, I was the number-one choice of both teams.

But my father had one desire in life, and that was for me to be an Olympic athlete of some sort. He always encouraged me, but he never pushed me. He never said, "I'd like you to do this or that." If I did something he would compliment me on it, but he never asked me to do anything, whether it be in sports or doing a chore around the house. He was just a wonderful guy.

Anyway, I graduated from Stanford in 1951 and played AAU [Amateur Athletic Union] ball for three years. One year I was with Stewart Chevrolet and we won the national championship and I was named Most Valuable Player in the AAU that year. The next year I was also MVP in the AAU, but we lost in the finals. The following year was the Olympics. I was told they had six AAU and six college players on the team and,

148

having done well the two previous years, I was assured of making the Olympic team and I was very tickled at that prospect.

At the time, I was playing at the Los Alamedos Air Station. We had a lot of good players and we played a lot of good teams. It was like playing in a summer league. Everybody was out to get me because they'd heard I was drafted by the pros and would probably be playing pro ball the next year. It was our last game of the year and we were ahead by about 40 points. I was sitting on the bench with the coach when he told everybody to go to the showers because there were only about thirty seconds left in the game. At that point, somebody fouled out and I went into the game. Almost as soon as I got in, a guy broke my hand in three places, so there was no way I could try out for the Olympic team.

I had given up three years of pro ball for a chance to play in the Olympics, but it was more than that. There was also the hurt to my father and mother. It was so disappointing for them, although, looking back on it, it wasn't so bad for me. I was recently talking to a fellow about my brother's son who was on the Olympic volleyball team until he was cut not long ago. This fellow asked me if anything like that had ever happened to me and I said, "No, I really can't think of anything that really hurt that much." But a day or so later I thought, Well, geez, the Olympics was a major thing. . . . But the fact that it didn't really hurt that much at the time was really indicative that my brother's son is not going to have a major problem. He's just got to go on with his life as I did and everything will be fine.

By the time this happened, there was only one league and so I went with Fort Wayne, since they held the rights to me. As far as a contract was concerned, I just stayed out here until I got what I wanted. Their first offer was $6,000 and I ended up with $9,500. Two thousand miles was a big advantage in those days. Communications were bad and they just called me up and said, "We'll offer you six thousand dollars." I said, "Fine, I'll stay here in California. I'll surf and do all the things I like to do. My family has money, so I don't have to go

149

and play basketball, even though I'd love to do it." That worked
fine. They just kept calling. I didn't like to practice anyway in
the fall. I was always in shape because I played volleyball all
summer long, so I didn't feel it was really necessary. So I
missed the first two weeks of training, but I did that every
year. I never went the first two weeks in the eight years I
played.

So I got the $9,500 and joined the club for the 1953/54 season.
They had Larry Foust, Don Meineke, Andy Phillip, Fred
Scolari, Frank Brian, and Mel Hutchins. They were a competitive team, but they were in the same division as Minneapolis, who, with Mikan, were always dominant. At the time,
the Lakers had a relatively slow team. This was about the time
when the jump shot was becoming dominant and you didn't
have specialists that were defensive men and passers, et
cetera. It was just getting to the point where everybody had
to score, although it took another ten years until it actually got
to that point. Speed was just coming into prominence. There
was the fast break, the real set, set, set game of five picks
before you shot. And if you didn't shoot a lay-up you had to
make a set shot. At that time, a team probably only had a
shooting percentage of just over thirty percent.

The jump shot was really the thing that brought basketball out of the backwoods. There were a lot of people who
died hard on that. They were the ones who thought that the
strategy of the pick and roll, among other things they did,
were a big part of the interest in watching the game, and they
probably felt this was lost when the jump shot came along.

When I got to Fort Wayne, there was a totally new re-
gime that had taken over the team. Paul Birch was our coach.
He'd coached one year and he had a certain amount of pride
in having his own selected players on the team. Those that
came from the prior years had a little rougher road. Originally, I'd been drafted by Carl Bennett [the general manager]
and Murray Mendenhall, who was the former coach. They
were high on me and that made it difficult for me with Paul.
I don't know that they had any plans for me. I was just kind

150

of left over from something that happened three years earlier when they drafted me. I don't think they selected me for any particular purpose.

We had a very well-balanced team. In fact, we had better games with our two squads than we did with some of our opponents. Mel Hutchins had been acquired from Milwaukee. Max Zaslofsky had been acquired from Baltimore. I was the fifth forward. There was Jack Molinas and Mel Hutchins, who were the starters at forward, and then there was Fred Schaus and Don Meineke, who had been the Rookie of the Year the previous year, as their backups.

I didn't start at the beginning of the season. In fact, I remember sitting out fifteen straight games. But then they traded Fred Schaus to New York, so I became the fourth forward. And then Jack Molinas got caught in the fix, so I became the third forward. And then Don Meineke got hurt, so I got to play a little bit. Once I was playing, I was better off. Birch then had the fans to answer to if I played well. You see, I played well in practice, but nobody knew about it. Our team consistently beat the first team.

Anyway, I did get to play a little toward the end of that first season because of the unfortunate circumstances, and then, the next year, I played most of the time.

Jack Molinas only played on the team for about two months. I did not like Jack, although all the other fellows did. I think he was a likable person, but we were competing against each other and he was not overly gracious to me, so I didn't feel I had to kiss his ass. He was marvelously talented. I don't think the whole front row combined had his IQ. It was over 150, I think, at least that's what they said, although there might have been a little literary license there. But he just had this incredible desire to bet on everything, like what time the sun would come out. He had to have some action at all times.

The story I heard from our owner, Fred Zollner, was that Jack was called in and told he was betting on games and that they were tapping his phone. They could not stand another scandal, already having had Kentucky and LIU, having caught Groza and Beard when they were already playing for the

Indianapolis team. They had the district attorney there, officers from the league, the owners from our team, and probably some local officials. Anyway, it was a pretty impressive group talking to him, and he couldn't have misunderstood what they were telling him. They said they would put him on a probationary basis and if he cleaned his act up, well, then, nobody would ever hear a word about it. The meeting was over at three and he went home at five and used the same phone and placed a bet. The guy was very smart and very talented, but he just had to do it. He was there and the phone was on the hook and so he took it off and made a bet. A few years ago, about five miles over here in the Hollywood Hills, he was shot and killed. He was in his backyard sunbathing and evidently the people got him, left his girlfriend watching him die. He was an immense basketball talent. He certainly would have been Rookie of the Year, and he was our leading scorer. The problem was that he was a destructive influence.

Molinas wanted to play with his back to the basket. Our man at center had to go out and play someplace else for him to do it. Jack was just as fast as could be and he would always run down the court, get in the middle, put his back to the basket; and that moved Larry Foust, our center, out of his spot. So we didn't do as well as we might have with Jack in there.

He was Paul Birch's number-one draft choice. He scouted him and he was really very high on him. He was a good player, but very selfish. He didn't rebound, he didn't pass—not that that's critical, because I didn't either. I led the team in rebounding but, as they said, my next assist would have broken my record. I'm not so sure I didn't have fewer assists per minute than any player in the league. But they were paying me to score.

People said I was graceful, but I couldn't verify that because I've never seen myself on film. I do know I was probably the best jumper in the league. There might have been others who were good jumpers, but I could move my body well to either side while in the air and still control my shot. Mel Hutchins could do it, too, but we were oddities at the time. This ability obviously helped my rebounding and it allowed me to take a jump shot over somebody who was not quite as tall as I was. I used the backboard a lot. I think you can throw the ball harder and more accurately using the backboard because you don't have to be exact in your distance since it's going to come off the board and go in. I also think it's a little easier shot from the point of view of touch. If you're off a little bit, it can still go in. I also happened to be in position to use the board a lot. Obviously, I didn't use it straight on, or when I was on the baseline, but anywhere in between I'd use it.

I didn't use a lot of trajectory in my shot, especially when I was playing poorly and my shot had less arch than it should have. Whenever I was in a slump the only thing I would try to do would be to arch the ball a little higher, so it would have more touch to it.

My nickname was "the Bird." There are two stories about how I got it, one true, one not. Everybody who ever wrote about it from the time I was a junior in college said it was because I could jump, that I just soared like a bird. It was propagated by John Hall, who was a sports columnist for the *LA Times*. He was at Stanford at the time. He and I were good friends and he took literary license with the nickname. The real reason I got the name came when I was in a fraternity at Stanford. I was only seventeen years old, while almost everybody else was three years older because they'd just come back from the war, in 1946. As a result, all the unpleasant tasks were mine. I mean, I had to do everything. A fellow I roomed with, Dave Davidson, was in the Army, and he said that the guys that did all the dog work there were called the yardbirds. Since my name was Yardley it was real easy to be Yardbird for a year. Because of the difficulty of saying Yardbird, it soon became Bird. It's not nearly as colorful as the first story, but it's true.

In my second year at Fort Wayne I was second on the team in scoring to Larry Foust. I led the team in rebounds and was last in assists. I was very consistent in that department. We did have an excellent team that year, a real good combination of players, though we were a little weak at guard. We had Frank Brian and Fred Scolari and Max Zaslofsky, but they were near the end of their career, though I think Frank could have played forever. He was a little erratic and I think he could have been better for us, but he didn't play very much. Max was older. He was a marvelous shooter, he just had so much heart, but he didn't rebound or pass. All he did was sneak through and shoot. Brian couldn't do everything either, but he could run. And the fast break had a real impact on the game. Nobody really went at it as they should have. We tried to be a fast-break team, but we weren't nearly as successful as the Celtics with Cousy and Russell. Jack Molinas started us on that fast-break thing. He would do it a lot.

That year we lost by 1 point to Syracuse in the finals. We were up by 17 at one point in the first half, then led all the way through the second half. We had the ball with thirty seconds to go, then fifteen seconds to go, and then we throw it right to George King, who goes in for a lay-up. I don't know about that. . . . Some of the players on our team were friendly with Molinas.

Two years later there was a scandal within the league. They decided that none of the suspected players would be announced. Instead, they would just unceremoniously retire. We had two men in that category from our team and I don't know whether it had anything to do with that scandal. . . . We all think that in our own minds we're great and we have a couple of stiffs out there that were hurting us.

Our main rival was, philosophically, Minneapolis. In the later years, it was probably the St. Louis Hawks with Bob Pettit. Our toughest opponents were always Syracuse and Boston because of the rat pits they played in. They played a real hard-nose, tough game. They would, like the Oakland Raiders, intimidate you. In Boston, the crowd was intimidating. In Syracuse, they played in a much smaller gym. It was small and intimate and the fans there were rabid. They were a hard-nose team and they attracted hard-nose fans. They had Al Cervi, Paul Seymour, and Paul Hoffman. You name the

154

ten toughest, nastiest guys in the league and Syracuse had five of them. They'd meet you at the locker room. They'd just walk over and not say a word. Just meet you at the locker-room door and walk out on the court with you. You knew it was not going to be a bed of roses that night. I've heard stories of fans carrying guns, intimidating people in the sense that, "If you win tonight, boys, it's your butt. . . . I've got a lot of money on this game. . . ." Things of that nature. I've heard a lot of stories, but I can't say I ever witnessed that happening.

I was the first to have a 2,000-point season, but I don't know how incredible that was because I think it's typical of winning teams that they don't have a scoring champion. You do one or the other. You either win or you have scoring champions. That year we didn't really have any good players. I was the only guy who could hold his own or have any respectability as a scorer. I also had Dick McGuire on the team, who to me was the finest, most unselfish basketball player who ever lived. If I had a chance to play with Cousy or McGuire, I'd take McGuire in a minute. He really looked for you all the time. He never shot the ball, and if you couldn't score with him on your team, then you couldn't score at all. So I had a huge advantage over everybody. Considering my talent, there were probably ten to twenty other guys in the league who could have changed places with me and scored 2,001 points. I was just in the right place at the right time.

I look back on it now and I can see that the following year it did place a lot of pressure on me. I had a number of problems the following years, physical problems that were mentally induced. I got hypoglycemia and asthma. I was a physical wreck the following year. They said at the time that it was psychosomatic, but I said, "Baloney, I've got a real problem." Now I know it probably was psychosomatic. My mind was doing that to me. I still have asthma, but nothing like it was then. It's something that will always be with me, but I'm sure it was induced by the strain put on me. And after I quit playing the hypoglycemia went away, too. I've never had a problem with sugar. But anyhow, the doctor said it was the pressure from trying to do the same thing I did before.

155

But I've got to say there was no pressure on me while I was trying to do it. We were a lousy team. We'd had two excellent years before when we'd gone to the final, but not that year. We had just moved to Detroit, and that was very disappointing because we all loved Fort Wayne. And personally, in the two years I was in Detroit I never found a saving grace. The games were poorly attended, the people were very cold and could care less about the team. But in Fort Wayne they couldn't do enough for you. If they saw you shopping, they'd pick up the tab. Even today, we send out about one hundred Christmas cards, and maybe sixty of them go to people in Fort Wayne.

There was never any animosity toward us in that city. It was a blue-collar town and the blue-collar workers just liked to see good basketball and they appreciated all the players. I'm sure if there were a crime center in the U.S., Fort Wayne would be the last choice. It was just an all-American city, the kind you'd read about in the *Saturday Evening Post*. It was just a wonderful town. I think it was probably pressure from the league that caused the move. A primary reason might have been because it was difficult to get to Fort Wayne for the other teams in the league. They had to ride overnight on a train, and accommodations were not good. It was real difficult for the league to have a team there. It was also not a money-maker like some of the other franchises. I don't know whether they shared gate receipts in those days or not, but Fred Zollner [the owner] also sold most of his product, pistons, to Detroit to go into General Motors trucks. So he felt if he moved the team up there'd he'd have a better political impact to sell his pistons to those people than if he were still located in Fort Wayne. I think those were the two reasons. I do think he would have preferred keeping the team in Fort Wayne because he had a home there, a plant there, and was popular there. But it was outside pressure that caused the move.

Fred Zollner made some unlikely choices. He hired Paul Birch as coach, and Charlie Eckman, the referee, to coach the team. It turned out to be a good thing because at least it released us from the drill-sergeant atmosphere that Paul Birch had put us under. Birch was a marvelous talent, a marvelous teacher, but every time we'd get behind in a game we'd say, "Well, hell, this is Birch's loss, the hell with him." Everybody was united against our coach. Then, when Eckman came in, he just cut the reins. "I don't care what you guys do, just go out and play." That was great for two years. You can always last a certain amount of time without any coaching. But that's the kind of thing Fred Zollner liked to do.

He was a very generous man, though. He paid the highest salaries in the league. He was always in the background and always very polite and generous in his everyday dealings. He was kind of like a second-class Howard Hughes, the reclusive type. He parted with his money very freely, very similar to Howard Hughes. But I don't think he was a very good businessman from the point of view of building a winning team. His team could have been a lot better had he had more knowledge of the game. He thought he knew all about it, as most owners do, but it wasn't true.

He liked players who fought. All his favorite players got in fights. They were roughnecks. They'd go out and get technicals. That was his type of guy. Maybe that was his frustration in life because he wasn't that type of person. But if I had my druthers, I certainly would have chosen him as my owner—or Mr. [Walter] Brown in Boston, who was a real gentleman. The rest of the owners were basically promoters and they had to scrape by, hand to mouth, sometimes not being able to pay the salaries. On the other hand, we always had our own plane, so we were well rested. We were the only team that had that. After a game, we'd just get on our plane and go home. It was specifically outfitted for us. Fred had the back half and we had the front.

From that point of view, he probably could have assisted us a little more. I liked to sleep and he let me lie down in the back with him. He never objected to it, but I know, in his mind, it was something detestable to him because I was not a first-class passenger. That always rankled him, but he never said anything about it.

157

I took about ten trains in my whole career, and that was generally when the plane was in the shop. Sleepers were not suited for tall men.

The year after I had my 2,000 points, I broke my hand halfway through the season and then I was traded to Syracuse. We were playing in the Boston garden. I broke my hand and Fred said, "Before you take him to the hospital, ask him to come to my box." So I go up there and he says, "You're through as far as I'm concerned. I never want to see you again." I said, "Fine." I was just one of the guys that got headlines and I wasn't this tough, hard-nose guy, and he didn't want me anymore. I never saw it coming, but it didn't really bother me. I got to go home and get out of that lousy Midwest snow a month and a half early. I was going to get my money and I'd come back the next year . . . maybe.

I always had a job during the off-season. I'm an engineer, and I always worked for an engineering firm. I was really more mentally stimulated by the summer job than the winter job. I really felt talking basketball with the players all your life was a bore. It stagnated you. In fact, my most enjoyable experience was having a relationship with Dolph Schayes, because he was an engineer also and at least we could talk about world affairs, or something like that. I don't think any of the other players were concerned with who was the premier of Russia, the welfare state, Social Security, or anything like that. They didn't go beyond the world of sports. I don't think they understood much of what went on around them. Some have been successful since, and we're still close friends, but most of them stayed in sports.

But I can't say enough nice things about Dolph. And it's funny, because before I played with him I couldn't say enough bad things about him. I just detested the way he looked on the court. He was always crying, complaining. He was the first one to go with the high-five. And he'd beat us all the time, which really didn't help our relationship. But once I got to know him, he was one of my favorite people.

*   *   *

It was a straight trade for Ed Conlin. Basically, I wanted to go home. I had gotten as far as Fort Wayne. The car was packed and ready to go back to California, and then I got a call from Paul Seymour. He asked me if I'd like to play for him the rest of the year and the following year. I said, sure. So I did go to Syracuse and about three weeks later we played a game on national television against Fort Wayne. Fred Zollner was in the front row. I had a big cast all the way up my arm, but I got about 30 points in twenty-two minutes and we beat their brains out. When I came out of the game I used my arm with the cast on it to give it to Zollner, just to tell him what I thought of him.

We had a very good team at Syracuse. There was Kerr, Schayes, Bob Hopkins, Hal Greer, Larry Costello, and Al Bianchi. In fact, I didn't even start for them. It was the best team I ever played for. We should have beaten Boston in the play-offs. We lost it in the seventh game of the series, and then they beat Minneapolis 4–0 in the finals, and we'd beaten Minneapolis sixteen straight prior to that. So it was a foregone conclusion that the Eastern Division winner would beat the Lakers.

The next year we also had an excellent team. We played Philadelphia in the play-off series. The pivotal game was down there. They wanted to take Kerr outside to get Chamberlain off the boards and I went into the middle. I was lucky if I shot fifteen percent that game. It's just the worst memory I have in basketball. Had I played a lick we might have done better that year. I just played horribly. I have no idea why. I didn't feel any different. The ball just didn't come off my fingers. It was too bad.

Going to a different team like Syracuse didn't mean I had to adapt too much. They knew what I was, a scorer, and they used me that way. It might have hurt Dolph a little. The only thing was, in going to Syracuse I had to take a cut in pay so that my salary was less than Dolph's. At the time, I thought we were stealing, anyway. I didn't think there was that much money in the world, so it didn't bother me. We'd have all played for nothing. The sad part of today's game, I think, is that the money has hurt it to some degree. I don't think they have the camaraderie between the players you might have if they'd been struggling together as we did. People go through their whole lives and don't have as much fun as we had on a road trip. Everything was always a high. Doing things with guys you enjoy, having fun, doing all the things people do when they go on vacation, getting notoriety out of it, and getting to play basketball. There were no drawbacks whatsoever.

Traveling was something like being in the military: the funny things are the tragic things. Things are fine as long as guys have something to complain about. I remember one time we traveled all night, didn't get to bed at all, and were playing Boston in the first game of a doubleheader in Madison Square Garden. All the guys were kidding around because Molinas had been with the team previously. They were saying, "Boy, if there's ever a time to bet on Boston, tonight's the night." And we must have beaten them by 25 points.

It was the same way if a key player was injured. If I was out a couple of games, we always won them. I know Larry Foust was hurt for eight games and we won all eight of them, not having won eight games in a row in the history of the franchise. It bothered Larry terribly, but he worried a lot to start with. He worried constantly. He was very funny, practical-jokewise, but as far as a sense of humor, I'd have to say he was way down the list.

I remember one thing Larry did when Paul Birch was coaching the team. Paul was a fanatic and very seldom did he come into the locker room at halftime without kicking the bag of balls. Sometimes he'd throw oranges against the wall, or at the players. He was a very physical, violent man. In those days, Fred Zollner was a great believer in crutches for physical things, so we always had a bottle of oxygen with the team. I don't know if we ever used it, but we always had one with us. It must have weighed seventy-five pounds. We also had a trainer with us full-time, who traveled with the team, which was very unusual. Anyway, the poor trainer had to carry that oxygen bottle around. So one day Larry put it in the ball bag at halftime. Birch came in, kicked the bag, and broke his toe. He never found out who put it in there, though he tried.

There are a lot of stories concerning Larry, especially when he went to Minneapolis with Hot Rod Hundley. Hot Rod just picked on him unmercifully. It was a real love-hate relationship. Larry did not like being made fun of in any way. He was very sensitive. Most times he'd act like a four-year-old, pounding his fists, getting upset, if the coach or anybody else made fun of him or criticized his play. That was one of his problems, his inability to take constructive criticism. Birch really made him into the player he was. Same with a lot of people. He made them very good. You didn't go out there and loaf, or you knew you were going to get the wrath of him. He was responsible for a lot of our success in the two years we worked as a good team.

For a time, I played with Sweetwater Clifton. I remember him coming to our house one Christmas and saying it was the first house of white people he'd ever been in. He wondered if we had any 7-Up or Coke. He explained that that was the reason he got the name Sweetwater, because he loved that stuff. My wife said she was sorry, but she didn't have any. It was winter. It was snowing like hell out. The kids and I were sick with the flu. Sweetwater disappeared, going out in weather like that. A little while later he came back with about four cases of soda and flowers for my wife. He didn't want to be without the soda and he wanted to bring back enough so that we'd have it in case somebody else came over to the house. He was just such a generous man. Diana, my wife, was very touched by the fact that he'd never been to a house of white folks before, and that he enjoyed us enough that he would come. It was very nice of him because he was a shy and bashful man.

One of the real characters I played with was Walter Dukes. He was always coming downcourt swinging those arms out uncontrollably, even in practice. He could really hurt someone. One day, somebody tied a bell around his neck on

161

a piece of leather so we'd know when he was coming downcourt in practice and could stay away from him.

He wasn't very attractive, but he would come in after a game, put on a blue suit, black shoes, same white sweatsocks he wore in the game, and go out with the most gorgeous women you ever saw. But he always smelled bad. Sweetwater's personal hygiene was better than anybody else that played basketball. He used to brush his teeth at halftime, he was so clean. So we had Sweetwater get some deodorant, toothpaste, and a toothbrush and give it to Wally. It was just about when Ban roll-on was coming out.

When Sweetwater gave it to him we were all there watching Wally. We made him shower and then, after he got out, we watched him trying to use the deodorant. The only person he'd ever seen use one like that, a roll-on, was a woman, so he put it on the inside of both thighs and down his chest. He just didn't know where to put it. It took Sweetwater about ten games to get up the courage to broach the subject with him.

When I decided to retire, I'd played one and a half years with Syracuse and five and a half with Fort Wayne. There were no physical reasons for my retirement, it's just that my kids were starting school and it was not an easy life for my wife, although she never complained. It just seemed like the time to go. I'd had a good year, but I'd finished horribly. It would have been nice to come back and do better, rub out the series we had with Philadelphia, but overall I'd had a good year. I'd made the All-Star team with Syracuse, which was probably more of a compliment than the other five years I made the team while playing for Fort Wayne, because it was kind of by default with them [one player from each team had to be chosen]. I had an opportunity to go into business, and so I took it.

For the first two years I was out of the game, I really poured myself into the business. I missed playing in the NBA, but I was working a sixty-hour week so I didn't think about it too much. I do remember that that year the Lakers had an exhibition game out here before they went into the play-offs and I played against them. I did very well and had thoughts that I'd made a mistake. Then, the following year, Abe Saperstein formed the American Basketball League and I played home games with the LA Jets, which didn't interfere with my business. I went on a few road trips, too, and so I made a lot of money. The bad news was that none of the checks cleared.

There were some dramatic changes in the game while I played in the NBA. For one thing, at the end, players could not be stopped by defensive specialists. Every team had a defensive forward and guard and maybe a third guy who could play defense both ways. As time went on, the teams could just not afford that luxury, because there was no way you were going to stop a guy with a good jump shot.

Mel Hutchins was by far the best defensive basketball player that ever lived, better than Russell and all of them. Russell could not play defense man-to-man. I scored 52 points on him twice. I just loved to see him coming. But when he was waiting for me there under the basket, well, I was lucky to get 10 points. But as an individual defensive player, Hutchins was the best. In our play-off series against Philadelphia Mel must have blocked seven of Paul Arizin's shots, yet he still got 35 points, which was monumental in those days. Hutchins totally destroyed him, yet he still got his 35 points. They wound up beating us by 15 points. If you could score on Hutchins you could score on anybody. So, if you could score on Hutchins, as Arizin did, then there's just no spot in the league for defensive specialists.

They talk about how rough the game is today, but I don't think there's any comparison with the way it was when we were playing. In the late forties and early fifties, it was much rougher, tougher, and nastier a game than it is now. I had eighty stitches in my head just from pro basketball. You never see guys getting stitched up anymore. Guys would physically abuse you just to intimidate you. As a rookie, you were taking your life in your hands. I took more punches as a rookie than I would have taken had I been a fighter. They hit you in the stomach, an elbow to

163

the head, and they wanted you to know that it was not unintentional. They wanted you to know they meant to do it and they'd do it again. An awful lot of good basketball players didn't make the NBA because of that intimidation factor.

There was a guy from Milwaukee [originally Tri-Cities and then St. Louis] named Bill Calhoun, who gave me the most trouble defensively. He was the kind of guy who wouldn't let you get the ball. He'd just hound you and you wouldn't get the ball, period. Once you had the ball, you were okay, but getting it was almost impossible because your teammates didn't want to pass it to you if there was the chance that it might get intercepted. He never scored much, but if I went to the boards and he took off a little early, I could never beat him downcourt. He was always intent on the basket—and me. He was going to be between us no matter where we were. He'd just hound you until you died. And he was the nicest guy. You couldn't get mad at him.

There were two defensive players that never got enough credit for it, Tommy Heinsohn and Jack Twyman. Both were real tough, but on them I could always get the ball and score. If you're having a good night, nobody's going to stop you. If you're having a bad night, anybody can stop you.

There's no question that Bill Russell's coming into the league changed the game. You just couldn't take a lay-up against him. He just took that portion of the game away from you. That meant that your man could let you go in for a lay-up. He could play up on you more and force you to go around him. Then, if you didn't stop to take a jump shot, you were going to get it blocked underneath. He was certainly the most intimidating, most dominant person that played sports. But there is one thing that always impressed me. Russell played in the 1956 Olympics and he didn't come to the Celtics until late December, at which point they were 18 and 1, with Tommy Heinsohn as an addition to the team. I've always felt that Boston would still have been the dominant team in basketball, even without Russell, because Heinsohn was exactly what Cousy needed. The disastrous team would have been St. Louis if Russell had never been traded to the Celtics. They might never have lost a game, what with him and Pettit on the same team. As a matter of fact, if I were starting a team and had my choice between Russell and Pettit, I would take Pettit over Russell. I think he was the better basketball player and could do a lot more things. He rebounded as well as Russell. He didn't block shots, but he scored considerably more. He was very unselfish and a much more likable person. Bob is one of my favorite people. Teammates always gathered around him. And, at the end of a game, he was just like Jerry West. He'd shoot the ball and then go after it. He seldom missed a rebound in the last few minutes of a game. He might take five shots, but eventually he'd get it into the basket. Had he and Russell played on the same team, it would have been outrageous.

When Bob first got to St. Louis, his skills were awful. We used to love to see him coming. St. Louis never came close to us his first year. He couldn't play defense. Alex Hannum was the man who made him.

On defense, I didn't have to play the tough guys because we had Mel Hutchins to do that. When I went to Syracuse and played alongside Dolph, that's when I had to play the tough guys. By then I'd learned that defense was important. I thought I played good defense, just based on Bill Calhoun's way of doing it: keep the guy from getting the ball. I think I did as good a job as anybody could on Elgin Baylor. The guy who used to kill me was Joe Grabowski from Philadelphia. He was about six-nine and he used to drive me nuts. Then, when I came to Syracuse, I had to guard Paul Arizin, which was a much easier job for me. It was funny, because Arizin was ten times the ballplayer Grabowski was.

You can't compare basketball players now with those that played years ago. They don't even look like the same physical specimens. I wouldn't even make a good college team now, that's how much of a dramatic difference in talent there is. The only recent player I could compare myself to would be Rick Barry; only he passed much better than I did. Basically, the thing I did better than most forwards at that time was rebounding. Very few players rebounded and were also in on the fast break. Dolph rebounded very well, but he didn't

165

fast-break. I feel that I gave the team I was playing for a big edge in that I could get a rebound and still make a basket at the end of a fast break. I wasn't fast, but I was quicker than most people.

By far the most disappointing thing in my career was never winning a championship title. I'd have given up the 2,000 points in a minute just to win one title. The 2,000 points didn't impact on me until recently. It didn't really affect me at the time. The thing that thrilled me was that I broke Hank Luisetti's record in college, and then breaking George Mikan's record in the pros. They were the number-one and -two players of the first fifty years of basketball, and to have broken both their scoring records was a big thrill.

The 2,001 just happened to be 2,001. The only good part of that was that we were playing Syracuse in the last game of the season and Paul Seymour, the coach, swore he would never allow me to get 2,001 points, no matter what happened. So he put Al Bianchi on me. The first quarter I got 14 points. Then they changed that system and put somebody else on me. Then I was 2 points shy of the 2,000. Then they put three guys on me and I didn't even get the ball for about ten minutes of the game. With about five minutes to go I was on a fast break. My team waited for me, gave me the ball, and I dunked it for my two-thousand-and-first point. I wish I'd known how much Seymour wanted to stop me from doing that. I would have loved to tweak him just a little bit.

But Paul became a good friend of mine once I went to Syracuse. He even told me how much he hated me. Paul's the strongest mental man I've ever met. He doesn't need anybody. Yet if I broke my hand today and needed his assistance, he'd drive from Syracuse here without taking a nap, just to help me. But if you plead with him, try to make him feel guilty, he'll just make you feel like a crumb.

When I was playing I was a real bitcher. I bitched all the time. What hurt me more than anything else were just little ticks on the arm. So if a referee didn't call a foul on that, I would be off. I was a moaner, just a spoiled kid when I was young. I'm still spoiled. I'll never get over it. You can be young once, but you can be immature forever.

But I don't think the referees gave me a tougher time because of my attitude. The best referee was Sid Borgia, and he let the game get completely out of hand. Obviously, I would have scored a lot more if I never played a game with Borgia refereeing, but I always felt that if I got 20 points in a game he officiated, that was as good as I could have played, because he'd make it real difficult for a guy to score. He gave the defense every edge. When Borgia was in there, we changed our style of play, and that's really something. You don't change your style for different teams normally, but with him you always rebounded stronger, played harder defense, and adjusted to his way of calling the game. And he's the only man I know that we did that for. We never even discussed referees other than Sid.

I may be the only scorer that ever lived who liked Sid Borgia. Pettit detested him. Everybody said they just hated to play with Borgia, but I really respected him. Didn't bother me a bit that he peformed all those gyrations. In fact, I enjoyed it. It was part of the spectacle of the game. He was putting money in my pocket by making it a better game, and that was fine with me. I would go into a game with him on the floor with a better mental attitude. I'd play better defense and pass better. I'd just be a much better basketball player with Sid reffing. He was going to negate my strength, so I would try to fit in with the team a little better than I would if somebody else were refereeing.

In my mind, Alex Hannum was the best coach I ever saw. He was strong, smart as a whip, logical, and I think he got along with people very well. They may not have loved him, but they got along with him. He was a Vince Lombardi–type coach that developed a team around its talent. He made Philadelphia the team they were when they won the National Championship. Schayes coached them, but Hannum was the guy that made them what they were. He was the only guy that had any impact on them. He coached them before Dolph and developed them into a team. Then Dolph took over. But Dolph was not a real good disciplinarian. Hannum was very similar to Paul Seymour. He would be my second choice as to the best coach I knew. He was also strong. Al Cervi was the same way. He coached Syracuse my first year.

I didn't think much of Red Auerbach as a coach. Cousy coached that team on the floor. Auerbach was just the right guy at the time. I think he's a pompous ass, which probably prejudices my opinion about him. He's never humble about the fact that it was anything other than his talent that got him where he was, and it was not his talent alone that did it. He wasn't that successful in other places he'd been. I think his baiting of referees might have lost him a game or two. Anytime a coach gets a technical thinking it'll fire his team up, the team's immediate reaction is, "That stupid ass is losing us a point."

The highlights of my career did not necessarily come in basketball. One of the things I really pride myself on is the fact that I won the Nationals and was All-American in volleyball two years, won five National Championships in tennis, and was able to play basketball at a high level. I think that's my biggest accomplishment, being at the top of three sports on a national level.

I have two bad knees from my basketball-playing days. One is real bad and the other is plastic and it's not too bad. The way I played, rebounding at both ends of the court, just wore them out. Didn't bother me while I played, but they did afterwards.

Because I have a prosthesis I get a lot of calls from people and requests to write articles, because doctors are very skeptical about having anybody do anything with a plastic device, for fear of liability. As a result, they ruin the quality of life for a hell of a lot of people who don't have to have that burden on them. I had not won a national championship in tennis with the plastic knee until this year and that was one of my biggest thrills because of the impact it had. If you can say you won a national championship with a plastic knee, then that gives people an indication that they can do a lot of things they're not presently doing. I greatly encourage people to disregard their doctor's orders and do what they want.

I like the game today. I enjoy watching it. It does get to the point where it's the same thing over and over, and I think they should make the floor bigger, the key bigger, and raise the basket.

I'd pay any price to watch Magic Johnson play. He's the only player I really enjoy watching. He and John McEnroe are my favorite athletes, and that's a dichotomy. I think McEnroe behaves like I did, so I have simpatico. I'm sure nobody liked me when I played, and there was no reason to. I'm not a despicable person and I get along with everybody, but I would not respect myself if I were on the other team, because I was a shooter and nobody likes the guy that doesn't play an all-around game. If somebody did like me it was probably because of something other than the way I played basketball. But the guys on my team were always very supportive of me. Now whether I just never heard their complaints or not, I don't know, but we always got along really well. The only time I heard anything contrary was during the era of Stokely Carmichael and Eldridge Cleaver and those people in the sixties. Walter Dukes wrote an article for one magazine that said I was a bigot and if it hadn't been for me hogging the ball and being opposed to him because he was black, his career would have been far different.

Nothing could have been further from the truth. I roomed with all the black guys from the time they came into basketball because I really enjoyed them. The sad part is, if you don't like a black man, then they tell you you're a bigot. I roomed with Sweetwater and with Chuck Cooper, and I had no bigoted attitude. If I didn't like a guy, I didn't care what color he was, and felt I had the privilege without repercussion.

169

Norm Drucker

Norm Drucker

Norm Drucker, who played a short time after World War II in the American Pro Basketball League, began his NBA officiating career during the 1952/53 season. Distinguishing himself as one of the finest officials in the league, he remained there until 1969, when he was enticed to the newly established American Basketball Association as a referee and supervisor of officials. He remained in that position for seven years, whereupon he returned to the NBA, refereed for one more year, and then became supervisor, staying until he retired in 1981. Today he and his wife, Shirley, live part of the year in Florida and part on Long Island, New York, where he has a children's summer day camp.

I first got involved in playing basketball in local community centers and neighborhood parks in Brooklyn. I played at Erasmus Hall High School and learned the game from Al Badain, a great coach. After being out of school for a year an assistant coach at City College, Bob Sands, motivated me enough so that I applied and was accepted at City. At that time, in 1948, I wasn't thinking of going to college, really. Mostly, kids in my neighborhood didn't go to college. But I did go and played for Nat Holman on the 1941/42 team that went to the National Invitation Tournament. That was Red Holzman's last year and we had a good team, with Red Phillips and Sonny Hertzberg. The following year, '42/'43, we had an up-and-down season. We didn't have any depth and the war draft depleted our roster.

In February 1943, like many others, I went into the Army and served for three and a half years. I was in the European Theater of Operations and was discharged as a first lieutenant. I returned to City College in September 1945, hopeful of completing my requirements for my degree and also to continue my basketball career. Prior to my Army service, I enjoyed playing for Nat Holman, who was a great coach, but after close to four years of Army service I found it difficult adjusting to Nat's basketball discipline and being close to players four years younger than I was. I was offered a contract by the Troy Celtics of the American Pro Basketball League, and accepted. Eventually, I was traded to the Trenton Tigers, where my coach was a legendary figure of those days, Herb Gershon.

I'm five-eleven and I played guard. I wasn't a great player, but I was a good-sized guard and considered tough, team-oriented, and a very good defensive player. While I was playing, I graduated and entered the New York City school system. I played until 1949 and while playing I started refereeing boys'-clubs and community-center league games. Very shortly, I was doing college games, and at this point I was assisted by John Nucatola, who conducted a basketball officiating school for the top prospects on the East Coast. The officiating supervisor for the American Pro Basketball League was Matty Begovitch, who was a former great player with St. John's, which was known as the "Wonder 5." I spoke to him about the possibility of officiating in the American Basketball League and he arranged for a trial schedule. Besides the games this meant car travel on icy roads to places like Elmira, Wilkes-Barre, and other difficult small cities. I also had the problem of knowing some of the players personally from when I played, and it took a great effort not to let friendship interfere with my officiating. But I was fortunate, and it worked out.

About this time I got to know Haskell Cohen, who was the publicity director for the NBA. He organized games and coaches' clinics during the summer and I worked some of these summer games. By the way, he was the originator of the NBA All-Star games. It's hard to believe that in those days he had to beg owners to sponsor the game. In fact, Walter Brown held it in Boston two consecutive years because they were afraid it would be a flop in any other city; and, of course, there was no profit attached to this game. Anyway, he was the one responsible for my working one NBA game in 1951 or '52—and, as it turned out, one of the most difficult games I ever had. But it whetted my taste for NBA ball.

I was teaching at J. H. S. 73 in Brooklyn in 1953 and about 1:00 P.M. I was told that I had a call from a Mr. Maurice Podoloff, who was then NBA commissioner, and who I had never met. I thought it was a gag. Today the commissioner, with a large staff, would never call a referee, but in those days he did many routine, day-to-day chores. Anyway, when the party on the line said, "This is Mr. Podoloff," I said something to the effect that I was Pat Kennedy, who was the number-one referee at the time. He said, "We have an emergency and Haskell tells me you are a good official and we need an official in Baltimore for tonight's game. Can you make it?" By this time I realized it was Mr. Podoloff, and of course I said yes, and immediately made arrangements to get to Baltimore by train.

I got to the arena and was directed to the dressing room, which was on the second floor. I waited for the other official to arrive. It was now about ten minutes before game time and still the other official was nowhere to be found. I reported to the scorer's table and the PR man for Baltimore said the game would have to start promptly, as they had some promotion at the half. I called the captains to the center of the court, and they were Chick Reiser from Baltimore and Al Cervi from

Syracuse, who were player-coaches for their respective teams. They both had never seen me in an NBA game and they both were tough—maybe vicious would be a better word—ball-players, and here I was going to work alone. As we are about to start the game, the other official, Max Tabacci, a real old-timer, suddenly appears at the ·table, takes his coat off—he had his uniform on underneath—and comes out to center court. We shake hands and he introduces himself, showing everybody that we'd never met previously. He says to me, "This is your first game?" I said, "Yeah." He says, "Let them play," which means don't blow the whistle too much.

We let them play and of course there were bloody noses, body bruises, players on the floor, and the game nearly out of control. He now got very angry and in the second half he said, "Let's call it tight." We called it tight and I don't have to tell you what happened. Everyone was mad at me. At the end of the game, he goes to the scorer's table, where he had deposited his coat, puts it on, and leaves me to fight my way back to the locker room. That was my introduction to NBA basketball. The one good feature of this experience was that I learned that officials had to be consistent.

I came back into the league during the '52/'53 season. During those days the league had some officials who only worked pro ball, such as Sid Borgia, Jim Gaffney, Arnie Heft, Mendy Rudolph, Stan Stutz, and Jim Duffy. Others, such as Julie Meyers, Lou Eisenstein, and John Nucatola, worked both college and pro ball.

In the early days, all referees had other full-time positions, as it was impossible to live on basketball earnings alone. In fact, many players and coaches had other jobs during the off-season and some during the regular season. It was a carryover from the old American Pro League, where you supplemented your job by playing ball on the weekends. I was in the New York City school system assigned to the Office of Continuing Education. Mendy Rudolph sold advertising for WGN-TV, Chicago; Arnie Heft was in real estate; Jim Duffy was a car salesman; Earl Strom worked for General Electric; Lou

Eisenstein was in the sports uniform business; Jim Gaffney was a golf pro at a country club. It went on and on. We worked around our main jobs, as the games were primarily on weekends and most of the teams were in the East.

When I came into the league there were only eight teams, so Fort Wayne, St. Louis, and Minneapolis were considered the Wild West. Traveling was easy. An example would be working a game in Boston on Saturday night and Baltimore Sunday night. Wherever you were, you could get home in one to three hours. We were paid by the game, and if you got hurt you didn't get paid, unless Commissioner Podoloff thought you deserved it. I think everybody started at $40 a game, and every year that you came back you got an automatic $5 raise. Expenses were paid separately. Of course, today referees would laugh at those expenses. For a while, we had to hand in our expenses to the penny, so you'd put down lunch, $1.25; dinner, $3.20; cab to the airport, $1.30. Later they changed it to where you got $10 a day for meals, do what you want with the money. But in those days, $4 would buy a good meal.

After my third year in the league, in 1956, I was making $50 per game. I was going to get an automatic $5 raise, but I thought maybe I should be getting a little more. So I called and asked to see Mr. Podoloff. He was about five-one, rotund, wore big red suspenders, and spoke very well. He could really intimidate you with his ability to speak. He sat behind a large desk that magnified his smallness. That desk must have been about 6' by 4', and when he sat down and you were sitting on the other side his head just appeared over the top. You constantly had to look to see if he was there. I got to know later on that although his outside veneer was brusque, he was rather sensitive inside. Anyway, he says, "Okay, what's on your mind?" No informality like, "You're doing a good job," nothing. I said, "I know I'm up for a five-dollar raise, but with all my financial responsibilities, I'd like a ten-dollar raise." Of course, in those days asking for a 20 percent increase was unheard-of. At this point, he pounded his desk, stood up to his full height, and said, "Are you trying to bankrupt the

175

NBA?" Repeating this story today sounds funny. I said, "Of course not," and he said, "You will get your five-dollar increase, the same as everyone else who has a good season." I walked out of his office thinking I did not get my raise, but in my first check I received the increase. To this day, I'm happy that the NBA is successful, because I may have been the cause of the league's demise.

From 1953 to 1960, the league usually scheduled back-to-back games. I guess this was done to save money and also to create more interest in each city. It was common for Boston to play in New York on Saturday night and the same two teams to play in Boston on Sunday afternoon or night. Usually, the same two referees worked both games. Of course, since 1970, you will find referees very rarely seeing the same teams more than twice a month. In fact, I once officiated four Knickerbocker games on the road in a six-day period and Ned Irish blamed me for the three losses. In all the years I officiated I was never blamed for a win.

Generally, the policy was for the referees not to travel with the teams unless one of the teams had a charter and then we were told to travel with them so as to save the fare. However, we were constantly thrown into the same traveling mode. An example would be if you had a Saturday night game in New York between Fort Wayne and New York, and a Sunday 2:00 P.M. game in Fort Wayne with the same two teams. Both teams and the officials would rush to make the 11:30 train out of Penn Station. Both teams and officials would meet in the club car trying to get some sandwiches or drinks before retiring. Because so much travel was done by train, referees and teams found themselves usually on the same trains because usually there was only one or two trains available.

Because there were only eight teams in the league and a handful of officials, it meant you officiated more often in each city. There were many referees who may have worked ten or twelve games in a city. It's rare today if a referee is more than four times in any one NBA city for the entire season.

In the social atmosphere of meeting on trains, airports, and hotels, the conversation was shop and small talk. Usually,

176

the teams and referees stayed at the same hotels, and after the game we would run into the coaches and ballplayers. There is very little of this type of contact today. When I was supervisor in 1977, the rules were already in effect that officials could not stay at the same hotels as the teams.

Except for the one game I worked in an emergency, I started in the NBA in 1953 and when I left to go to the ABA for the '69/'70 season, I had seen many changes. Over the years, the overall improvement has been in the shooting, coaching, and the change from good individual defensive play to team defensive play. This change was necessary because of the improvement in the offensive play of individual players and the inability of a defensive player to stop a good offensive player in a one-on-one situation.

In the early days we had players who were considered good shooters if they were completing thirty-five percent of their attempts. Over the years this percentage has been climbing and we now see shooters in the forty-five-percent-and-above bracket. The athlete has become better and bigger, which has changed the game. The game used to be played below the basket and now it is being played above the basket.

The 24-second rule wasn't in effect when I started, and the game became boring during the final three minutes. It should be the most exciting time of the game, but it wasn't. This was because the rules paid a premium to the team that could freeze the ball and not attempt to score when they were ahead. Players like Al Cervi and Bob Cousy could freeze the ball by themselves while other players stood around doing nothing. It may have been good strategic basketball to freeze the ball because the object was to win the game, but it was boring.

The league tried different rules in an attempt to improve the game. One year we had a jump ball after each basket in the last five minutes of the game. On each jump ball each player had to line up with his man. It was the referees' responsibility to see that each pairing took place. The last five minutes took an eternity. This rule was an attempt to give the losing team their opportunity to get the ball back and score. At the time, they thought it would be a good idea. This change created a little more excitement because it gave the losing team the chance to get the ball back, but a jump ball after each basket? I don't have to tell you that this rule went quickly by the boards. Another change was the rule which gave the ball back to the team that was fouled in the last two minutes of the game. They tried all of these Band-Aid solutions that really didn't work. The game needed continuity of play without a parade of foul shooters; and rules which would insure that the game could be played in the same way throughout the contest.

Then they came up with the idea of having the offensive team play with a 24-second shooting clock. A practice scrimmage was held and, according to Eddie Gottlieb (the Philadelphia owner), Dan Biasone (his counterpart at Syracuse) came up with the idea of the 24-second clock. They timed the offense, and the average time it took the offensive team to attempt a shot was 16 seconds; and so Dan said, "Let's add eight seconds and work with a twenty-four-second clock." That's how the 24-second clock was born and in the estimation of many it saved pro basketball. The games became much more exciting and spectators did not leave the arena during the last two minutes of the game. The art of freezing the ball became a thing of the past. The clock was now a psychological advantage for the losing team. Teams soon learned that when they were ahead it was poor strategy to try to use up eighteen to twenty seconds of the clock before shooting because they usually ended up with a poor attempt or because of lack of time the wrong player was attempting the shot. Boston was the first team to realize this, and Bob Cousy once said that you always had to play the game as if you were losing. However, the more talented teams are able to use up more of the clock and still attempt a good shot.

The clock also changed the officials' way of working. The clock speeded up the game and demanded the officials stay in better shape. During a game, with the 24-second clock, an official runs between five and six miles. Of course, it's not the

178

same type of running as a ballplayer does, but if you aren't in real good physical shape it may be reflected in your judgment and inability to get into good positions. Officials started to stay in condition all year round. You rarely ever see an NBA official who doesn't look physically fit. It's not so in sports that do not require running, such as baseball and sometimes football.

As ballplayers became faster and more agile, and all teams went to the running and fast-break game, officials had to make an additional effort to keep themselves in the best of shape, both mentally and physically. As an official becomes more experienced he learns tricks of the trade, which permit him to be more effective with less running. You get to know the patterns of teams, and this permits you to get better angles and positions. Another important part of officiating—besides intestinal fortitude—is the ability to concentrate and relax. Most of your good NBA officials have these attributes.

When there were fewer teams in the league, officials got to know the teams pretty well, as we saw them very often. Today, that has changed; with twenty-three teams in the league you just can't know them all. I think that because of this and some other reasons it is more difficult to officiate today. All officials enjoy working the better games, although it's not said publicly. The better teams have more finesse and the games are like a ballet; while the poorer teams usually make up for the lack of finesse with aggressive play, which usually lends itself to a game which is known as a game with a "stevedore's touch."

Were there any particular players I liked or disliked? Well, psychologically, certainly. Any player who deliberately or constantly gives you a hard time, you may dislike him and subconsciously, if you do, it may show up in your calls. All pro referees try not to let this dimension come into the game, but I rather doubt that it can be eliminated from your mind. The one player I did not get along with was Rick Barry. This was only on the court, and since those days we have become friendly. He was a great competitor and quite vocal. He also expected to or hoped to get each and every call in his team's favor. We had constant problems in the NBA and ABA. He complained, and this type of reaction to calls gained him the distinction of having many technical fouls called; and he got his share of ejections.

Usually, the superstars have very little to say to the officials. They play and are not distracted, no matter what the call may be. Over the years, I heard very little from such players as George Mikan, Slater Martin, Paul Arizin, Tom Gola, Frank Ramsey, Bob Pettit, Bill Russell, Wilt Chamberlain, George Yardley, Artis Gilmore, and Julius Erving.

The coach that comes to mind that I had many a confrontation with was Red Auerbach. He was always trying to get an edge, and I wasn't going to give him any in games I worked. Most of the officials felt the same way. Sid Borgia and Mendy Rudolph and others made him live by the rules. Some of the others did not. Did his attitude and behavior spill over into other games and did I subconsciously react negatively to his team? I don't know. At the time I thought not and, hopefully, I was professional enough to treat each game as a new one.

In the early days, up to 1964, we were afforded very little security from the time we entered our locker room until we left the arena. You got onto and off the court yourself. Later, we were afforded a security guard, and the league rule was that he had to be in uniform. I remember in St. Louis the guard was about eighty years old. He was a former usher and in no condition to defend himself or the referee as we had to walk through the twenty-five rows of fans to get to the court in Kiel Auditorium. Most referees told him to remain in the locker room, as it was more prudent for us to get through the crowd ourselves. He was happy and of course some of the beers that were in the locker room were consumed before we returned.

There were many incidents between referees and fans throughout the league. It seemed that there was one every night there was a game in Syracuse. Of course, here again you had to walk through the crowd to get to the locker room. In Boston, one night, Earl Strom and I had a donnybrook with two fans as we were coming off the court. Luckily, after the first punches, the police were there to break it up. In Los Angeles, Earl and I were again involved with some fans who blamed us for the loss. Come to think of it, Earl Strom seemed to be in many of those battles. One night Mendy Rudolph was attacked by a fan as we were leaving the court in Cincinnati Gardens. Here again, the officials had to walk through about ten rows of fans to get to our locker room. Because of these problems it was a common practice for referees when leaving the court to take off their belts and wrap them around their hands, leaving the belt buckle out in case some guy came at you. That was a common practice, and it gave the appearance that the referees were "ready."

I recall in Syracuse they had a guy named "the Strangler." Guys like him roamed all around the court, about a foot and a half off the sidelines. Today at least they move the fans back some. I remember Sid Borgia had a fistfight in Syracuse and was later sued by the fan. And I understand "the Strangler" tried to strangle a college referee one time. I think that's where he got his name. One time Boston was playing in Syracuse, and they were really hated by the Syracuse fans. "The Strangler" was doing more and more crazy things and he was rather close to the Boston huddle, screaming at the Boston players. The story goes that Jim Loscutoff grabbed him and pulled him right into the huddle and they took a couple of shots at him. He came out bleeding from the eye, at least that's how the story goes.

I guess it's an identification with the team that makes the fans so rough. Fans are not objective, and in their effort to help motivate their team they see the officials as the enemy. Not only were we in the same city ten to twelve times a year, but sometimes confrontations with coaches made us well known in each city. Many times, we had arenas where the fans would shake the guide wires of the baskets while the visiting team was attempting a foul shot. One night, going off the court in Baltimore, a fan came at us and Earl Strom punched him and he broke his thumb. Referees are poor fighters. We used to complain to the league office, but very little security was put in place. Of course, today this is not a problem.

We usually had a good relationship with the players and

often some of them, after a particularly tough game, would say to the officials, "Hey, walk off the court with the team," which would afford us greater protection.

I never had more than the normal problems with players. Over twenty-four years of officiating I had several players run into me by accident, I think. There was only one player that deliberately ran into me because he did not like the call and that was John Brisker. He said it was an accident, but I knew it wasn't.

In the old Madison Square Garden on Fiftieth Street, the fans used to bet in the lobby. You would actually see money changing hands and people asking other people for bets. It was small amounts of money. Today the gambling is more sophisticated, but gambling on all basketball is growing. I don't think it can ever be eliminated, and that is the reason the league constantly stays on top of this potential problem. The NBA tries to make certain that players, coaches, and referees are not involved in any way. This security department was started years ago and was headed by Jack Joyce, a former FBI agent. There should be an awareness of the potential, and it's reasonable to assume that a player, coach, or referee could determine the outcome of a game. The close supervision of the league nearly eliminates this problem. However, a devious official could influence the outcome of a game. It doesn't have to be outrageous. It could be a subtle call or no call during the game. As precautionary measures the league has a security section and security representative in each city. Games are observed by the league office and supervisors. Officials are requested not to go to racetracks, frequent places where bettors would congregate, and in general not make easy friends.

After twenty-eight years in pro basketball I'm intelligent enough not to tell anybody that every call I made was correct. I'd like to think that ninety-nine percent were good calls, but there were some real clinkers. However, even when you know you made a poor call you don't compound it by trying to make up for it. You hear broadcasters say, "That is a makeup call." I'm not saying it doesn't happen. If it does happen, though, it is attributable to a poor official or a rookie. If you make a mistake the immediate basketball family knows it, and you don't compound it by making another error. A referee establishes his reputation by demonstrating to the coaches, general managers, and players that he is impartial, fair, and honest.

Who do I think were the greatest players over the years? I would say the best players I saw were Wilt Chamberlain, Bill Russell, Bob Pettit, Jerry West, Elgin Baylor, Kareem [Abdul] Jabbar, Julius Erving, and Larry Bird. They performed on the same high level each night and had the ability to make better players of their teammates. There are loads of players who could have outstanding games but couldn't do it consistently. These players also had a great desire to win. A man like Bob Pettit is probably most outstanding because he was a poor passer and dribbler. Yet because of his great shooting and rebounding ability, he was a superstar. Elgin Baylor was one of the trickiest players and nearly impossible to stop. Oscar Robertson was and is the greatest guard I ever saw and for a long time I rated him as the greatest ballplayer. I have changed my mind after watching Larry Bird. Julius Erving brought the game onto another planet and, of course, Wilt Chamberlain, besides being a scoring machine, may be the strongest basketball player of all time. I think that because Wilt was so mild it saved a great many other players from physical harm. The only time I ever saw him get angry was when he chased Bob Ferry up into the stands and the time he decked Clyde Lovellette, who was playing for Boston at the time. San Francisco was playing Boston in the play-offs, and Clyde was the backup for Bill Russell. The game was in Boston and Lovellette was muscling Wilt. After a few elbows Wilt turns and tells Clyde to stop—now! Clyde suddenly raises his fists à la Jack Dempsey and makes a motion as if to throw a punch. Wilt hit him with a short right and Clyde starts his descent to the floor. After about four seconds, he begins to get up, and George Lee from the San Francisco bench yells, "Clyde, I've seen you fight—stay down and take the full count."

Another very strong man was Sweetwater Clifton. When

he played, the league had very few black players and many of the white players were reared in the South and had some built-in bias. I wasn't in Boston, but the referee who worked the game told me that Bob Harris made some comment to Clifton and also made a physical challenge. Clifton hit him and Harris lost several front teeth. The Boston bench started to come toward Clifton, and when Sweetwater started to meet them, they all retreated. It could have been that they didn't agree with Harris's comments, or that they used good judgment in not testing Clifton.

There was an incident in St. Louis. In 1958, Walter Dukes and Sweetwater were playing for Detroit. St. Louis was not a very cordial city for the black players. Dukes went for a ball behind the basket and ended up in the first row. Suddenly, Dukes is in a fight with some fans. At this point, Clifton runs towards the stands and with his humor yells, "Walter, you take the first row, I've got the second row."

I did not encounter any anti-Semitism in the league. The early black players had some problems and most of these were with fans. The one city in which fans yelled obscene remarks at players was St. Louis. As the years went on and the black players started to enter the league in greater numbers, there was a steady decline of this bigotry.

As far as which game was the most outstanding and most vivid in my memory, it's difficult to pinpoint. There were so many, but if I had to pick the one outstanding game I would say the seventh play-off game between Boston and Philadelphia in 1969. Philadelphia, with Chamberlain and Hal Greer, was leading in the series three games to one; and Boston won the next two games to tie the series. The final game was to be played in Philadelphia. Russell and [John] Havlicek led Boston. Mendy Rudolph and I worked the game, and I don't have to tell you the place was wild. The Philly-Boston games always had an extra dimension, and play-off games became more dramatic. It was a great game, with no team able to get a lead of more than a few points. Bill Russell pulled out the victory in the last few seconds. Getting off the court was going to be

184

a problem as the Philly management, in their wisdom, sold what seemed to be ten thousand standing-room seats and we had to get through that crowd behind the basket. With three seconds to play, Mendy and I decided not to go the usual route, and joined the Boston club in getting off the court; later we made our way to our locker room. It's very interesting to note that referees feel a psychological lift when the game is more important, and you feel that you've been chosen to work an important game.

Red Auerbach never impressed me with his mode of behavior. He tried to portray the image of being brighter and more intelligent than the other coaches in the league. I was more impressed with the quiet coaches who did their job and didn't blow their own horn but were recognized by their peers. Red has said the reason he carried on during the game was to intimidate the officials and get the calls at the end of the game. He has told stories how he used this weapon. Most of this is his imagination. He has been successful because he is a good coach, has had great players, and is able to evaluate talent. Anyway, I didn't allow this type of behavior in games I worked and therefore he received many technicals and a batch of ejections. In fact, one of his suspensions was attributable to me because he had been warned by Commissioner Podoloff not to be ejected from another game as that would cause a suspension. Sure enough, I had to eject Red; and Podoloff suspends him. The referees didn't help Red, but the greatness of Russell, Cousy, Sharm, Jones, and Havlicek did the job.

The very good coaches in the league have been Red Holzman, Alex Hannum, Jack McMahon, Dick Motta, Pat Riley, John Kundla, Jack Ramsey, Doug Moe, John MacLeod, Lenny Wilkens, and K. C. Jones.

When I came into the league there was a certain style of officiating that was acceptable. It was a carryover from the Pat Kennedy style. It called for making the calls at the top of your lungs, using hand gestures, and being overly demonstrative. It was a lot of show, and as the league matured it was frowned upon; a number of coaches and players resented this type of officiating. Through the years the league has eliminated this type of officiating. It may have helped the league in the early years, but everyone recognizes that only the ballplayers sell the product. Interestingly enough, the way each official referees is an extension of his personality. The best referee I ever saw was Mendy Rudolph. He enjoyed the respect of all the players and coaches. He had great judgment and style. Sid Borgia, who was a very strong official, was part of the new league in '46/'47, helped the league in its early days, and was a carryover from the Pat Kennedy style. He also was an exponent of "letting them play." Later Sid would become the supervisor and became famous in the league for his philosophy of "no harm, no foul." In fact, I think that in different ways George Mikan, Bob Cousy, Mendy Rudolph, and Sid Borgia are the four individuals that had the greatest impact on the development and growth of the league in the early years.

When I began officiating in 1953, the principle was, "Let them play." This meant, Keep the game in control and don't let anyone get killed. There were people that thought the fans wanted to see physical mayhem with basketball. Over the years, it began to change for the better and, starting about 1973, there was the elimination of this type of play. It was difficult to get new and young officials to referee this way as there was no training ground for this type of ball. It was so unlike college basketball that college officials found it difficult to make the change. Today the game is more open and less physical, which lends itself to more efficiently refereed games. During my formative years as a young official I was most impressed with three officials I observed: They were Matty Begovitch, Jocko Collins, and Lala Eckstein. Begovitch was a top college and pro official in the early forties. Jocko Collins was also a college and pro official during those days and eventually supervisor of NBA officials. Lala Eckstein worked in the American Pro League. All these men had a style and exerted control over the game, which made them stand out on the floor.

The evolution of pro basketball keeps jumping to higher

horizons. Although there have been great players throughout the history of the league, the present-day players are no doubt faster, bigger, and stronger. I don't think the teams of the fifties and sixties could play as a team today. However, the individual stars, such as Oscar Robertson, Jim Pollard, Wilt Chamberlain, Tom Gola, Paul Arizin, Jerry West, Bob Cousy, Bob Davies, George Mikan, Bob Pettit, Bill Russell, Nate Thurmond and Rick Barry, John Havlicek, and Elgin Baylor—and a host of others—could very well fit in and be stars in today's game.

I remember the first pro games that were on TV. The NBA games were on Saturday and Sunday afternoons. I heard the teams that were on TV were paid something like $5,000. The good teams that drew well, like Boston and New York, didn't want to play in the afternoon and lose the big house in the evening, so they usually traded their games to another team, who didn't draw well and wanted the $5,000 guarantee. This meant that the public did not see the more skillfull teams and got a poor impression of the type of basketball played in the pros. Of course, this has changed over the years; and in fact one year the league decided to put their best foot forward and scheduled popular teams like Boston, New York, and Los Angeles more often.

In the early days, all the officials knew the owners because they were in many cases part and parcel of the operation. In those days, some of the owners were coaches and some sat on the bench as observers and as assistants. Eddie Gottlieb of Philadelphia was a coach. Lester Harrison of Rochester was a coach. Danny Biasone sat on the bench and growled. Irish sat in the stands. Ben Kerner sat in the first row opposite the bench. Fred Zollner of Fort Wayne was at every game, home and away. The owners identified with their teams. Today I don't think any of the officials know the owners and if they do, it's from far away in a loge box seat. Of course, in light of the many teams in the league and the big business revolving around the league, I think the present situation is a better one.

*   *   *

187

In 1953, I broke in with a Rochester road game, and Lester Harrison was the coach and owner. The Rochester team won the game and while I was in the locker room Lester Harrison opened the door and said, "Drucker, good job. You're going to be a good referee." Sure enough, the following night in Minneapolis, he won again, and he told me in the runway, "You're going to be as good as Pat Kennedy." Being a rookie, I was taken in by this flattery. About three days later, I officiated a game in Rochester and they lost. Lester knocked on the locker-room door and when I opened it he said, "Drucker, forget what I told you the other two nights." That was Lester Harrison. There are a million stories about Lester. One is that he coached the team so as to save a salary. With all the great players he had he really didn't need a coach. I saw them once deliberately huddle so that their shoulders were touching in the huddle, and they wouldn't allow Lester to get in there to talk to them.

Probably the greatest defensive game played by a big man was the game in which Walt Bellamy made his debut with the Chicago team against Wilt Chamberlain. I guess Wilt took it as a personal challenge. Bellamy, who went on to become a good player, received a lot of hype and there was a big crowd in Chicago. Well, Chamberlain blocks about eight straight hook shots and on offense, as usually was the case, scored with ease. Chamberlain blocked a few more in the second period and Bellamy stopped attempting shots. Of course, Chamberlain was making a point that no rookie was equal to the king.

A few years later I had an incident with Walt Bellamy that has been told many times. Walt had a way of speaking in which when he made a comment he used his name in [place of] the first person. For example, if he complained that Russell had fouled him he would say, "Norm, Russell just fouled Walter." As the game continued he kept saying, "Norm, Walter just got fouled again." I became tired of his complaining and told him to stop or I would call a technical. Sure enough, on another play, he once again said, "Didn't you see that Walter was fouled?" I blew my whistle, walked past Bellamy, and said, "Bellamy, tell Walter that I just called a technical on Walter."

In 1969, I went to the ABA together with Joe Gushue, John Vanak, and Earl Strom because they offered us a great deal. Mendy Rudolph decided at the last moment not to switch. Who would've ever thought in those days that they would be offering bonuses and $50,000 salaries for officials? I think that led to the total improvement in referees' salaries and working conditions that are now enjoyed by pro officials.

Before I signed with the ABA I went back to the NBA but Walter Kennedy wouldn't negotiate. I remained in the ABA for seven years as an official and supervisor. We were treated very well. The NBA play was tougher, as the new league did not have the big men and therefore it was a more guard- and forward-oriented game. There were some great players in the ABA, though, and some of them are still in the NBA. There was Julius Erving, in his prime, Moses Malone, George McGinnis, Billy Cunningham, Artis Gilmore, George Gervin, Billy Melchionni, Dan Issel, Rick Barry, Roger Brown, and Mel Daniels.

After the merger, I returned to the NBA in 1977 and the following year I retired from active officiating and became the supervisor of referees until 1981.

In all, there were twenty-eight years of great times. I made lasting friendships and, above all, it allowed me a freedom of personal expression which I was able to express through my officiating.

*Johnny "Big Red" Kerr. Knicks versus Syracuse, January 4, 1961;
Kerr is number ten. (N.Y. Daily News Photo)*

Johnny "Big Red" Kerr

Johnny Kerr, playing with the Syracuse Nationals, the Philadelphia 76ers, and the Baltimore Bullets, totaled more than 10,000 points and 10,000 rebounds in his career. He was also the first coach of the Chicago Bulls, guiding the expansion team into the play-offs, which earned him NBA Coach of the Year honors for the 1966/67 season. He also coached the Phoenix Suns and was involved with the American Basketball Association. Today he lives just outside of Chicago, where he does radio and television commentary of basketball games, and is a partner in Kerr Financial Services.

Putting the cart before the horse, I've had a dream come true. I was born and raised in Chicago, played there on the city championship team, took the Big Ten championship with the University of Illinois, the NBA championship with the Syracuse Nats, and then came back here to coach the professional team. I've made the big circle, and it was kind of neat.

I grew up in Chicago. My dad played soccer in Scotland and so I played it for three years in high school. But from my

191

junior to senior year I grew eight inches. One day in my senior year the basketball coach saw me coming through the hall and said, "Come out for the team." I said, "I can't do all those things." He said, "Let me be the judge of that." So he got me out there. I was a pretty good athlete, so he put me on the team and, gee, we went undefeated until the end of the year and when we went to the state tournament there was a big hullabaloo about this kid they found on the soccer field.

I graduated in the middle of the year, in January of 1950, so I came back and played the rest of the season and we won something like fifteen in a row. All of a sudden, scholarship offers started coming out of the wall. And remember, this was my first year playing basketball. Anyway, it was printed in the program that I'd accepted a scholarship to Bradley, but a kid named Irv Bemoras called me from [University of] Illinois and said, "Why don't you take a ride down here and see the campus?" I said okay, went down there, fell in love with the school, and said, "I'm gonna go here."

I wound up leading the team in scoring for three years and I didn't really start until I was a senior. I might have been one of the first sixth men in the game, and I was All-American my senior year.

After the season ended I was at an East-West All-Star game in New York. Danny Biasone, who was the owner of the Syracuse Nationals, tells the story about how he and Jack Andrews, who was a writer for the *Post-Standard*, were at the game, waiting for it to begin. Andrews says, "What do you think, Dan? Do you think we'll see anyone down here?" And Biasone says, "I already know who I'm gonna draft." Andrews says, "What do you mean?" Biasone says, "I know just from watching him warm up." Now today, the scouting system is so intricate, there are no sleepers anymore. Everybody knows who's out there. But at the time Biasone says to Andrews, "I've been watching this kid and this is the one I'm gonna draft." It was great. I think I was the sixth pick overall. That was the year Pettit went to St. Louis; Hagan went to Boston and then was traded for Russell later on; Gene Shue was picked up by the Knicks; and Larry Costello was picked by Philadelphia. But Larry went into the service and when he came out Danny Biasone said to Eddie Gottlieb, "You know that kid you got, well, you're not going to use him and he's from nine miles from out town, so why not let us have him?" I think he got him for something like $500, and of course the rest is history, with Larry making the All-Star team.

So I was drafted by Syracuse in '54 and I had no idea where the hell Syracuse was. I went out there to visit, but before I went my roommate told me to be sure and get a bonus. "Don't sign unless you get a bonus," he said. I said okay, but I didn't know anything about anything at the time. So I went out there and negotiated with the general manager, a guy named Leo Ferris, who offered me $5,000 as a yearly salary. That was it. I said, "I can't sign for five thousand. I need more money." He said, "Well, that's more than a lot of guys are getting. I can't pay you as much as Dolph Schayes."

I wanted to call Harry Combes, my college coach. He says, "Yeah, go ahead and call him." So I went into the other room and called Combes in Champagne and told him my situation, that I was out there and they'd offered me $5,000, what should I do? He said, "There's really no other place to go if you want to play professional ball because they're the ones who drafted you." I said, "Okay, thanks, coach." He hung up and then I heard the click of another phone. I came out and Ferris was all smiles and he says, "Well, what did he say?" But you know, he was listening on the other phone. Anyway, I said, "I can't sign for just that. I gotta get a bonus." He says, "How come you need a bonus?" I said, "My roommate told me, Don't sign without one." He said, "Okay, I'll give you five hundred dollars." Big deal, you know.

At that time, they used to negotiate a contract by raising them from $500 to $1,000 each year. I mean, it was really weird, those numbers. I remember Jack McMahon telling me in St. Louis that he was going to negotiate a contract and there was a $300 difference with Ben Kerner [the owner] and Kerner says, "I'll flip you for it." Nothing to lose, right? Today, you set up a suite in a hotel room, you fly in with your agent, they fly in, you meet, and you spend about ten grand just setting the thing up. I remember signing many contracts with Danny Biasone—who was the inventor of the 24-second clock, by the way—at the Greyhound bus station over a cup of coffee. One time I remember signing a contract with him and we never even mentioned dollars. I wanted $18,000 and he wanted to give me $16,000, but the figures never even came up in the conversation. Danny says, "Well, what do you think?" And I said, "Well, you know what I want." He said, "I know what you want but you know I can't give it to you. You know what I want to give you." And I said, "Yeah, but that's not enough." He says, "Well, if we make good at the end of the season I'll give you what you want." I said, "Okay," and I signed a blank contract. We both knew what we were talking about. When I got my contract back it was for $16,000. It was sort of a make-good contract. But that doesn't mean that you had to play good to fulfill the contract. What it meant was that if they made money you'd get some extra money. Anyway, at the end of the season the team was sold to Philadelphia, and Danny called me into his office and said, "You know, I told you I'd give you what you wanted if we did good. Well, I didn't do that good but I made a few bucks selling the team and so I'm gonna give you what you wanted." And there was a check for $2,000. So it was funny. I signed a contract, with both of us talking, and neither of us mentioned a figure, but we both knew what the other guy had in mind.

There was no such thing as agents then. You just came in and you were petrified because you were talking to an owner; you didn't say very much. At that time the owners were not like the conglomerate owners of today, those who have other big businesses to run. Back then, it was their only business and they either owned the arena or were directly involved in running the team. They'd come down to the locker room and talk to you. Today I have the feeling that some people invest in a team so they can bring their friends down to the locker room to meet the players and say, "This is my team." Sort of like a toy. But then every one of those owners derived their main income from the team. Danny had a bowling alley and a restaurant, but a big part of his income came from making the team work. And I think we were one of the first community-owned teams, because he'd sold shares in the team.

When I got to Syracuse for my first training camp, it was held at a place called Manlius Military Academy, which was about fifteen miles out of town. Of course, the big thing was to find out who was going to drive, because you got paid mileage. I think it was about 5¢ a mile.

The year before, the Syracuse team had had a great deal of success. They'd been beaten by the Lakers in the play-offs, but they'd played them well and strong. But what I hadn't realized was that they were a team that played without a center. They had what they called a "Syracuse weave" and a fast break that everybody talked about. There was no true center. Now the only position I'd ever played was center and so I had no idea what was going to happen to me. They had another big kid on the team, I think his name was Jim Neal, from Wofford College. He was big, six-eleven, and he was the center. Earl Lloyd, who was one of the first black players in the league, was sort of their roving forward center. So I came in and I didn't play much.

It was a good team, but they felt they were lacking a big man. I remember I played sporadically the first fifteen or sixteen games. About sixteen games into the seasson—we were playing in Rochester—I had a talk with the coach, Al Cervi. I was very dissatisfied with the amount of playing time I was getting. I said to him, "If you give me a chance I think I can prove to you that I can play."

Now, this guy was a psychologist. They called him "the Digger." He was a real competitor. After practice he'd say, "Come on, kid, we'll play one-on-one, a game of five." If you beat him in a game of five, he'd make you play another game of five and you'd keep playing until he won, then he'd say, "Okay, take a shower." The veterans would say, "Hey, rook, let him win the first game." Anyway, I got into a confrontation with Al and said, "Hey, coach, let me play a little. You got me running in and out with Lloyd and we're doing the shuffling boogie, so nobody can play here. Just give me a litle bit of time and I'll show you what I can do." He says, "You're starting." So I started against Arnie Risen of the Royals and I remember I had big numbers. I can't remember exactly, but

I think I had something like 22, 23 points, 17 rebounds, you know, starting. Anyway, I played extremely well and my confidence got better, and he started me and played me longer and longer. I think I ended up averaging about 10 points my first year, and I was a strong complement to Dolph Schayes, who was our leading rebounder and scorer. I also blocked a lot of shots.

That year we ended up in first place and played the Fort Wayne Pistons for the championship. Fort Wayne was coached by Charlie Eckman, who was an official during the season and was later made coach in a changeover. And now he had his team in the play-offs. By the way, the 3–2 situation that they're playing now, where you play two games at home, then go away for three, and come back for two, is not new. I didn't realize this until recently, but that year we played our first two games at home in Syracuse, and then we went to Fort Wayne—only we didn't really go to Fort Wayne because the American Bowling Congress was there, so we went to Indianapolis. We played three games there and we lost all of them. That may have been the first time a city in a championship round didn't have their own team. So we won our first two games at home, lost our next three games on the road, and then came back and won the next game at home. The last game was a great one. We all had a good game. Matter of fact, I think the high scorer on the team was a reserve named Billy Kenville who had something like 15, and I think six or seven of us had from 10 to 15 points, something like that. And we won the game, 92–91. So in my first year in the league we won the championship. But I never did get a ring. You know what we got? We got a plaque from the Optimists' Club that said, "Congratulations, World Championship." But I've always threatened to get a ring because we did win. So one day I'm gonna have that plaque mounted on a ring and I will have the biggest damn Championship ring you ever saw! But yeah, we won the Championship and it was tremendous to win it my first year in pro ball. I played twelve years and never got to the final round again. Of course, it was only a couple of years later that Bill Russell and Wilt Chamberlain came into the league.

We always played Boston tough, though. We were in that one famous game where Havlicek stole the ball. Somebody even made a record of that game. I think it was the '64 season. We were playing the final game in Boston and they had a 3-point lead. Then we go down and score and it's a one-point lead. Russell takes the ball out under his basket with five seconds to go. We were pressing them, and Russell throws the ball up and hits the guide wire on the backboard and it goes out of bounds. It's our ball now. Everything was quiet. Auerbach put out his cigar. Heinsohn had fouled out and I think he was on the bench with a jacket over his head. We called a time-out. Schayes was coaching and he said, "What are we gonna do, what are we gonna do?" Someone said, "Put John in to set the screen." I was out of the game by this time and Chamberlain was in. Everybody said, "Give the ball to Wilt." But Wilt says, "No, they'll just foul me." Everybody just looked at him. So Schayes decided to put him in on the other side of the basket, out of the way. I was to go down to set a screen. Hal Greer was to take the ball out of bounds and throw it to Chet Walker, and then I was to come down and set a screen for Greer, who would just duck behind me, get a pass, and shoot. We'd worked that play out about a hundred times a year. It was a sensational play. So Schayes says, "Let's make the play work for Hal." Fine. So I went down and I'm holding both K. C. Jones and Sam Jones down low, by their jerseys, and the ball goes over my head and I hear 13,909 fans screaming at the old Boston Garden because suddenly Havlicek is dribbling away with the ball. He'd intercepted the pass and was running away with it. Now they've even got a record out with Johnny Most screaming, "Havlicek stole the ball," or something like that. Yes, we had some great battles with Boston.

My second year in the league I think I got a raise up to $6,500. But you've got to remember that it wasn't like it is today, where you get paid in a year-round situation. We played seventy-two games, I think, that first year, but got paid for six months. So that $5,500 I made in six months was really kind of neat because you could go out and get another job for the other six months. At that time you either worked for the club or you could, if you could talk in front of a crowd, make some speeches and do some promotional work for maybe $100 a week, which wasn't bad in those days. That way you could supplement your income. But the problem was, you made $5,500 in a six-month period and you spent it like you were making $11,000. All of a sudden the season's over and you say, "Where is it? Where's that check that's supposed to be coming in?" But remember, things were different then. Costs weren't as high.

Another thing that was different then was that the ballplayers were a lot closer than they are now. After a ball game you could say, "Let's go over to my house," and the guys would come over and somebody would bring a case of beer and you'd get a couple of pizzas or chicken and before you knew it you had sixteen, seventeen people over and you were having fun, talking about the game. I don't know if they talk about the game as much today. About who they're going to play that day. I don't know if they talk about the game at all. It's funny, when I was coaching the Bulls I went back to the locker room to go to the bathroom one afternoon when the team was out on the floor. I was looking for something to read and the players had left a few bags open. I found a *Wall Street Journal* in one bag, a James Bond novel in another, and a *Playboy* magazine in the third. I had my choice; they were that varied in their reading.

My second year with Syracuse the team changed. I think George King wanted a bigger raise, so they traded him to Cincinnati. Billy Kenville wanted more money, so they traded him to Detroit. As I recall, we ended up third in the division, tied with the Knicks. That was the year Tom Gola came in with Philly, and they had a good year. In the play-offs that year I was voted outstanding player in the *one* game that was on TV. I got a watch. We beat Boston that year but lost to Philadelphia, and we never really had the success again that we had my first year there.

In 1964, the team moved to Philadelphia. I'd been in Syracuse nine years. Money made the decision to move. The sport was getting big-time, teams were moving to the West Coast, and travel was getting more expensive and the gate couldn't handle it. There was no revenue source except for the season tickets and in those days you're talking about $5 a ticket in Syracuse, so forget it.

Speaking of travel, it's funny, I set the consecutive game mark which stood for nineteen years. Recently, somebody said to me that it was much tougher for Randy Smith to beat that record than it was for me. I said, "What do you mean?" He said, "Well, now they've got to go out to LA, over to Portland. . . ." I said, "Wait a minute. We had to travel, too, and our closest trip, after Rochester and Cincinnati, was to New York City, and we were on a train for eight hours and we never even left the state. That was to one of our *closest* foes. And talk about getting sleep on a train, especially when you're over six feet tall. We'd leave early in the morning because they didn't want to have to put up anybody overnight at a hotel. It was economics. For instance, they'd hire a trainer for two bits wherever we were. We had a guy named Art Van Auken, who was a great trainer, but he only worked the home games. We never had a full-time trainer traveling with us. Economics. That's why it was very popular to have player-coaches, so you could keep your staff way down when traveling.

When we'd have a game in Fort Wayne we'd get on a sleeper at night, the car would be there waiting for us, and then we'd get something to eat. Sometime during that night a train would back up and hook onto us, pick us up, and away we'd go. All of a sudden—it had to be five, five-thirty in the morning—there'd be a knock at the door, and they'd say, "Waterloo coming up." We'd never even stop in Fort Wayne. Waterloo, Indiana, that's where we'd stop. We'd get out, and it looked just like the town where Spencer Tracy stopped in that movie *Bad Day at Black Rock*—the station with the little potbellied stove and everything. We'd walk over to a place called the Green Parrot restaurant—I'm not making this up—and there'd be three kids sitting there having a cup of coffee. One kid would say, "Are you ready?" and we'd say, "Yeah." You see, they knew we were coming. They had the schedule. Then they would drive us to Fort Wayne. I don't know how long it took, but we slept in the car. Maybe the kids would get a fin apiece for driving. But that's the way travel was.

And how about going from Syracuse to Minneapolis? We'd take a sleeper again, travel all night to Chicago, get into Chicago, and then transfer to another train and travel all morning till five, five-thirty, jump off the train there, take a deep breath and freeze your lungs. We stayed at the Nicolette Hotel. I remember going down to the lobby and seeing a guy perform down there. Everybody was making a fuss over him, and his name was Liberace.

By the way, that first year I played against Mikan. That was another thing I relished—getting a piece of some of those other guys' careers while they were still playing. Guys like Bobby Davies, Max Zaslofsky, Carl Braun, some of the great names. But in Minneapolis they'd have on the floor Clyde Lovellette, Vern Mikkelson, Jim Pollard, Mikan, and they were just waiting for us. We'd go out and it was funny, we'd have good success there. And then when the game was over we'd get back on the train and go to our next destination. We didn't fly anywhere for years.

For amusement we'd play cards, an awful lot of cards. Matter of fact, one year Dick Barnett was on the team and when he got traded and wound up with Los Angeles it cost me a lot of money. That reminds me of the time Barnett jumped our team and went over to Cleveland in the ABL, I think. Danny Biasone was very upset. He wanted to get a lawsuit going to keep Barnett from playing. I remember that Cleveland team went on to win the championship and we asked Dick how much money he made for winning and he said, zero, no money. Anyway, he wanted to come back to Syracuse. They'd gone to court and Biasone wins the case and they say he's got to return to Syracuse. But Danny says, "Well, I won the case, but I just wanted to prove a point. It's obvious you don't want to be here, so we don't want you here." So he moved him out of our division, over to LA. The owner of the Cleveland team, by the way, was George Steinbrenner.

In those days the coach had a rule about having only two cans of beer on the train. Well, my roommate and I, Billy Kenville, found out that Fosters put out beer in a big can—it was a quart—so we had a couple of those before we'd go to sleep. But it was tough, those sleepers, they were never quite big enough to handle guys over six feet, so we'd stay up and get really tired.

In those days, the fans were really something else. We were tough in Syracuse. We were really a first-quarter team. We would just blitz the other team. We'd come out and get 35, 40 points. For years they used to say that Cousy had the Syracuse flu because he liked to miss those games in Syracuse. They talk about the fans today, but you've got security which controls a lot of them. In those days I don't think they did. There was a guy they called "the Strangler," who once grabbed Eddie Gottlieb on the bench and put a strangle hold on him. Gottlieb says, "I'll put fifty dollars in an envelope in Philly and we'll get rid of you." We had fights with guys coming out of the stands. It was rough. Johnny Nucatola, who was head of the officials, was working a game one time and he got beat up going from the game in Syracuse. Charlie Eckman, who'd heard about what happened to Nucatola, changed at half-time—he was leaving. He changed into his dress clothes and he was gone. I mean, it was a little tougher in those days. We had a lot of fights at different places, and they could care less about it. In other cities they'd throw things at you. The fans got caught up in a frenzy.

It was goofy. Like when we played Tuesday nights at Madison Square Garden. One time we were playing the Cincinnati Royals with the Knicks and Boston to play the second game of the doubleheader. There'd be maybe six thousand people watching the game. There'd be about a minute to go and maybe we were beating Cincinnati by 7 points. Schayes would score, putting us up by 9, and three thousand people would stand up and cheer. Then Jack Twyman would go downcourt and score, and the other three thousand people would stand up and cheer. See, they were betting on the game, on the point spread. They didn't care who won. Tuesday in New York was called "Get Even Day," and it was a doubleheader and you'd always have someone cheering for you. You didn't know who they were or what was going on, but you knew they'd bet on the game and they were gonna bet on the game to follow. Betting is big now, but I think the gamblers were tougher in those days. They used to meet under the stands and exchange money. The fan was a little rougher, too. I can remember playing in Madison Square Garden and I'm getting ready to shoot a free throw and all of a sudden the basket starts shaking like hell, it's moving, going around in circles. The ref says, "Shoot the ball. You got ten seconds." I say, "The basket's moving." They look up and sure enough some guy in the balcony is wiggling that thing, the guide wire, and the basket's moving like hell.

I had the Iron Man record that went 844 regular season games. The truth is, I didn't think anything different my first three or four years. I thought you were supposed to play every game. I mean, there came a time when guys would get very upset about playing every game, but if you tried to take them out they'd want to play longer. Harry Gallatin had the record—"the Iron Horse," they called him. I think it was six hundred something. Then Dolph Schayes had it. We were playing together and neither of us missed a game, but Dolph had been there so many more years than I had, so he broke Harry's record and it was kinda neat. I just kept playing games along with him. One day, we were playing Philadelphia, I think, he ran into Al Attles and broke his cheekbone and the streak ended. But he'd played in the play-offs in Boston where he broke his right wrist and he just shot left-handed. He shot that whole series left-handed and averaged 15 points a game. But I just thought that's the way things were supposed to be.

So he was the new record holder but he stopped at 706 games, I think, and I broke the record. I never thought he'd miss a game, but all of a sudden he stopped and I passed him. The funny thing was, Dolph was my coach and here I was going to break his record. The owners of the 76ers gave me 707 uncirculated John F. Kennedy half-dollars for breaking the record. Walter Kennedy [league president] said it was a bonus and that it was against the rules, but he was going to turn his head away on this one. In fact, he was there for the presentation. With all those uncirculated fifty-cent pieces, the truth is I don't have one of them left. My kids took them for lunch, for school.

The record stopped at 844 during my year in Baltimore. My coach decided not to play me. It was Paul Seymour, who was a teammate of mine on the world championship team. When Chamberlain came to the Philly team, I said to Dolph, who was the coach, "You're gonna start playing me at forward. I know you're gonna want to get me in the game and," I said, "that's not the way I want to play." I said, "I still think I can play, so why don't you trade me if you can." So he said, "Okay," and I said, "The new kid needs a chance anyway." The new kid turned out to be Billy Cunningham. I talked to Irv Koslof, and he said, "John, I want you with the team as long as I've got it." And I said, "That's not the point, Kos, I just want to see if I can play another year." So he said, "Okay, in that case." They arranged to trade me for Wally Jones. But they couldn't find Wally Jones. They ran an ad in the paper: "Wally, come home, all is forgiven." I went on to Baltimore and I figured I could play fifteen minutes a game behind Walt Bellamy. Only when I got there, they traded Bellamy to the Knicks for Johnny Green and Johnny Egan and Bad News Barnes. I thought I was gonna be a backup and suddenly I'm a starting center.

Anyway, we were playing Boston and Seymour thought he would go with Bad News Barnes and Bob Ferry. It upset me. Absolutely. I thought somewhere along the line I could run one thousand games or whatever. If I was hurt, I could understand not playing, but I was fine. I remember the fans were hollering for him to put me in, but it got to the point where I didn't want to go in. So the record stopped, and of course I thought back over the years on how many times I was hurt and kept playing. But Seymour said it had to end sometime.

I always thought it was the kind of record nobody will care about. Nobody will know what goes into this record except the guy who breaks it and his wife. My wife knew I was sticking my foot in the snow, trying to get the swelling down so I could play the next day. Today I read about an athlete who can't play because of something. You know, I've had broken bones and broken noses, and you just play.

I played some after that, but I had a back problem, spasms, and a couple of other injuries, and then the coaching job opened in Chicago. Actually, Paul Seymour had recommended me for the job in Baltimore, but there was no way I was going to coach a team I'd just played with, had a few drinks with, partied with.

One of my old buddies I grew up with in Chicago had a petition signed by twenty-two hundred people who wanted me to coach there and I ended up getting the job. I thought it was an outstanding chance to do something.

Did I miss playing basketball? No. Because I went from playing to coaching, to television and radio. I can still do everything I did before, except play. I can go into the locker room, go out with the guys, go to practices. I just can't go over the lanes. Somebody said, "Do you miss coaching now?" and I said, "as much as I can." I really enjoyed that first year because we had an expansion team and, as a matter of fact, I don't know anybody who had the success we had the first year, what with us making the play-offs. No expansion team has ever done that. I was coach of the year. I had so much fun because we took guys that were the eighth and ninth players on their teams. It was Al Bianchi's and my first coaching job and I was coming to a team in Chicago that had been a graveyard for basketball. They'd had the Packers, the Zephyrs, but nothing worked right. It was my city, my hometown, and I didn't care what happened; I wanted basketball to stay here so I could come back and watch it. I was the P.R. man, the good-time Charlie who handled the press, and sold the fans and the press on the team; and Al was the whip, the man in the trenches, the guy who molded a lot of that team.

My last year as a player, '65/'66, I was making $24–$25,000. I'd played twelve years and gone from $5,000 to $25,000. At that time, $25,000 was probably enough to put me as one of the top fifteen money-makers in the league.

The two most dominant players I played against were, of course, Bill Russell and Wilt Chamberlain. Being in the same division, I still made the All-Star team three times, which I thought was thrilling.

Russell gave me more trouble on defense; he was not that strong an offensive player. And Chamberlain, well, you just had to try and hold him to under 70 points. One of my favorite stories happened after a game in Syracuse when we went to a lounge we used to go to. We'd just played Philadelphia. A guy said, "John, how'd you do tonight, playing against Chamberlain?" I said, "I got 38." He said, "Set 'em up, my boy got 38." Everybody got a drink and then he said, "How did Wilt do?" I said, "He got 63." You know, you could always score against him, but when he had the ball you never knew if he was going to score 100. One year he averaged 50 points a game, and that's phenomenal. Yes, he was unstoppable. He was so strong. Thank God, he was docile. I think the guy only had a couple of fights and they were very much provoked. Tom Heinsohn had one with him, I think, and Clyde Lovellette, too, who was always knocking you around. But the guy I had the most battles with was Wayne Embry. I was the second smallest center in the league, and Wayne was the smallest but the strongest. Coach would always say, "Hold your ground," and I'd say, "I am." And there was Wayne leaning on me, pushing me out across the floor. You could smell the rubber from my sneaks burning.

As far as backcourt men were concerned, I played with two of the all-time best: Costello and Greer. There's no doubt about those two. Greer had the best fifteen-foot jump shot in the business. We had a play that we worked on rookies where we'd say, "Let's weave it," so Greer would come down with the ball, Costello would make one move to him to get the ball, and then I would break out the high post and Greer would hit me with the ball, and Costello would just shoot down the lane. All I had to do was see his jersey go by me and I'd bounce the ball between my legs. Lay-up! It was fantastic.

But I would be remiss if I didn't say I saw two of the best backcourt men in Cousy and West. Cousy was good, but West was the best offensive guard that's ever been around, and I don't care what they say about Walt Frazier.

It's hard to pick out an individual game that stands out for me. The most I ever scored was 42 against Cincinnati. But the

205

big thing was I learned how to play the game. The biggest thrill is when I hear someone, some of the old-timers, describe a new player by saying that's the kind of pass Kerr used to throw, or so-and-so reminds me of Johnny Kerr. I haven't played since '66, so who the hell remembers me except when you hear older people talk about it?

I had a big thrill not long ago. I was doing a game down in the stadium, and Billy Crystal and Gregory Hines were there. At halftime, I went into the private room to go to the washroom and Gregory Hines turns around and says, "Jesus Christ, Johnny Kerr, my old man took me to see you." And then Billy Crystal says, "We're junkies. We love it, man. My Dad took me to see you at the Garden how many times!" Those guys made me feel like a million bucks. That's the way it is when somebody remembers you out of the past.

Who would I compare myself to today? Well, he's so much better, but I would like to think I had the alertness of the game that Bill Walton has. If Walton had played ten years he might be known as the all-time center. I've always been impressed with the way he has such a zeal for the game, his observations, he's always watching what's going on.

The biggest change in the game while I was playing was the widening of the lane, which put some guys out of business. All of us were hook shooters, but now the lane was moved out and it was a lot longer for shots. After my fifth year in the league, I learned to play facing the basket. I could play down low and post-up and score from there. I could then go outside, play the wing, play the top of the key, face the basket, and shoot. And if I didn't, I would have been out of business. Neil Johnston led the league in scoring with the hook shot, but he threw two of those hooks up and Russell just snuffed him, and that was the end of that. They widened the lane just because players were getting a little too big. Chamberlain was the cause of that as much as anybody else.

Another big change I've noticed is that when I played we were always talking about the game. Wherever we were, we were talking about let's try this or let's do something different. I guess I'll always be a practical joker and doing something new, coming up with a new wrinkle and using it on the other players, was the same as pulling a practical joke. I really enjoyed that. The game just doesn't look like fun anymore. It's just a way to make some money.

Speaking of practical jokes, I used to drive my roommate, Al Bianchi, nuts. He was a handsome-looking guy who wore a lot of dark clothes, and he had the worst case of dandruff. He was always using shampoo, trying to get rid of it. I would take a little bit of salt and flip it on his shoulder. He'd come down and we'd say, "Jesus, Al, I don't know what you're using this time, but it's not working." Just goofy little things like that that we'd have fun with.

I think now the season is probably too long. I think everybody would like to see some games out, except for the monetary consideration. The players don't want to lose that income, the owners don't want to lose that income, and for some reason the fans still come out.

Leonard Koppet, who is a good friend of mine, and I are for a rule change. We don't want to lower the basket or raise it or widen the court. We are both proponents of eliminating one man from each side. We think it'll open up the game, make it a little more exciting. There would be more things to do, the game wouldn't be so clogged up. And anyway, the way the game is played, it's only three men. Five is too many to have on the court. You rarely have five guys involved, and on the rare occasion when there are four they're just going through the motions. I'm not on a cause, though, like letting women have the vote; it's just something somebody asks me, what do you think should be done with the game, I say.

But like I said, I've been very lucky and sometimes I see the past; I see Costello's jersey go by me as I'm getting the ball.

Cal Ramsey

Cal Ramsey

After an illustrious high school and college career, Cal Ramsey played only two years in the NBA, after which he spent three years in the Eastern League, trying to play his way back up. A knee injury dashed that dream and Ramsey taught school for a while, then broke into broadcasting, working as a color commentator for the New York Knicks, one of the teams he'd spent a short time playing for. He has worked for the Urban League and today is involved in the Mobil Summer Games and is Assistant Director of Alumni Relations at New York University, where he played his college ball.

My mother bought me a basketball for Christmas when I was eleven years old. At that point I was really more into baseball, but when I got that Christmas gift I started going out to the park and playing with it. I liked it, and that's how it all began for me.

I was born in Selma, Alabama, came to New York when I was eight years old, and I've been here ever since. I went to junior high school in Harlem and I still live in Harlem. I played basketball, baseball, and softball and I was also the best typist in junior high school.

I went to Commerce High School in Manhattan, and while I was there I made All-City my senior year and was a high school All-American, chosen for the second-team All-Star team. I played against Wilt Chamberlain and he and I became very good friends from that point on. It was unbelievable, because I think he was the first of the athletic big men. There were a lot of big men around, like Walter Dukes, Swede Holbrook, Ray Felix, and George Mikan, before that, but they weren't real athletes, they just played basketball. Wilt was different. He was a real athlete. He ran track, threw the javelin, he did everything. He was just a great athlete and a real nice person. We spent a lot of time together during the summers playing 3-on-3 half-court basketball. He was sensational, even then. He was getting 50, 60, 70 points a game. Just incredible. There was no opposition. When we played a New York team against the Philadelphia team in the All-Star game, I think me and Wayne Davis—who, by the way, is an FBI agent today—were the biggest guys on the team. We were six-four and we had to play against Wilt, who was seven feet. So it was tough.

After high school I had several offers to go to college and I opted for New York University because my coach at the time, the late Herman Wolf, sat down with me and we discussed the various offers. He kinda felt that I would be better off at NYU because I'd probably get a better education in a school with more stature, and that I'd also play in the Garden—all NYU's home games were there. So, after careful consideration, I narrowed it down to Seton Hall and NYU, and NYU won hands down.

I played three years of varsity ball, since you couldn't play as a freshman. I was captain of the team in 1959 and I made the All-American team, too.

I had some exciting moments in college ball, and three of them stick out. The first one was my sophomore year, when we played North Carolina. They had the number-one team in the country, they'd won thirty-three or thirty-four straight games, and we played them in the Garden to a big crowd. We lost to them by 5 points, but we were in the game to the bitter end, and I think I had 27 points and 17 rebounds. Another game that sticks out in my mind was against Cincinnati when they had Oscar Robertson, who I consider to be the best all-around player of all time. Bird is creeping up there, but Oscar did it for a long time. We played against Oscar and I guarded him. I scored 18 and I held him to, I think, 56 points in that game. It was quite an athletic display by Oscar. He was really a great player. One of the things that you have to remember about him was that people talk about triple-doubles— getting double figures in rebounding, scoring, and assists. Well, Oscar Robertson in 1961, for the entire season, averaged triple-doubles—31 points a game, I think, 11 rebounds, and over 10 assists. Bird will have to match that.

The last game that sticks in my mind was against West Virginia when they had Jerry West and they were ranked number three. This was my senior year, and nobody thought we could beat them; we weren't even ranked nationally at the time. I had to guard Jerry head up, and we beat them in overtime, and I think I scored 30 and had 20 rebounds. So that game will always stick in my mind.

I averaged over 17 rebounds in my collegiate career, averaging 19.7 rebounds in my sophomore year. I was in the top seven or eight rebounders in the country, which I was always very proud of, even to this day. When I left NYU I'd set seventeen records, all of which have been broken with the exception of all my rebounding records—that's rebounds for a game, for a season. I once had 34–35 rebounds in a game against Boston College. So I still tease the kids by saying, "You can break all my records, but you cannot break my rebounding records."

Senior year, when I was All-American, I played in a couple of All-Star games. I was drafted by the St. Louis Hawks, the tenth player selected overall. I didn't play very long in the league and I was really kind of demeaning myself one day when I was talking to Wilt Chamberlain. I was saying I wasn't really that good a ballplayer and Wilt says, "Do you realize that when you came out of school you were the tenth player selected? Today you would have been a number-one draft choice and gotten a couple hundred thousand dollars." At that time there were only eight teams in the league, with ten players on each team, so only eighty players could get a job playing basketball. So, even to be considered on that level, I had to be a pretty good basketball player.

So I went to the Hawks. When I was drafted Marty Blake, who now has a scouting service, was general manager. I met with him in a hotel room in New York. I had to go by myself and sit down to talk with Marty and Ed Macauley [the coach of the Hawks], trying to negotiate a contract. I wanted $10,000 and a no-cut guarantee. Marty and Ed told me, "Well, Cal, we have Bob Pettit and Cliff Hagan. We'll give you seven thousand dollars, if you make the team." And that was the end of the discussion.

I didn't go to rookie camp initially, because I wanted to stay on for my graduation. They had a summer camp, and it was at the time of my graduation, so I missed two days of it because I'd worked too hard not to be there for that day. Afterwards, I went out to rookie camp. I went with Alan Seiden, from St. John's, who should have played in the NBA a lot longer, but he just talked too much. We went out and the first thing we did in rookie camp was start running a backdoor play, like we ran in the playgrounds all the time. Macauley stopped the practice and said, "Hey, this is not New York. You guys got to do things the way I want it done." So we had to stop running all those backdoor plays.

I had a pretty good training camp that year, but the fact that I was playing behind Pettit and Hagan limited my time considerably.

A couple of things surprised me about St. Louis. I was told that it was a racist town; and, sure enough, the first day I got there, I was staying at the Sheraton Jefferson Hotel and it was late. I got in late after my graduation and I wanted to eat. So I went across the street to a restaurant and I ordered some steak and a baked potato. The guy said, "To take out?" I said,

"Listen, I don't want to take it out." He said, "You're not gonna eat it here. You can't eat here." So I said, "Oh, well," went back to the hotel, ordered room service. That was in 1959.

There were two occasions when we were traveling and we stopped at a restaurant in St. Louis to eat. Sihugo Green and I were the only blacks on the team and they would not let us eat in the main dining room. They took a room and partitioned it off for us to eat in.

I'd also heard that some of the players were racist. They particularly talked about Bob Pettit and Cliff Hagan. But I found them to be extremely helpful to me, and I'd like to make that very public. I can recall one time we were playing a preseason game someplace in the Ozarks and Sihugo said, "I'm not even leaving my hotel room." I was sitting in the room and Hagan came down, knocked on the door, and said, "Come on, Cal, let's go out and have a beer." And he took me out. And then Pettit used to work with me in practice, because I guarded him a lot, and he helped me a great deal. Those two guys were very helpful individuals and I saw no racism with them, with any of the players on the club. But I did encounter quite a bit moving around certain parts of the country.

I was a small forward at that time and that was one of the difficulties I had. I couldn't play the guard position because I couldn't dribble that well. I was a good rebounder, obviously by the records I set, and I did a pretty good job at small forward, but I was playing behind two really great, great forwards. Actually, I would have had a chance to stick on the team, but as the season progressed I wasn't playing much. But I was playing well in practice and I'd do well when I got into the game.

As fate would have it, I was cut. They said they might call me back, they thought I was a good player. I was home for a week and sure enough they did call me back when they released somebody else. So I was pretty well set.

About a week or two passed and Clyde Lovellette, the center, got hurt. I'll never forget it. We were sitting in the locker room and Sihugo was sitting across from me, and Macauley came in and said that Clyde was going to be out a while and that they needed a backup center. Si looked up at me and I knew what was coming. I had to go.

So that was the end of my career with St. Louis. I came home and I was keeping myself in shape and I got a call from the Knickerbockers, asking me if I wanted to try out for the team. They said, "Look, you're a local kid, you played your games here at the Garden, if you do well and the fans like you, you'll have a job for a long time." So I went to a practice session. Willie Naulls, who was a friend of mine, was guarding me for the tryout, only he was half-guarding me, letting me do anything I wanted. I did pretty well and they gave me a contract. I played well, but I didn't play very long. It was a good offensive team, but we didn't win many games. We didn't have a dominant center, and that was the problem. Willie Naulls was a great offensive player, and Kenny Sears was very good, kinda frail; I used to call him "the Zipper" because he was so skinny. But it wasn't a great team by any stretch of the imagination. I did very well coming off the bench. As a matter of fact, the coach wanted to keep me, but someone made a decision they didn't want me for some reason. It was not the coach's decision, I know that for a fact, because he made me his first player off the bench. He liked me. Actually, right before I was released they had a three-on-three game with the guys who were expendable, and I outplayed everybody on the floor. A couple of reporters were there and they said, "Wow, Cal, if someone has to go it certainly won't be you." But sure enough, they let me go. I was shocked, absolutely shocked. Because it wasn't that I was playing poorly. I was playing and playing well. So I had to grin and bear it, because there was nothing I could do about it.

I decided to get my military obligation out of the way, so I went into the National Guard and did six months so I could be out in time for the next season. Sure enough, the Syracuse Nats contacted me and invited me to try out with their club. I did and played pretty well, but again they said I was too small. That was the big thing. It's a tough game. I don't want to knock Alex Hannum, but decisions are made by coaches and general managers. I was playing pretty good and we'd been on a road trip and the last game we played was against Cincinnati. Oscar and I were good friends at this point and the game had gone into overtime. I hadn't played at all. Then we went into double overtime and I finally came out. I was guarding Oscar and he said, "Damn, Cal, I thought you were doing real well and you're not playing." I said, "Zero"—that's what I called him—"I don't know what the hell is going on."

We came back to Syracuse and we had a practice. Since I hadn't played very much, after the guys left the court I did calisthenics and I shot free throws and I did some jogging. Alex just sat there and watched me. I did this about twenty-five to thirty minutes, then I came in. He said, "Cal, we've got to cut you." I said, "You should have told me before I did all that work."

I've been told at the time there was a quota system in the league. It could have been one of the reasons I didn't stick with one of those teams, if at the time they only wanted two or three blacks on each team. Of course, now that's changed. But I think I should have stayed with one of those teams. I was not a great basketball player, but I was a good one and I was better than some of the players that stayed ahead of me. So there might be some credence to the fact that there was a quota system.

After being cut by Syracuse, I went down to the Eastern League and played there for three years. It was traumatic, to say the least, because first of all your ego is shattered because you feel you could be in the NBA. And you're used to flying someplace, staying in a nice hotel, and getting meal money. I played with only one team, Williamsport, which was like a six-and-a-half, seven-hour drive into the mountains of Pennsylvania. We went five guys in a car and left at 12:00 P.M. to get there by 6:30. We'd get out of the car, change, go out and play a game in the high school gym, come back, go to a little hotel someplace, get up the next morning, travel to the next town, do the same thing, and then make a six-hour drive back home. It was a real comedown, but it got to be fun because I met a lot of good friends and it was very competitive. There were a lot of players who could have played in the NBA.

At the time I was playing in the Eastern League I was also teaching school from eight-twenty to three-thirty, then working in the after-school center from three to five, the evening center from seven to ten and playing in the League on the weekends, and then going to graduate school at NYU in the summers. It was a lot of hard work.

I was doing very well in the league, averaging over 20 points and about sixteen, seventeen rebounds a game over a three-year period. But the third year I went up for a lay-up and Ed Warner tried to block the shot, tripped me up, and I went down and tore my knee up very badly. It was a Bernard King–type injury. Ironically, about a week later Satch Sanders of Boston called me. Red Auerbach was talking about me coming to camp and having a tryout with the Celtics. Also, Dolph Schayes had taken the job as coach of Philadelphia and he'd sent word that I could try out. But at the time my knee was torn up so badly I would never play basketball again. So that was the end of my basketball career at twenty-five years old.

In retrospect, I think it was the best thing that happened to me, because I was never going to be a great basketball player. If I hadn't been hurt I probably would have kept trying to play in the NBA. But now there was no question that I couldn't play anymore, so I immediately took a teaching job, went to graduate school, and have been able to do a lot of things in the world of education and the world of sports. Had I pursued that basketball dream, it might have been detrimental to me. So I kind of feel that hurting my knee was a blessing in disguise.

I'd been working in teaching and other things but I was going to all the games in the Garden and someone said they needed a statistician. I did that for two years, and I used to go to the press room and talk to the local sportscasters. They said I ought to be on TV and I said, "I'd love to."

Finally, they decided to make a change and I auditioned

with Marv Albert at the NBC studio. We did a game simulation without an actual game going on, including the half and an interview. I was actually auditioning for radio, but they liked what I did, so they put me on TV. I did that for ten years, working as a color commentator with Bob Wolf, Dick Stockton, Andy Musser, and Marv Albert.

The major change that I've seen is that the players are much better athletes today. We have guards like Magic Johnson, who's six-eight, and we have Ralph Sampson dribbling the ball down the floor in a fast break, which he should not be doing. I think the quality of the athlete has changed a great deal. They're bigger, better, quicker, stronger, but I wouldn't think they're more cerebral. I think the players in my era were more cerebral and we had more of a team game than you see nowadays. That's the big difference, I think. It might be that the players get so good individually in high school and college. I think the advent of television gave players the opportunity to look at others. When we came along there was a game on TV maybe once a week. But kids coming along now get a chance to look at Dr. J, Larry Bird, all those guys, and they learn so much more and they become stars individually. By the time they're professionals they want to score, they want to be a star, because that represents a lot of money. And that might be a reason why players might be a bit more selfish rather than team-oriented.

I think the teams were closer when I played. Let me tell you, the little time I played, there were few blacks on those teams, but there was a feeling of camaraderie. We all knew one another. When we went to Boston to play we would have dinner at Bill Russell's home and listen to jazz. If we went to Philly, we would go out with Wilt. But there's a reason for that. There are so many players in the league today you can't go out with everybody. But when we played, every black player in the league knew each other. We would often get together. I don't think you see that any longer. I remember being with Syracuse, playing a game in Fort Wayne, it was preseason. We went to a bar, me, Larry Costello, Swede

217

Holbrook, and Johnny Kerr. I was the only black in the crowd. We got to the bar, a big place, like a nightclub, and the guys sat down with some girls. I went to the bar to have a beer. I was standing there waiting for the guys because I wasn't going to fool with the girls, and some guy sitting down at the end of the bar said, "Boy, I ain't seen a nigger around here in years." I looked around, not knowing, really, that I was the only black in the whole place. I said to the guys, "I'm going back to the hotel, I'll talk to you later on." And I left.

But we would often go out together. In New York, I brought all the guys up to Harlem, to Small's Paradise, which Wilt owned. That camaraderie existed then. Maybe one of the reasons for Boston's success, besides the fact that they've always had great athletes and a great leader in Red, is that there's always been a feeling of camaraderie, even in the days I played. I'd go up to Boston to visit Satch [Sanders], even after I stopped playing in the league, and we'd have a party and all the guys would come and go out together. They still do that to this day. Those guys are very, very close. Few teams have that kind of relationship among the players. It doesn't happen very often, but it's been in Boston for years.

The Knick team of the late sixties and early seventies had that reputation, but it wasn't true of them. The team was very, very bright, very talented, but they were very individualistic away from basketball. [Dave] DeBusschere and [Bill] Bradley would run together. Clyde was out there doing his Clyde thing. Willis was really into hunting and fishing. So they did not run around a lot together. But on the court they were the perfect team. Off the court, not at all. People might have thought that, but it was not the case.

Over the years there are a lot of players who impressed me, going back to Elgin Baylor, who I thought was one of the greatest players of all time, an amazing athlete. Jerry West, a tremendous shooter. Walt Frazier, I thought he was one of the tops. Oscar. A player I had a lot of admiration for was Bob Pettit, because he wasn't the most talented player, but he got more done. You know, he was almost like a Larry Bird, except

218

they played a different style of game. He was not a great jumper, he was not fast, he couldn't dribble, but he would get the job done. I mean, he would get 30 points and his twenty rebounds, and he was very consistent. But he was not an athlete. I can recall a game where we were down by one point and we called a time-out. A play was called and John McCarthy gave the ball to Pettit about eighteen feet from the basket and he didn't get a shot off. After the game Pettit said, "Damn, John, why'd you give me the ball all the way out. I can't do anything out there. I can't dribble." You know, he wanted the ball close to the basket. But he was smart and very much like Larry Bird.

Another guy I thought was amazing because he was my size was Cliff Hagan, because he had the uncanny ability to get his little hook shot off and this twisting little lay-up off against Russell and Chamberlain. Nobody else could do it except Cliff.

Of course, Russell was just incredible. I can still see it. One time I was playing against the Celtics and I think Heinsohn was guarding me. Tommy went to the basket and I had a clear range, couldn't see anybody. I put the ball up and from nowhere Russell came up and knocked the ball away. I'll never forget that. And then one time I was playing Heinsohn and Cousy had the ball and I saw them give the backdoor sign and he went right behind me and Cousy threw a perfect bounce pass right between my legs and he went in for a lay-up.

There were two other guys I used to love. I called them the Bobbsey Twins: Bobby Wanzer and Bobby Davies. They were ahead of me, but I used to watch them play with the Rochester Royals. They were a great combination.

For his time, Cousy was the greatest guard. He couldn't do things that maybe Isiah Thomas could do, because Isiah is a great athlete and because times have changed. For instance, if you go to a practice, even high school, almost every kid can walk dribbling between his legs. When we played nobody ever dribbled between their legs. I don't believe Oscar Robertson ever threw a ball behind his back or through his legs. He was just a basic, fundamental player. I think TV has

had something to do with that change. We just played basketball the way we knew it. We didn't have any reason to
think we could do these different kinds of things. TV show-
cased the guys who were fancier ballplayers. I think TV has
helped players develop at a younger age. The other change
TV has brought about is the advent of big money.

When I played all my contracts were for $7,000. Willis
Reed, when he first came to the NBA, made $11,000. K. C.
Jones played on the champion Boston Celtics and the most he
ever made was $25,000. That's the way it was. The guy who
changed everything was Wilt Chamberlain, because Wilt came
along and demanded $100,000. If Wilt hadn't made a stand it
might have been a long time before salaries changed. But
Wilt got $100,000 and then Russell decided he wanted $1
more than Wilt, and that was the beginning of the large contracts. But Wilt was the one who changed things and I think
every player playing today should be thankful to him.

Wilt and Bill are good friends of mine, so I don't try to
pick out the best between them. If asked, I say, Wilt Russell
was the best. But you have to consider that Russell was not an
offensive player. He was the best defensive player of all time.
But when you consider that the best playmaking guard at that
time, the early and mid-fifties, was Bob Cousy, the best
shooting guard was probably Bill Sharman, the best sixth men
were Frank Ramsey and later Havlicek, the best defensive
players coming off the bench were as a guard K. C. Jones and
as a forward Satch Sanders, and the best coach in the game
was Red Auerbach, so Russell had the opportunity to play
with the best players in the game. All he had to do was
rebound and block shots and occasionally he'd score. Wilt had
to try to do everything.

I love Wilt and he'd do what he had to win. We used to
play cards, dirty hearts, the loser drinks a quart of water. Wilt
hated to lose. I think the key to that Boston team was the
chemistry between the players and I think Wilt was the kind
of person who could have blended in with that group. He
didn't have to score 50, 100 points a game. I think he would
have blended in because, remember, at one point in his ca-

reer he averaged 50 points a game and then decided he was going to be the best shot blocker in the game and he blocked more shots than anybody. Then, the last couple of years, he said he was going to lead the league in assists in the center position for the first time and he did.

Wilt is so strong. After my career was over, we were going up to Kutscher's for the annual All-Star game. When we got out of the car he said, "Cal, get my bags, I'll meet you in the room." I lifted his bag and said, "Damn, this thing is heavy." So when we get to the room, we start playing cards. He says, "Let me have that bag." So I give him the bag. He had weights in the bag and we're sitting there playing cards and he's doing arm curls. He was very strong and still is. He hasn't changed that much.

Wilt wasn't the first to make the dunk shot, but I guess Wilt and Russell were the ones that really began to make it popular. When I was in high school, Boys' High had a team where everybody could dunk the basketball. They used to have a drill for it. That's why they were called the Kangaroos, because the whole team could dunk the ball. I could dunk, but I never did it in a game. I guess it was probably considered showboating, and I guess a lot of players just couldn't dunk. Not trying to cast any racial slurs of any kind, but most of the players at that time were white athletes and they were not great jumpers.

The game itself has become flashier. There's a lot more scoring, less defense. They way it is now, it's almost impossible for one man to stop another man. No one is going to stop Irving or Thomas or Bernard King or McHale or Bird. These guys are talented offensive basketball players and no matter how good you are defensively you're not going to contain them.

I think the game is less physical now. I mean, there are more fights, but it's a less physical game. When we played, a five-ten guard did not go down the lane for an uncontested lay-up. It was unheard of. I mean, you paid the price. You'd get an elbow in your head. Nobody was trying to hurt anybody, but that was a no-no. So the players nowadays might get into more skirmishes because there's all that ego involvement in the game now. When we played, there were not a lot of fights but it was definitely a more physical game. I can recall a game in Syracuse when I went down the middle for a lay-up and somebody cracked me right across the nose. I couldn't see for about five minutes.

They beat Wilt up unmercifully when they went to get the ball. Broke his nose once. I remember when I was with the Hawks they talked about him. "Hey," they said, "when he gets the ball let's go get him." So I told Wilt, because we were good buddies. I said, "Look out, because they're coming after you." So it was definitely a more physical ball game.

Travel was different, too. I can recall when the Syracuse Nationals came down to New York to play a game at the Garden, we'd put five six-footers in a car and drive down here to play, then drive back. I can recall taking charter planes, which is really interesting because we'd get into the charter and we'd have cheese sandwiches, Cokes, orange juice. When I was with the Knicks as a broadcaster and we had charter flights we had our choice of chicken, steak, turkey, shrimp appetizers, wine, all the beer you'd want. Back when I was playing we'd get soda and ham-and-cheese sandwiches. That's a big change.

We were also more into basketball in those days. Between games we'd play basketball. If I had an off day I went to the gym and played basketball, usually with Willie Naulls. It was exciting. It was fun. Particularly to be a Knickerbocker, even for so short a time, since I was from New York and everybody knew me. Unfortunately, it didn't last long, but it was a lot of fun while I was doing it.

Fans are interesting. There's a difference between college fans and pro fans. The college fans were mostly bettors, it seemed to me. They loved me, since I was a great rebounder. I'd get a big round of applause when I did something good. Then one day I hurt my knee and was playing against Tommy Hawkins of Notre Dame and he just annihilated me. I had a bad game and they booed me off the floor because we didn't cover the points, I guess.

The Knicks didn't draw an awful lot in those days, but they had a lot of doubleheaders, so there'd be a lot of fans in the arena, although they'd be there to see Boston or Philly or one of the other teams. They weren't really Knick fans. That's because the Knicks weren't winning then. It wasn't until the early seventies when the Knicks had a great team that the Garden was packed. Everybody wanted to be there. But there was none of that when I played.

The three greatest teams, in my estimation, were the Philadelphia teams with Wilt; the Boston teams with Cousy, Russell, Sanders, K. C. Jones, Sam Jones, Bill Sharman, and Frank Ramsey; and the Knicks with Bradley, DeBusschere, and Reed. There were other good teams, like St. Louis with Pettit and Hagan and McCarthy, and the Nats, and Cincinnati, but there weren't any other great teams like Boston, Philadelphia, and the Knicks, primarily because of Russell and Chamberlain, and the team play of that Knicks club.

Offhand, I can't think of any player playing today who reminds me of me, because primarily my game was rebounding and shooting the jumper and I was only six-four and I couldn't dribble very well. They tried to make me a guard with the Knicks and I wanted to play the small forward on defense. That would have meant that Carl Braun would have had to guard Hal Greer. So he said, "No, Cal, I'll play the forward, you play Greer." Greer ran me into more picks in one minute . . . he almost broke my back.

Jerry West. (Courtesy Basketball Hall of Fame)

Jerry West

Jerry West joined the Los Angeles Lakers for the 1960/61 season, after an illustrious college career at West Virginia. He played for the Lakers for fourteen years and was voted to the All-Star team every year with the exception of his rookie season. During his career he was consistently among the top-ten scorers in the league, but he was also known for his tenacious defense and his intense desire to win. Today West is vice-president of the Los Angeles Lakers.

In the beginning, I remember I used to watch the other kids play basketball around the dirt courts back in Chelyan, West Virginia. It wasn't until I was about five or six years of age that I first picked up a basketball myself, and then it was just because it was something to do. In my particular case, a neighbor's house had a basket and a hoop and I used to go over there and after the big guys were finished playing I would give it a try. In fact, I can remember not being able to get the ball up to the basket, having to shoot it between my legs, and even that didn't always do it. That's how small I was.

You go through the progression of watching other people

play and then you try to get people your own age interested in playing. Finally, you get to the point where you can get the ball up to the basket, and that's an accomplishment.

As a kid, I was very small and I wasn't very good, but I did have an interest in the sport. As with most kids, when I wasn't able to play very successfully at an early age, I got discouraged. It was almost embarrassing for me because I couldn't play well. Then, all of a sudden, in junior high school, when I got into the ninth grade, I grew a little bit and I got a little better at basketball. Still, there was nothing major about my game. I was just someone who liked to play and once in a while I had a good game.

In high school, I started to grow rapidly, from a small kid to one who was real gangly, extremely skinny, with no strength at all. But then, suddenly, I began to develop a real interest in the game. In fact, during the summer, on the real hot evenings, I can remember shooting baskets in front of our house. But still, it was more because it was something to do rather than my having a great, intense love for the game.

Your mind is a wonderful vehicle. You can, as a kid, put yourself in any arena, in any player's body you want, just by using your mind. Sometimes, I used to shoot ten times just to make a last shot which would, in my mind, win a game. But that's the wonderful thing about being a kid. You have the enthusiasm, the ability to go out and immerse yourself in something for hours at a time.

But in many ways I almost feel as if I was cheated just because I didn't really have a lot of formal training at that time in my life. Basketball was just something you did because you enjoyed it.

As a kid growing up I had no dreams of playing professional ball. I had no aspirations that I would ever be that good. My biggest goal was just to be on the high school team. I played on the JV team in high school, and I played pretty well, so they asked me to move up to the varsity. But I broke a bone in my foot and wound up playing in only one game, one real good game, where I had a very big last quarter. So I play one game against our archrivals and I break a bone and they put my foot in a cast. I can remember going to basketball practice, playing with a cast on my foot, and breaking that cast on numerous occasions.

In my junior and senior years in high school, I played varsity. In my junior year I became pretty good, averaging somewhere in the high twenties. But again, I was very thin, I caught a lot of colds, and I was always tired. My junior year, the team had a .500 record, but in my senior year we won the state championship. We were a team that wasn't supposed to win. By then my notoriety had spread and in the state tournament I did some things that were very attractive to people. I got a huge amount of scholarship offers, but still, I was a virtual unknown.

When I was a high school junior I thought I played real well but I think I only made honorable mention on the third team All-State. Other people in the same conference as ours, guys that I played against, would make All-State and I didn't, and I think that was the most depressing time of my life. I didn't think the reward system was very good, and suddenly I realized there was an awful lot of politics involved. I couldn't understand the fact that I didn't get considered. It made me feel like I wasn't very good. After something like that, you have the tendency not to give yourself much credit.

In West Virginia, as in many states, they have what they call Boys' State, where they select kids from each district based on your schoolwork and your civic responsibility. I was selected to go and there happened to be a lot of basketball players there, some of whom had made the All-State team. I went there thinking I wasn't as good as any of them but instead I found that they weren't as good as I was. That was proved to me when, after all the work was done, we'd go out, choose up teams, and play basketball. My team never lost and I suddenly realized how good I was when I found that I was always the first one to be chosen. It was then that I realized I had a real good chance to be a decent player. Between that year and my senior year an awful lot was done for my confidence, being that I could play successfully with players of that caliber. And so, as a result, I had an incredible senior year.

It was a long learning process for me. I had a very fine coach in high school who stressed the teaching of defensive play. He was very good, but the fundamental parts of the game I had to learn by myself. I was always a poor ball handler by my standards, even after I became a professional. I learned to become an adequate ball handler just through experience, by playing against better people all the time. But I think I certainly could have been a lot better earlier if I had been exposed to some of the things kids are exposed to today.

I could always anticipate, steal balls, and block shots, when people were unsuspecting, and I always had a move for the ball around the basket, picking up rebounds and stuff. But it was something you just took for granted. Shooting-wise, I was the kind of shooter who improved with years in the league. I learned more about what a shot was all about. Again, I had nobody who taught me how to shoot. I was self-taught.

I was college All-American two years. I was sure I was going to be drafted, but I had no idea I would be good enough to play in the pros. Even though in most postseason tournaments I played against some of the best people in the country, I was shocked when I was the second player chosen in the draft, after Oscar Robertson. I had no idea I'd be good enough to play because I thought there were so many holes in my game. I had good athletic skills, I could run and jump, but I didn't know if I could play successfully in the pros.

There were no contract negotiations at that time and so, basically, I played for very little money. My first contract with the Lakers was for $16,500, but at that time I wasn't worried about the money. Later on, though, when you get on in your career, you want to get paid for your status in the league. But with me it was never the case with this franchise. I don't think I was ever paid what I was worth. Looking back, I only regret that I wasn't represented by someone other than myself. I took people for their word and it wasn't the best of situations from my standpoint. The players were taken advantage of, for sure. They were abused, mistreated, and I think the owners took great delight in doing it. But still, I'd have to say that everything else was very positive.

*　　*　　*

When I walked into my first training camp I was scared and intimidated. I didn't want to ruffle any feathers of the veterans. I was a gifted athlete, but I didn't know how to play basketball. I'd read about these guys and so I deferred to them. As a result, I let some of the veterans hold me and shove me around more than I would after I'd played a few years.

The Lakers had a poor team when they moved to Los Angeles, and that was my first year in the league. Players on that team included Rudy LaRusso, Ray Felix, Frank Selvy, Bobby Leonard, Jim Krebs, Rod Hundley, and Elgin Baylor. I don't remember an awful lot about those early years, but I do know that I didn't start until midseason and that was only because we were losing. I did have a very good last half of the season for a rookie, and I played particularly well in the play-offs. I think those play-off games provided an impetus for the next season. The play-offs always bring out the best in a player. If the average players fall down, somebody has to be there to pick them up, and I liked being in that position.

It was a big adjustment going from college to the pro game. There's the number of games you have to play, living away from home, the completely different kind of life-style, and the physical part of playing. I was an aggressive player but I never really understood why people fought. To this day I don't understand it. One of the responsibilities as a professional is to learn how to play when you're mad and frustrated and not let it get the better of you.

In my second year in the league things changed. I went from a decent player to an All-Star player in one year. I think confidence made the difference. I also had a lot of energy as well as the athletic ability.

I was lucky in being able to play with Elgin Baylor. It was a great experience. Not only was he a great player, but he was also a great person. He treated me with respect. We both liked to win, and that made it nice.

Later, I got to play with Wilt Chamberlain. I think everyone who ever played with Wilt either loved him or hated him. He was terrific with me. He prolonged my career from a mental standpoint because I'd grown tired of having to be so involved in all phases of the game with this team. I put so much pressure on myself that if we didn't win every night it was a traumatic experience when we lost. You try to forget it if you can, but I couldn't. So Wilt gave me a little different mental outlook on the game. He also provided something we never really had. We always had centers who did a credible job, but never a dominant one we could look up to and know would get 20 rebounds and maybe 100 points. With Wilt, we'd never know what he'd do on any given night.

There was no one player who gave me the most trouble defensively. There are always players who bother you and sometimes one player is better than another, but if you're a scorer and you score 28 and your average is 30, everyone will say what a great defensive job the other guy has done. I remember I had back-to-back ball games against the Boston Celtics where K. C. Jones played me great. I score 48 and 50 points. We go back to Boston, he played me just the same, and I scored 17. So he did a great defensive job that night, right? But the other two nights, did he do a great job on me? Probably not. But those things are going to happen. When you give a basketball to people, you've basically given them an in because they know what they're going to do with it. If the guy is good enough, you'll never stop him. The best you can do is make him work harder, and there are always people who are going to make you work harder for a basket.

I would say that the toughest player for me to guard was Oscar Robertson. If you did a decent job on him, he got his average. Basically, if he wanted to score, he scored.

I guess I always seemed to play pretty well against Boston. There were also certain arenas I liked to play in and others I didn't like. I simply could not shoot in Milwaukee. Even in practice I shot the ball flatter and never shot well. Even when they didn't have very good teams there, I still couldn't shoot well. But, on the other hand, I always seemed to shoot the ball real well in Boston and Detroit. I don't know why that was, but there are always places you seem to do better.

Fans can be tough in some places, but it's all part of the game. After a while, you don't pay too much attention. On the whole, I was very well received all over the league. In LA, the fans weren't really very enthusiastic when we first moved there. They sat there and watched and they wanted you to prove to them that this was a game for them to come out and see. Now, of course, there's a remarkable interest in the game, but it wasn't always that way.

It was very frustrating being in the play-offs as many times as we were and not winning the championship. It's like you failed. In the 1969 series against Boston, we should have won. It's a real frustrating situation when those things happen and you don't know why. I have no idea why we lost it that year. It's funny, the series we did finally win [1971/72], I didn't play very well. I knew if we didn't win that one it was going to be the end of the line for me, because I wasn't twenty-six years old anymore. I would hurt when I'd wake up in the morning. I knew my career couldn't go on indefinitely and here I was playing terribly. It seemed so ironic because I'd play so well in other series and here I was, when it really counted, not doing well at all. But I guess it was meant for us to win. I'm a firm believer in luck and being in the right place at the right time. After we won it that year I have to say it was a nice summer, but I'll tell you, it would probably never make up for all the other heartbreak of summers I'd spent when we didn't win it.

The players on the Lakers were close and we had some good times together. Sometimes we'd have to take the train to a game and we'd bitch and complain, but in the long run we always had a good time. Those are the things you remember. There were just so many wonderful things that kids today simply cannot have an opportunity to participate in. I think the money has made more of a difference in the way players approach the game. If players today get a bump or a bruise, they think how it's going to affect their career tomorrow. We never thought of anything like that. Money has also put a division between players.

During my career with the Lakers we had a thirty-three-game streak, which set the record. There was no pressure involved. Actually, it was easy. There weren't many close games in there. It was just a special team that combined all the elements you need to have a team of that caliber and dominance. We probably shouldn't have lost but three or four games that entire year. We just kept going. It was that easy.

It was my decision to end my career. I'd gotten hurt the year before I retired—that was the '74/'75 season—and it was probably one of the worst things that ever happened to me. My injury just wouldn't get any better. I'd just come off a contract hassle and hadn't gone to training camp. The owner [Jack Kent Cooke] felt there was nothing wrong with me and he told that to two or three people. I'd like to say that I had played many games where these people stuck needles in me to play and I was perfect then when I would agree to that. But now, suddenly, I was being questioned as to my ability to play and I could not take that, especially when I'd played so many times when I'd been injected just so I could get out there on the court. I thought it was very unfair. I signed a contract, came to camp, worked very hard that summer, but I was still bothered by the injury. There was still some pain, not great pain as it was before, but the pain was there. I knew there would be times during the season when I probably wouldn't be able to play. But, all in all, I could have played, but they put so much pressure on me to perform. Today some of the players say that they're being played too much and they're talking about thirty-eight minutes a game. Well, then I had to play forty-eight minutes a lot of nights. At my age I simply wasn't going to be able to hold myself together. With me, it was just a little extra pressure I put on myself. People paid to see me play and if I didn't play I felt I was cheating them.

When I left it certainly wasn't under the best of circumstances. Instead of being treated with some respect, I was persona non grata. My last year, 1974/75, I only played about thirty games because of the injury. I signed a contract to come

232

back the next year and I went through training camp and even played in one exhibition game, but then I decided to retire. I didn't have any regrets, although it would have been easier for me if I'd decided to quit at the end of the season rather than waiting until after the summer.

I played fourteen years in the NBA and in those years I saw the game change. I saw more better athletes come into the league, beginning with the early sixties. The one major difference I see today is that more big kids are in the game and the coaches are much more involved. It's like a chess match today. Everybody has become very sophisticated in their coaching methods. Sometimes I think this is at the expense of the game.

Overall, I think there is, collectively, some improvement in the shooting ability of the players. I think one thing that has contributed to this is the new baskets that have been installed. The change in the baskets has to do with the rims. They've been made so that the rim can be pulled down in order to keep the backboard from breaking. As a result, they give a little more. A ball hits up there and bounces around. You shoot balls that hit right in front of the rim like a rocket, but it will go up and bounce in. I think this has had a definite effect on the shooting. I also think the post-up shooting has become really good and this might be attributed to better college coaching.

I think that today it's definitely a less physical game than it was when I first came into the league. Most people who watch think it's the other way around. But the truth is, there are fewer fights. Players are more in control of themselves. It's the nature of the athlete today that he's not going to stand there and slug it out. He's going to use his athletic ability to get away from people. I think it makes for a better game.

Collectively, I'd have to say that today the players are better than ever. For one thing, there's more exposure to the game. Basketball is a relatively young game and every time you have a great star, someone who improves on something, you'll have another kid come along who improves on that.

233

When I was first playing, we had no role models and very little instruction. In effect, you taught yourself how to play the game. If you were blessed with some special instinct to play the game, it showed up.

Of today's players, I'd have to say that I love to watch Michael Jordan play. His ability to defend and make the jump shot are things I felt I could do. He takes the ball to the basket. The difference between us is that he's such an enormous jumper, with huge hands, that he makes some spectacular plays around the basket. He has creativity and great desire.

When I was playing, I didn't pay much attention to the referees. I think they have the most difficult job of all. I've never seen a basketball player yet who has felt the call against him was correct. And those things tend to upset you as a player. To me, a guy who had a softer personality always made for a better official.

I've never really thought much about coaches. Almost every coach I played for I've liked. Even though some of them were fired, I still liked them personally. I think players who are going to blame coaches for lack of success better take a good look at themselves in the mirror.

I think that basketball today is a great and beautiful game. The league office has done an incredible job. I think it's due to the advent of a lot of good teams, new, young, exciting faces, television exposure, and things of that nature which have helped change the perception of the game. I'm a baseball fan in some respects, but I don't think there's any comparison for thrills and excitement to basketball.